More critical praise for *How the Left Lost Teen Spirit:*

"Rock, rap, reactionaries, and liberals all get a thrashing in ...ldberg's insightful book."
—**VANITY FAIR**

"Danny Goldberg has written ... nt memoir filled with fascinating ... ccess into the corridors of power—b... ...ton insiders or the Hollywood elite—Danny provides the reader with an eyewitness account of history as it unfolds. His searing insights and straightforward recommendations for the future of the left should be required reading for anyone concerned with the state of democratic politics in this country."
—**REVEREND JESSE L. JACKSON**

"We can't know where our culture is headed if we don't know how we got to where we are. This book can get us there."
—**NORMAN LEAR**

"In this lively and intelligent report, Danny Goldberg reminds us once again how the battle for freedom of expression needs to be re-fought every day. I don't know for sure if God is on Goldberg's side, but after reading this book, I sure am."
—**ERIC ALTERMAN**, author of *What Liberal Media?*

"Goldberg authoritatively dissects the disconnect between progressive politics and younger voters."
—**TIME OUT NEW YORK**

"An effecting memoir of Goldberg's experiences within the clash of popular culture and politics . . . The great value of his book is as an insider's tour of American cultural life from the sixties to the present."
—**LIBRARY JOURNAL**

"Danny Goldberg's memoir contains the powerful reflections of the most progressive activist in the recording industry. His candor, vision, and sense of humor are infectious. It is required reading for those concerned with transforming America into a genuine democracy."
—**CORNEL WEST**

"What was the sixties? It was 'I am the Walrus' blaring from the record store in Chapel Hill. It was hearing some guy yell, 'No pictures!' at an antiwar meeting. It was the smell of trampled grass on the Washington Mall during the March on the Pentagon. It was hearing the word *fascist* spoken in regular conversation. It was the zip in the air knowing the draft was coming to get you. It was seeing *Hair* your last day in New York on the way to Africa and the Peace Corps. If you want to get a feel for the sixties—in fact, if you want to keep the spirit alive—just read this book."
—CHRIS MATTHEWS, host of MSBNC's *Hardball with Chris Matthews*

"This is the history of the world that I have lived in all my life; the planet where the atmosphere is composed of equal parts: politics and art."
—STEVE EARLE

"[A] riveting report from the frontlines. Whether you stand to the left, right, or center in America's culture wars, Danny Goldberg's book is a must-read for anyone who cares about civil liberties, the First Amendment, and rock and roll."
—ANTHONY ROMERO, Executive Director, ACLU

"Danny Goldberg has spent thirty years fighting for your rights. It's about time you got up off your ass and joined him. Reading this book is a good start."
—PAUL BEGALA, cohost, CNN's *Crossfire*

"An important book by a wonderful writer we all thought was a record company executive. A litany of missteps and disasters which is, thank God, a page-turner."
—PETER CAREY

HOW THE LEFT LOST
TEEN SPIRIT

HOW THE LEFT LOST
TEEN SPIRIT

(...and how they're getting it back)

Danny Goldberg

RDV Books
New York

Published by RDV Books/Akashic Books
Copyright ©2003, 2005 Danny Goldberg
Originally published in hardcover under the title *Dispatches from the Culture Wars: How the Left Lost Teen Spirit*, Miramax Books, 2003

ISBN-13: 978-0-9719206-8-2
ISBN-10: 0-9719206-8-0
Library of Congress Control Number: 2004115732
Printed in Canada
First paperback printing

RDV Books/Akashic Books
PO Box 1456
New York, NY 10009
Akashic7@aol.com
www.akashicbooks.com

The author and publisher gratefully acknowledge permission to reprint the following previously published material:

"Love Me, I'm a Liberal" by Phil Ochs, ©1965 by Almo Music Corp.
    on behalf of Barricade Music, Inc. All rights reserved. Used by permission.
"John Walker's Blues" from *Jerusalem* by Steve Earle, ©2002 by Steve Earle,
    published by Sarangel Music (ASCAP) and administered by Bughouse, a
    division of Bug Music, Inc. All rights reserved. Used by permission.
"The River" by Bruce Springsteen, ©1979 by Bruce Springsteen (ASCAP).
    All rights reserved. Used by permission.
Excerpt from "The Ballad of the Skeletons" from *Death and Fame: Last Poems
    1993–1997* by Allen Ginsberg, ©1999 by The Allen Ginsberg Trust.
    Used by permission of HarperCollins Publishers, Inc.

For Rosemary, Katie, and Max

CONTENTS

ACKNOWLEDGMENTS

I first would like to thank my partner in Artemis Records, Michael Chambers, whose vision and friendship have given me a home in the record business during the years that most of this book was written. Without the vocation that he and I work so hard on together, I'm not sure I would have had the confidence to embark on this project.

Similarly, I thank my other colleagues at Artemis, including Michael Krumper, Sage Robinson, Ken Walsh, Adrian White, Carise Yatter, and especially Daniel Glass.

Jack Newfield, who recently passed away at the age of sixty-six, bugged me for years to write a book such as this, and his encouragement was indispensable. He was a great writer and a great friend.

Andrew Wylie, my agent, not only shopped and sold my proposal but has been an extraordinary source of support in all ways. Andrew is a cosmic grand master at his craft. He has been a great friend and agent during this process. I thank him from the bottom of my heart.

At Miramax Books I want to thank Susan Mercandetti, whose initial leap of faith is something I will never forget. JillEllyn Riley has led me through the process with care, attention to detail, and support the likes of which have continually delighted and surprised me. I also want to thank Tina Brown, whose blessing was so helpful, and

Harvey Weinstein, whose blessings remain essential. And especially I thank John Burnham for welcoming me into his world.

JillEllyn introduced me to Harper Barnes, my editor. Harper worked tirelessly on the narrative flow. To the extent that the book has a coherent structure, much of the credit belongs to him. In places where it rambles on too much, it's probably because I failed to take his advice.

Several people spoke to me at length about the themes of this book, and I thank especially Harry Belafonte, David Fenton, Tom Hayden, Gary Hart, Paul Krassner, Norman Lear, Michael Lerner, William Schneider, Marge Tabankin, Jack Valenti, and Dr. Rosalyn Weinman.

I appreciate the feedback on an earlier draft from Michael Des Barres, Patrick Goldstein, Earl Katz, and, again, Jack Newfield and Marge Tabankin.

My assistant of many years, Robin Klein, was helpful in countless ways, and no expression of appreciation can possibly suffice.

I have been blessed with many cheerleaders, makers of contacts, confidants, and partners in political mischief. Among that number I especially thank Stanley Sheinbaum, Ken Sunshine, and Chuck Blitz.

In developing the confidence to write I am grateful to several editors over the years who have given me the space to express myself in opinion pieces, including Michael Lerner, Victor Navasky, Katrina vanden Heuval, Bob Kuttner, and especially Allison Silver.

These books were of particular help in clarifying my thoughts:

Edward DeGrazia, *Girls Lean Back Everywhere: The Law of Obscenity and the Assault on Genius*
Jib Fowles, *The Case for Violence on Television*
Marjorie Heins, *Not in Front of the Children*
Jack Newfield, *Somebody's Got to Tell It*

Eric Nuzum, *Parental Advisory: Music Censorship in America*

Paul Slansky, *The Clothes Have No Emperor*

Thanks to musicians and to the music business, for giving me a place in the world.

My political consciousness was born in my childhood. I thank my parents, Victor and Mimi, for their inspiration and love, and my sister Rachel, brother Peter, sister-in-law Lola, and nephew Benjamin, for constantly setting an example for me to live up to.

Thanks to Hilda Charlton, whose blessings I am grateful for beyond description.

Love to my kids, Katie and Max, who graciously put up with my disappearances to the basement.

For their help in preparing the paperback edition I'd like to thank my RDV colleagues Johnny Temple, Robert Greenwald, Johanna Ingalls, and Victor Goldberg; as well as Scott Ritter, Jon Sinton, Jenny Toomey, Scott Goodstein, and Jeff Cohen, and my new assistant, Jacqueline Sproles.

For their generosity of spirit in supporting the original addition I also want to thank Kelly Mearkle and Sandy Mendelson, Jaimie Horn, Ann Hornaday, and Don Imus.

More than anyone I am indebted to my wife, Rosemary Carroll, who has not only encouraged me in every way imaginable and led me through many dark passages, but also read every draft and version and gave me continual notes and comments, without which this work would have been infinitely more embarrassing.

Introduction 2005

Last night I had a dream
That the world had turned around
And all our hopes had come to be
And the people gathered 'round
They all brought what they could bring
And nobody went without
And I learned a song to sing
The revolution starts now.
—Steve Earle

DON IMUS HATED the title of the original hardcover edition of this book, *Dispatches from the Culture Wars,* and urged me to change it to the subtitle, *How the Left Lost Teen Spirit.* "*Dispatches* sounds like you're a member of the Communist Party or something," the talk-radio superstar grumbled.

Besides being my personal homage to Kurt Cobain, I appropriated the phrase "teen spirit" to refer to the energy that a political movement needs—not only to mobilize young people, but also to touch older people who make political decisions based on emotional and spiritual reasons rather than purely intellectual ones, and who are thus more affected by the language of popular culture than by the language of editorial pages. In the quarter-century since Ronald Reagan was elected president, Republicans and conservatives have understood such populist emotions better than Democrats and the political left.

This book is a rant in the form of a memoir. The rant is against a particular kind of liberal self-destructiveness that masquerades as pragmatism but has been, instead, one of the main causes of the decline of progressive political power despite widespread support for progressive political goals.

I have been in the music business for more than thirty years as a PR guy, a personal manager, and, for the last decade, a record-company president and owner. I have worked with rock legends such as Led Zeppelin, Neil Young, KISS, REM, Warren Zevon, and Nirvana, with pop icons such as Diana Ross and Madonna, with politically committed musicians like Joan Baez, Bonnie Raitt, Jackson Browne, Bruce Springsteen, and Steve Earle, and with gangsta rappers, singer-songwriters, boy bands, heavy-metal icons, classical tenors, country divas, jazz masters, and critical darlings, as well as with counterculture icons such as Allen Ginsberg, Timothy Leary, William Burroughs, and Cornel West. I am fifty-four years old, a "baby boomer" and an "aging hippie." I am also a businessman. I live in New York now, which is where I was born. But for most of the 1980s I lived in Los Angeles, and when I visit there I am still a "Hollywood liberal," and have worked with such conservative targets as Norman Lear, Barbra Streisand, and Jane Fonda.

My wife, Rosemary Carroll, and I are parents of a girl and a boy, which, contrary to conventional wisdom, hasn't made us any more politically conservative. We have hosted fundraisers for, among others, liberal Democrats like Hillary Clinton, Russ Feingold, and Ted Kennedy, and worked with independent progressive leaders like Jesse Jackson and Ralph Nader (although not in 2004!).

To some establishment Democrats, it is people like me who have screwed up the party. I was against the war in Iraq, and I met with and supported Howard Dean in the early stages of the primary campaign, thinking that he was a strong vehicle for that opposition. I have been involved with political fundraising concerts, I'm an ACLU board member, and I'm a friend of Michael Moore. To me, it is the conventional wisdom prevailing in Washington, D.C. that has screwed up the party.

In November 2004, many Washington pundits began reviving the term "culture wars." Post-election polls indicated that "morality" was the number-one issue for voters. Of the 22 percent who said that issue motivated them, more than 80 percent voted for George Bush. Democratic soul-searching began in earnest and focused primarily on three areas, all of which have long intrigued me: youth, spirituality and religion, and cultural positioning.

YOUTH

In the days just after George Bush was reelected, the political media repeatedly claimed that one of the reasons for John Kerry's defeat was the supposedly disappointing turnout by young voters.

Kathleen Seelye in the New York Times wrote, "The much discussed first-time voters did not really materialize." Tom Curry on MSNBC.com chimed in, "Contrary to much ballyhoo and self-promotion from Democratic-allied groups such as Rock the Vote, voters aged eighteen to twenty-nine did not show up in unprecedented numbers and accounted for the very same percentage of the electorate that they did in 2000, 17 percent." On MSNBC, Joe Scarborough (who claims to be a big Nirvana fan) dismissed young voters: "They take you to the alter," he solemnly intoned, "but they don't vote." Newsweek's website said that only 10 percent of eighteen- to twenty-four-year-olds turned out. CNN cited the "low turnout" as one of the disappointments of 2004. John Tierney in the New York Times listed "the youth vote" in the category of "losers" and smugly wrote, "The unprecedented get-out-the-vote campaigns turned out so many young Americans that their share of the electorate went from 17 percent in 2000 to 17 percent in 2004." *Washington Post* columnist Donna Britt mocked "young, 'PlayStation-beats-standing-in-line' non-voters."

The left-wing press was even harsher. Alexander Cockburn wrote derisively in *The Nation*, "So much for Rock the Vote and Eminem. The youth vote stayed the same as in 2000." *The Nation*'s Katha Pollitt claimed, "Young people constituted their usual pathetic proportion of the total vote, and this is after the best efforts of P. Diddy."

These reports were all either completely misleading or outright false.

The total votes cast by people ages eighteen to twenty-nine was 20.9 million, which is a 4.7 million *increase* from 2000. The turnout rate for those under thirty increased from 42.3 in 2000 to 51.6 in 2004, the highest since eighteen-year-olds got the vote in 1972.

So why did those pundits say the youth vote was "the same" as 2000? Because *overall* turnout was up significantly, the *ratio* of the young vote to the overall vote was the same. (The *Newsweek* website got these facts mixed up. Eighteen- to twenty-four-year-old voters were 10 percent of the *total electorate*; their turnout *rate* was around 50 percent—the best it's ever been.)

If one were rooting for Kerry to beat Bush, it would be worth noting that Kerry carried the eighteen- to twenty-nine-year-old vote by 54 percent to Bush's 45 percent—and lost the vote of those thirty and older by 53 percent to 46 percent.

In 2000, with Al Gore and Joe Lieberman dampening youth support with their attacks on culture, the under-thirty vote went 48-46 for the Democrats. In 2004, young people gave Kerry a margin of over 2 million votes, more than *quadruple* the margin of 2000. If that shift hadn't happened, Bush would have won by 5 million instead of 3 million.

African Americans, women, elderly voters, Latinos—all showed a decline in the percentage of votes for the Democrats. No other Democratic leaning group came close to increasing turnout and support the way young voters did.

In battleground states, under-thirty turnout was around 65 percent and their share of the electorate was 19 percent of the total, a significant increase over previous years. In Wisconsin, first-time voters gave Kerry a margin of 58-41, which swung that state Democratic. In Pennsylvania, voters under thirty supported Kerry by a margin of 61-39. Both states would not have gone to Kerry without those younger voters.

By what twisted logic does a bright spot become a disappointment? Why, of all the statistics about young voters, did so many in the media focus solely on the meaningless "percentage of the overall vote"? What causes such distorted thinking? Is it middle-aged jealousy of the bravado and energy of young people? Is there some kind of anti-hippie hatred or former-hippie self-hatred infecting my fellow baby boomers who make up such a large chunk of the political media elite? Whatever causes this neurosis, some sort of collective therapy is required to get rid of it. Young people and those who rallied them should be congratulated and thanked by the Democrats, who, while they're at it, can also apologize for a campaign that failed to attract the support of older Americans.

SPIRITUALITY AND RELIGION

I wholeheartedly agree that progressives and Democrats need to incorporate religion and spirituality more substantially into their politics. The most important progressive leader of the twentieth century was Martin Luther King Jr., who weaved his political agenda seamlessly into his identity as a Baptist preacher. For years, many progressive writers, including Rabbi Michael Lerner and Cornel West, have been eloquently suggesting a spiritual framework for progressive politics.

One approach, which is *not* a good idea, is to address moral concerns by trashing core values. As a creature of rock and roll and Hollywood liberalism, I have been yelled at for years by culturally tone-deaf economic liberals who have urged Democrats to drop "social issues," such as affirmative action, feminism, and gay rights. Shortly after Massachusetts Governor Michael Dukakis lost the presidential race to the first President Bush in 1988, I attended a conference, similar to those happening post-2004, about how Democrats could possibly win again. Pat Cadell, who had run President Carter's campaigns, strongly advised Democrats against "being distracted" by divisive social issues, such as abortion rights. Marge Tabankin, who then was running the Hollywood Women's Political Committee and who later would run foundations for Steven Spielberg and Barbra Streisand, responded by saying, "To most women I know in politics, choice on abortion is the equivalent of the civil rights movement. So if you want a party that includes women, you can't ignore this issue." I passionately agreed, and in response, Cadell, a large and striking figure with a salt-and-pepper goatee and a wandering eye, rose like a biblical prophet, face flushed and finger waving, and shouted at me, "It's people like you, Danny, that have ruined the Democratic Party!"

So-called pragmatists like Cadell want to turn the clock back to the 1930s, when Franklin Roosevelt could unite bigoted and tolerant voters around labor issues. Such an approach is neither moral nor pragmatic.

The partial-birth abortion vote was brilliant strategically for Republicans and aggravating for Democrats. Very few women actually get the procedure they were defending, and yet Democrats paid a price for appearing to be insensitive to depictions of the practice as inhuman. Bill Clinton was able to explain his concerns about the health of mothers, veto the bill, and still leave office with record-breaking approval ratings. To have failed to oppose the bill would have, in fact, indicated acquiescence in the ultimate erosion of *Roe v. Wade,* and would have cost the Democrats by alienating feminists, *Hardball*'s Chris Matthews, a Catholic, frequently asked anti-abortion politicians if they were in favor of executing women who had abortions or doctors who performed them. This may be a better way of framing the issue.

It would be easier for Democrats if gay marriage were not a high-profile issue. But to suggest (as Clinton was said to have advised John Kerry) that Democrats should join Republicans in support of ballot initiatives banning gay marriage is a triple loser. First, it would be morally wrong. Second, it would contradict the value of inclusion that has been one of the primary animating beliefs of Democrats for decades. It would further reinforce the very perception that has hurt Democrats the most: that they don't believe in anything except winning and that they sway with the changing political winds. (Several weeks before the election, a *Time* magazine poll asked people if the candidates were good at "sticking to their positions." Bush got a yes from 84 percent—Kerry only 37 percent. The single most effective line George Bush uttered in his stump speech was, "You may not always agree with what I do but you will always know where I stand.") Finally, abandoning gays, and feminists for that matter, on such emotionally charged issues would create a revolt in the party that would dwarf the impact of Ralph Nader's 2000 run. As filmmaker Robert Greenwald says, "The answer isn't to whore it up and change our positions to ones which we think will get us votes. It's to express a moral basis for the positions which we do have."

So how to do it? It's important to recognize that religious faith is not inherently conservative. Reverend Jesse Jackson and Reverend Al Sharpton ran primary campaigns with extremely progressive domestic agendas, but gracefully contextualized their positions in the framework of Christianity. Jimmy Carter, especially during his post-presidential years, has been a strong progressive on foreign policy, but always does so in the voice of a man who for years taught a weekly Sunday school class in Georgia.

There are many clues in George Lakoff's books *Moral Politics: How Liberals and Conservatives Think* and *Don't Think of an Elephant: Know Your Values and Frame the Debate*. Lakoff, who is a linguistics professor, crystallizes feelings I've long had when he contrasts the moral framework of conservative politics to the "shopping list" approach liberal politicians have taken to issues. He explains that in order to resonate, Democrats need a moral narrative that connects to and animates their positions. Conservatives already do this, based on what Lakoff calls a "strict father" concept of morality. He makes a convincing case that liberals can do so by using a "nurturing family" construct. Lakoff also makes the point that the "framing" of issues usually determines their outcome, and he gives many examples of conservative success at framing, such as calling a bill that cuts taxes for the wealthy "tax relief."

Liberals are often baffled that members of the middle class frequently vote against their self-interest on economic issues. The voters do it because they have bought into a worldview that says it's morally wrong for people to be penalized for success. It is pigheaded for liberals to insist on selling every idea on the basis of self-interest, since so many wealthy liberals vote against *their* self-interest by supporting higher taxes—and we do it for moral reasons, as well. We want to live in a society where we take care of each other. The way to counteract the anti-tax view isn't to accuse people who vote for tax cuts of being idiots, but to engage them in a positive argument about the moral role of government.

As an executive in the music business, I need to acknowledge that there are indeed aspects of popular culture that alienate some religious people. However, the two interests are not mutually exclusive. One thing that many religious people and fans of pop cul-

ture have in common is a preference for emotional and spiritual energy in politics instead of a purely intellectual approach. And both
religious people and pop-culture fans share the view of the Washington elite as condescending and tone-deaf to the meaning in
their day-to-day lives.

As I discuss in more detail later in this book, no election cycle
would be complete without lamentations from politicians and the
political media about the "coarsening of the culture." On MSNBC's
Hardball, Pat Buchanan insisted that the prevalence of trashy pop
culture was part of what "moral" voters identified with Democrats.
Former Clinton labor secretary Robert Reich, usually one of the
most cogent liberals, defensively responded by noting that Bill Clinton had pushed through a law mandating a "V-chip" in TV sets. In
a post-election *Washington Post* column about Kerry's loss, Donna
Britt explained, "I'm one of millions of Americans who click off
shock-jocks' radio obscenities, who was angered by Janet Jackson's
crude, failed attempt to sell albums, and whose careful monitoring
of my nine-year-old's entertainment often feels futile. Citizens such
as I exist in every political party."

As a longtime defender of pop culture, I should say that I think
what Janet Jackson did was wrong. It's not appropriate, under any
code, to spring a surprise like that on a mass audience or on an established TV network. But the political media's reaction to the incident was totally irrational and out of proportion. Shortly after the
2004 election, *New York Times* columnist William Safire said on *Meet
the Press* that Jackson's flashed boob was the "social, political event of
the year." I had watched the Super Bowl with my son Max, then ten
years old, and we barely noticed the soon-to-be-infamous breast
flash. What we could not avoid, however, were the countless commercials for the erectile-dysfunction drug Cialis, thanks to which I
and millions of other parents had to provide an explanation for the
meaning of the word "erection." Why is it so easy to question a

naked breast, but not the moral obligations of pharmaceutical companies? The moral frame that pertains to the Janet Jackson incident should be the concept of corporate accountability to the public in general. This would put conservatives, who amorally support the corporate imperative to make profits above all else, on the defensive and introduce a vital new paradigm into many political conversations. It is no coincidence that Sumner Redstone, CEO of Viacom (which owns CBS and MTV, the networks responsible for the controversial Super Bowl half-time show), announced in the summer of 2004 that he was voting for Bush because the president was "a citizen of Viacom" and his administration's policies were best for the company.

People of goodwill disagree about precisely which parts of the culture have become "coarsened." Some readers of this book may think that I am somewhat extreme in my defense of the marketplace of ideas and the vigor with which I resist those who demonize pop culture. Despite its many disgusting and materialistic elements, I prefer raising my children in today's culture rather than the sexist, racist, homophobic, repressed cultural environment in which I grew up during the 1950s. That era featured a network-TV schedule dominated by westerns in which every human problem could be solved by pointing a gun at the bad guys. I can't figure out a set of rules to eliminate the parts of Howard Stern's show that I dislike that would also continue to allow Allen Ginsberg's seminal poem "Howl." And I vastly prefer an American culture with Stern and Ginsberg than one with neither of them.

It is worth noting that the American public is not always honest with itself. Voters may have liked the idea of the V-chip—but 90 percent of parents never use them. Janet Jackson's brief flash of flesh was the most downloaded footage in the history of the Internet. The coarseness hasn't, for the most part, been caused by liberal politicians, or even by corporate media, but by our own collective fascination with sleaze.

The political-taste police went after Whoopi Goldberg for a silly pun based on the fact that the president's last name is also slang for genital hair. A thousand more tasteless jokes go unnoticed, but this one was told at a Kerry fundraiser at Radio City Music Hall in New York City. After the election there were even pundits who listed this trivial controversy as one of the ways in which Kerry disrespected middle-American values, and who counseled Democrats to be wary of Hollywood. But it wasn't Whoopi's joke that provided George Bush with a line for his stump speech, it was Kerry's remark after the event that the entertainers "represented the best in American values." Believe me, it would have been okay with those of us in showbiz if he hadn't said *that*. A simple "thank you" would have sufficed.

CULTURAL POSITIONING

Many people felt that George Bush was a "regular guy" and that John Kerry was an "elitist." Since both come from upper-class families and both went to Yale, the blame for this disparity has to, in part, go to an ailing political culture on the Democratic side. The job description of someone seeking to be president should include the discipline and ability to emanate cultural empathy with a majority of voters. Reagan, Clinton, and Bush did this effectively. George Bush Sr., Dukakis, Mondale, Gore, and Kerry did not.

As isolated incidents, it's not that big a deal that John Kerry referred to Lambeau Field, the Green Bay Packers' famous stadium, as *Lambert* Field; or that the self-proclaimed Red Sox fan badly mangled the name of Sox World Series hero Manny Ramirez; or that he looked like he was trying too hard when he ostentatiously dressed in a camouflage outfit on a widely photographed goose hunt just before the election; or that he looked like a rich guy when he was photographed wind-surfing during the Republican convention. Nor is it determinative that George Bush is always filmed on vacation clearing brush, that he looks comfortable in cowboy boots, or that he delivers simple lines effectively. However, the aggregate effect of these symbolic moments and many others makes it clear that there was insufficient attention paid to cultural language by the Kerry campaign.

It has now become part of Arnold Schwarzenegger's mythology that he became a Republican because, shortly after he arrived in the United States, he saw and liked Richard Nixon on TV. But it is not uncommon for people to change parties as they grow older and become more involved with politics. Wesley Clark went from being a Republican to a Democrat, and Ronald Reagan went from Democrat to Republican. Given that Schwarzenegger is pro-choice, pro–gay rights, pro-environment, pro–stem cell research, and married to Maria Shriver, it seems clear that in this particular instance, Shriver's uncle, Ted Kennedy, who met Arnold before he entered politics, dropped the ball. Democratic political pros who worked with Kennedy didn't take Arnold's political aspirations seriously, while Republicans like former California governor Pete Wilson and former Los Angeles mayor Richard Riordon mentored him. Only rarely have performers made good politicians, but given that the Republicans got the one actor who became a president and another who has inspired legislation that would make it legal for him to run, it would be a good idea if Democratic power brokers decide now that they won't let the *next* Reagan or Schwarzenegger slip through their fingers.

At the core of Democrats' cultural disconnect from working-class people in Middle America is the party's failure to advocate enough political positions that matter to their targeted audience. Thomas Frank's vital book *What's the Matter with Kansas?* brilliantly identifies the alienation that has aided the cultural right. Of course, I don't think that Democrats can or should oppose gay marriage or abortion. But Frank eloquently explains how Democrats could have at least *some* connection with the anger and frustration of many Middle Americans if they publicly reclaimed their historical position on the side of workers against giant corporations. For example, most Democratic leaders in recent years have followed the counsel of supposedly pragmatic "moderates" by supporting NAFTA and other "free-trade" laws. During the initial phase of his primary campaign, John Kerry railed against "Benedict Arnold corporations" who outsourced American jobs to foreign countries, but at the request of financial supporters in the banking business, the line was dropped for the general-election campaign.

There is no more effective cultural populist on the left than Michael Moore. He is emotional. He speaks about class issues through the prism of his own childhood. He knows how to make complex subjects understandable to average people. Yet Michael's very populism, his gift for expressing political ideas with humor and emotion, is resisted by some of the liberal snobs who, to me, are part of the problem. Shortly after the election, *New York Times* columnist Nicholas Kristof, wrote, "Firing up the base means turning off swing voters. Governor Mike Johnson, a Nebraska Republican, told me that each time Michael Moore spoke up for John Kerry, Mr. Kerry's support among Nebraskans took a dive." The *Los Angeles Times'* Patrick Goldstein quoted former Clinton chief of staff Leon Panetta as saying, "The party of FDR has become the party of Michael Moore, and that doesn't help the party."

Of course, Nebraska is not a swing state, and it is implausible that there were polls that measured the effect of Michael Moore's utterances. It is also pretty silly to ask Republicans for advice on how Democrats can win. They want Democrats to lose and they know that anything they say in the media is part of what political pros call "the permanent campaign." It seems likely that the Republicans who counsel Democrats to put Michael Moore and Hollywood liberals at a distance are trying to psyche out their opponents—the way they did when they convinced Al Gore to steer clear of Bill Clinton in 2000.

Panetta's comment is even more absurd. Michael Moore did not run for president; John Kerry did. Michael Moore did not run John Kerry's campaign; Washington- and Boston-based Democratic campaign "experts" did. The analog to Moore is William Buckley, who created a vigorous and unapologetic conservative presence in the media during the 1960s at a time of liberal ascendancy. Franklin Roosevelt was very close to a number of entertainers and people in the media, such as columnist Walter Winchell, whom he regularly invited to the White House, actor and comedian Will Rogers, and director Frank Capra, whom he commissioned to make a series of films to explain to American servicemen and their families why the United States was fighting World War II.

Panetta and his ilk seemed to think that "rallying the base" was a political mistake, despite the fact that this was the primary strategy of Karl Rove, the mastermind of Bush's victories. It is unimaginable that conservative columnists or politicians would suggest that Rush Limbaugh did more harm than good for Republicans . . . and that is one of the reasons they won.

THE LEFT

Tom Hayden and Jack Newfield both suggested that I title this book *How the Democrats Lost Teen Spirit*. But I feel that there has been plenty of cultural tone deafness on the entire left side of the political spectrum, not just in the Democratic Party. Countless college students were seduced by campus conservatives because they opposed speech codes on campus that had been implemented by leftists. The term "politically correct" was used as a cynical ploy by conservatives to delegitimize noble programs such as affirmative action. And it resonated because of misguided progressive excesses. In the run-up to the war in Iraq, progressives limited their appeal by unnecessarily aligning publicly with radicals whose agendas had nothing to do with Iraq. Comparisons of Republicans to Nazis also hurt the left. Martin Luther King Jr. gave a sermon in which he cautioned against "non-transformed non-conformists" whose personal bitterness interfered with their ability to work for progressive goals. I often thought of this construct when I tried to get the increasingly bitter Ralph Nader to reconsider his run for president in 2004.

In his book *All the Power: Revolution Without Illusion*, Mark Andersen, a longtime grassroots progressive activist, makes an impassioned moral plea for reassessment of left-wing politics to make sure that actions lead to progressively desirable results. For example, the public protests in Seattle that focused attention on the inhumanity of many global trade agreements had an important energizing and educational effect. But the same thing cannot be said about all the dozens of subsequent marches, some of which seemed to have been organized with little or no thought for the real-life political consequences. For those who tire of endless talk about process and strategy, and who long for a spiritual context for progressive political action, Andersen's book is healing and inspirational.

HOW THEY'RE GETTING IT BACK

In many discussions with fellow activists over the last few years, the example of Barry Goldwater has come up often. Goldwater lost in 1964 by the biggest landslide in American history. But because Goldwater took such passionate and coherent conservative positions, he galvanized a generation who soon took over the Republican Party and led one of their own, Ronald Reagan, to the White House sixteen years later. In the sixteen years since Jesse Jackson's run for the Democratic nomination in 1988, there has been no prominent progressive leader in the Democratic Party. Maybe, we mused, we need our own Goldwater to shake us loose from the confusing and ineffective identity into which Democrats had devolved. Although Bill Clinton's victories were inspiring, much of his success was based on his personal charisma and supernatural political skills. Clintonism without Clinton failed miserably, as demonstrated by the loss of both houses of Congress.

In 2004 there were two campaigns. Although John Kerry is a brilliant and decent man who would have made a fine president, it must be acknowledged that his campaign failed and that he personally did not leave many footprints.

But if Kerry was not Goldwater, the 2004 campaign nonetheless produced a movement that is analogous to the conservative movement of the sixties through an explosion of new non-governmental messengers. *This* will be looked on as the beginning of a new progressive movement: the campaign animated by Michael Moore, Air America, and dozens of best-selling books; the campaign organized by MoveOn.org and hundreds of other websites; the campaign of countless new activist groups that helped fill the vacuum and spoke to the yearnings of the one-third of Americans who were truly progressive and whose voices had been ignored by both the national Democratic leaders and the mainstream media. An awakening took place among established Democrats as well, as think tanks like the Center for American Progress at long last began to play catch-up with conservative institutions.

Additionally, after years of overlooking successful conservative efforts that have influenced the news media, a progressive media critique has finally gained momentum. Fairness and Accuracy in Reporting (FAIR) and its founder Jeff Cohen were among the trailblazers in pointing out conservative bias. Eric Alterman's definitive book *What Liberal Media?: The Truth About Bias and the News* exposed the rightward drift of the media culture, which had been facilitated, in part, by the canny claims of conservatives to the contrary. David Brock's Media Matters, *The Daily Howler*, and Al Franken's Air America radio show were among those that began to turn the intellectual tide.

For the first time in a quarter-century, there is a vibrant, energized progressive movement in America. Maybe one of the reasons I'm less depressed than a lot of my friends is that I was so much more depressed than they were until recently. Democratic losses and progressive decline over the last several years have been caused in large part by the virtual absence of coherent cultural and youthful energy on the left. With the current resurrection of populist energy on the left, electoral victories will return, notwithstanding the continued but ever weakening ravings of the same myopic, discredited "experts" who have helped steer Democrats and the left away from youth and moral energy since the Reagan years. Yes, the left is getting its teen spirit back. Help, indeed, is on the way.

Introduction (to Hardcover Edition)
Rock, Rap, Reactionaries, and Liberal Snobs

It's always the young that make change. You don't get these kind of ideas when you're middle-aged. The young have daring, creativity, and energy— they have impatience. So you take your young legs and your eagerness and your natural feelings for justice and peace and a better deal for our planet, and you go out and you make tomorrow better than it is today.
—Abbie Hoffman at age fifty, speaking to a college audience

I T MAY SEEM a little ridiculous for someone like me, a guy in the music business, to be criticizing the Democratic Party and the American left, but I'm sick and tired of watching the ideas that I believe in lose political ground. Like other people in my field, I've been able to meet many of the intellectual and political leaders whose beliefs I share. I usually come away inspired by their policy ideas and deeply depressed by blind spots that doom those ideas. A political ideology that's purpose is to help and empower ordinary people is often directed by leaders and strategists to whom the public is an alien beast and to whom young people seem to be, astonishingly, irrelevant.

Even though majorities of the American public regularly tell pollsters they want national health insurance, tighter gun control, better pay for schoolteachers, energy independence, and stronger environmental regulation, advocates for these causes seem unable to translate this public support into political results. Not only has the Democratic Party grown considerably weaker over the past few decades, but mainstream Democrats have moved steadily away from progressive causes. The 2002 election was merely the latest example of Democrats walking away from millions of their supporters and potential supporters, supposedly for politically pragmatic reasons, but with toxic political results.

The weirdest thing about the political shift to the right is that it has occurred during a time when virtually every cultural battle in America has been won by the left. People who have fought for abortion rights, free speech, gay and lesbian rights, and racial equality can look at a country transformed in their image. Yet most leaders in the political left and the Democratic Party have profoundly mixed feelings about their cultural allies.

People in the entertainment business, especially the music business, are linked in the public mind with profound cultural changes over the last several decades. So, without ever planning it that way, I've become an enemy in the "culture wars," not only in the minds of conservatives but to many Democrats and others on the left whose policy goals I passionately support.

What exactly is "my" side? In previous eras there were more clear-cut definitions of what "left" and "right" were. Today there are dozens of variations. On economic issues I'm a typical liberal. Having run my own businesses and having worked for big corporations, I have a basic belief in capitalism, but I think that government, representing the collective will of the citizens, has a special obligation to balance out the excesses of the marketplace. I wouldn't mind paying higher taxes to have national health care, better paid schoolteachers, smaller class sizes in public schools, and more jobs programs to help lift people out of poverty and help average-income citizens deal with their lives more easily. It seems to me that many Western European countries have been better at supporting people on the low end of the economic spectrum than Americans have, and the extent of poverty here seems immoral to me given our country's wealth. Although I've never been a member of a labor union, I believe they should be stronger. Corporations have so much power that it seems healthier to me for there to be a strong counterweight on behalf of workers. I also think our country should be more generous with foreign aid given the immense poverty around the world.

Conservative rhetoric implying that private charities can replace government doesn't ring true to me. I know that governments tend to be inefficient, but there are some things that only government can do, such as build highways, protect the environment, provide police protection, etc. The environment is an area where it's particularly important for government to enforce the public interest when it clashes with the economic interest of businesses. And by the way, there's plenty of corruption and inefficiency in the business world as well. I'm fascinated by the antiglobalization movement and I suspect that important moral leadership will emerge from there, but I'm not particularly sophisticated about many of the underlying issues.

Although some of the artists I've worked with have been involved with a wide array of issues and I try to read on a variety of topics, my primary interest is American culture and my primary field of activism has been about individual rights. It drives me crazy, for example, that the United States has so many of its citizens in prison, most of them for nonviolent crimes. Many of the people I know in both the business and political worlds would have spent time in jail if these laws were enforced against everyone.

I am an ardent civil libertarian and have been an officer of the ACLU since the mid-1980s. The ACLU was started in the 1920s as an advocacy group for the Bill of Rights, with special emphasis at that time on the right to unpopular criminal speech in the wake of opposition to World War I. During World War II, the ACLU defended Japanese Americans who were interned by the Roosevelt administration. The ACLU has been involved with many landmark legal cases, including the court decisions that legalized abortion, that banned prayer in public schools, that gave accused criminals the right to remain silent and the right to an attorney, and virtually every case in which the government has attempted censorship of the arts.

It was the latter area that drew me to the ACLU when the music business was attacked, but I soon found myself enthralled with the organization's deeply idealistic vision of democracy, and it's the one political place where I've been involved as a participant as well as a supporter.

A belief in progressive economic policy doesn't automatically go with a commitment to civil liberties. For example, there are many left-wing Catholics who favor making abortion illegal. There are progressive college professors who favor "speech codes" on campus. There are members of "identity groups" representing the interests of gays and lesbians, feminists, African Americans, Jews, and so on who support boycotts of media offensive to some members of their groups.

I am an absolutist on free speech. I believe strongly in protections for those accused of crimes. I am against the death penalty, I am pro-choice, and I am in favor of affirmative action to get racial minorities and women into positions that have been historically closed to them.

Having been associated with the ACLU as an officer since the mid-1980s, I am often getting into arguments with progressive friends who disagree with the ACLU on one issue or another, none more than the organization's position that many campaign finance laws, such as McCain-Feingold, interfere with freedom of speech. (The ACLU supports complete public financing of political campaigns as the solution to this problem, and I agree.) Paradoxically, there are numerous conservative libertarians who agree with the ACLU on these issues but with whom I personally disagree on a wide array of economic issues.

Similarly, foreign policy in the post–Cold War period does not lend itself to traditional left-right divisions. I don't know much more about foreign policy than what I read in the newspapers, so I'm not inclined at this juncture to give a shopping list of every superficial foreign policy opinion I've ever had, but growing up during the Vietnam War has certainly made me suspicious of convoluted government rationales for military action. However, I am not a pure pacifist and I agree there are rare occasions when killing people with the military is the least bad course of action.

There are millions of people who share this set of beliefs. My lament is that the political culture whose role it is to advance the progressive agenda has grown increasingly elitist, snobbish, and removed from huge chunks of the American people, including most young people. This cloistered retreat is largely responsible for twenty years of regression for progressive policies after decades of progress during most of the twentieth century.

The silver lining of the 2004 election is the emergence, finally, of a new progressive culture which is manifest in groups like MoveOn.org, media such as Air America, a robust stream of best-selling progressive books, the long-overdue development of progressive think tanks, unprecedented organization of young people, and new Democratic faces on the national political stage such as Barack Obama, Howard Dean, and, more prominently after his reelection, Russ Feingold.

But there is still that neurotic resistance on the part of many Democrats and progressives to young political energy.

Although I've supposedly been in the middle of one, I've always found the phrase "culture war" bizarre, especially as it applies to entertainment. No one ever talks about a culture war in the music business. We talk about "great records" and about "hits." We talk about "artists" and "fans," and we talk about the ways to connect those two groups: radio, record stores, TV, concerts, press, and recently a lot about the Internet, CD burning, and new economic models.

And we talk about how much money everyone risks and everyone makes. We don't think of ourselves as being at war with anybody, except maybe metaphorically with one another. We just want to get our ideas and products out. If people don't like them or want to criticize them, no problem. No one has ever suggested passing a law mandating exposure to dirty movies or rap music or beatnik poetry, nor boycotting retailers that choose not to carry R-rated videos, nor "shaming" people in bow ties who want to return to the culture of the good old days.

Having been a teenager during the Vietnam War, I have connected rock and roll with politics as long as I can remember. By the 1970s, after attaining enough success in the music business to be able to help political causes I believed in, I began by working with rock artists who did benefits for environmental groups. I later got involved in efforts to prevent a Reagan-era war in Central America.

It never occurred to me that the way I made my living would itself become a political issue, but in 1985, when I read of Tipper Gore's efforts to intimidate record companies into instituting a ratings system for lyrics, I felt compelled to defend my colleagues in the music business and the adolescents who loved and helped create the culture that was under attack. Since then, a substantial amount of my activist avocation has focused on the intersection between popular culture and politics.

This book is a memoir based on seventeen years of experience at that intersection. At every place in the ideological spectrum, from moderate Democrats to movement radicals, again and again, in dozens of different ways, my experience is that the left avoids reaching out to large masses of Americans. If one is a classics professor or art critic, there is nothing wrong with having tunnel vision and an aesthetic or philosophy that ignores popular taste and trends. Such independence of thought can be a virtue in those professions. But for the vocation of politics, the goal of which is to move majorities to support policy goals, such parochial myopia is outrageous. Without mass public outreach, politics, especially progressive politics, cannot succeed.

The phrase "culture war" is itself deceptive. It seems to me that several different culture wars have been going at the same time.

1. THE REVENGE OF THE CULTURAL CONSERVATIVES

The "culture war" most commonly described is driven by attacks on popular culture by conservative cultural critics. Cultural conservatives believe that American society reached its moral zenith in the early 1950s. Then a supposedly dreadful decline began with the advent of the beatniks, hitting bottom in the late 1960s with the hippies and the antiwar movement.

One archetypal cultural conservative is Jerry Falwell. After September 11, 2001, Falwell joined fellow conservative Christian Pat Robertson on *The 700 Club* and blamed gays, feminists, and the ACLU for the tragic attacks in New York and Washington, claiming that left-wing libertines had driven an angry God "to remove his protection from America." Even President George W. Bush criticized Falwell's remark, but there's no denying that the reverend spoke for a certain constituency that remains part of America's cultural mix.

Similarly, George Will, Lynne Cheney, Pat Buchanan, William Bennett, Robert Bork, and Norman Podhoretz all talk about a "coarsening" of American culture since the fifties. Their opposition to pop culture has been perfectly consistent and can be traced back to attacks on early rock and roll and Beat poetry by conservatives in the fifties, and to Vice President Spiro Agnew's demonization of the Beatles in the sixties.

Cultural conservatives like Bennett claim that high divorce rates, drug addiction, and teen violence are all the result of modern culture. They want a return to the authoritarian America of the 1950s, when the Catholic Church could make books "banned in Boston" and J. Edgar Hoover and the acolytes of Senator Joseph McCarthy could marginalize and terrorize any kind of unorthodox political or cultural thought. Not surprisingly, cultural conservatives frequently bemoan the state of the popular entertainment culture. It was ever thus.

2. THE ASCENDANCE OF THE LIBERAL SNOBS

Most of my own battles, however, have been with liberals and Democrats, many of whom I've supported in political campaigns. Starting in the mid-1980s, Democratic politicians and left-wing intellectuals began agreeing with cultural conservatives about the supposedly negative effects of popular culture.

The Democratic Party's commitment to culture bashing was exacerbated during the Clinton era and reached a new pinnacle with the national ascendance of Senator Joseph Lieberman of Connecticut. But it's not only so-called New Democrats who have embraced attacks on pop culture. So have important voices on the political and academic left, including, at times, Ralph Nader and Reverend Jesse Jackson.

Most liberal snobs are from my own generation, the so-called baby boomers. Cultural conservatives want their children to grow up like they did; liberal snobs are afraid theirs will.

Conservatives attack pop culture going back to the turn of the last century. Liberals will extol the virtues of pop culture well into the sixties and conveniently claim that "something changed" shortly after they themselves came of age.

Liberal snobs tend to focus on violence and bigotry, cultural con-servatives on sex. There are very few Democratic voices sticking up for youth culture. Although conservative Christians are a vital part of the national Republican coalition, many Republicans are actually more open-minded on the issue of free speech and pop culture than some Democrats, and I'm not just talking about libertarian conser-vatives such as P. J. O'Rourke and Ann Coulter.

President George W. Bush was seen on magazine covers with U2 lead singer Bono following a meeting about debt relief in the third world, and Bush cracked jokes while welcoming rock/reality-TV star Ozzy Osbourne to a White House dinner. There are no policy implications to any of this, but politically it sends a message that Bush is a "regular guy," whereas Democrats, whose actual agenda is far more relevant to young people, come across as uptight, preachy elitists.

One problem seems to be that many members of my generation, the generation now in power, have a basic resentment toward young people. This is a particularly foolish position for people to the left of center, since no progressive change has ever occurred any-where in the world without the energy and inspiration of young people, who traditionally have provided the shock troops for the left.

Liberal snobs and cultural conservatives alike are often what free-speech activist Marjorie Heins calls "metaphorically chal-lenged." Usually educated in law, journalism, political science, or sociology, politicians and pundits spend decades viewing human be-havior in a linear, literalistic way. They frequently interpret art and entertainment as if they were devoid of metaphor, humor, irony, or Aristotelian catharsis. Looked at through this lens, neither fairy tales nor Greek tragedies nor classic opera would pass moral muster.

3. THE WASHINGTON DOMINANCE OF TONE-DEAF MAVENS

The same snobbery and insensitivity to young people that drives culture bashing has created a Democratic Party and a public-interest left whose leaders appear unwilling or unable to communicate with the "unwashed" masses who do not read newspaper op-ed pages or watch public television. This isn't exactly a culture war so much as a disconnect between progressive political leaders and the culture of the people they want to lead.

By tone-deaf mavens, I mean the self-insulated consultants and pundits who have enormous influence on American politics and who, for the most part, are much more tuned in to other mavens in Washington than to what Americans are really thinking.

Conservatives, who control far more media than left-wingers, are clever enough to promote the spokespeople who have "working class" styles, like talk-show propagandists Bill O'Reilly and Sean Hannity. Although in the lead-up to the 2004 election there was, at long last, the emergence of some populist liberal media, it is still a mystery why so few progressives do the cultural homework that has so empowered conservatives.

The fact that academics with radical new ideas no longer reach out to a mass audience was lamented as long ago as 1986 by Russell Jacoby in *The Last Intellectuals*. By contrast, he cited Galileo, whose "crime" was not to have revolutionary thoughts about the solar system, but to publish them in colloquial Italian instead of academic Latin. Most progressives today express themselves in language that might as well be Latin. And it's not just Democrats like Al Gore using incomprehensible insider jargon like "Social Security lockbox."

When I interviewed Gary Hart for this book he speculated that American politics was less progressive now because more of the public was "less compassionate" than they had been in the 1960s. If Hart were correct, George W. Bush would not have described himself with the poll-tested phrase "compassionate conservative." The moral lessons of the 1930s and 1960s have been ingrained in the majority of the public. There is a consensus against racism and for fairness. The debate that conservatives have cleverly constructed is not about compassionate goals but about whether or not progressive programs actually work. The failure of progressives has been their inability to explain to average Americans why their particular solutions are better or even how their ideas are different. On the weekend before the 2002 midterm election, the New York Times published the results of a poll of Americans in which they asked people about their sense of the vision of each major political party. Forty-two percent felt that the Republicans "had a clear plan for the country," if they gained control of Congress. Only 31 percent felt that the Democrats did. (Sadly, the same syndrome affected the Kerry campaign in 2004. Six weeks before the election, a New York Times poll asked, "Do you think the candidate has made it clear what he wants to accomplish in the next four years as president?" 50 percent said "yes" regarding Bush, while only 38 percent said so of Kerry.)

Organizations on the far left are even less likely to communicate in the cultural language of mass America. "The left likes to talk to itself," says my old friend David Fenton, whose PR firm Fenton Communications has represented a Who's Who of progressive organizations over the last twenty years, including Greenpeace, Amnesty International, the NAACP Voter Fund, and MoveOn.org.

"The do-good sector," says Fenton, "is filled with wonderful people who don't have business backgrounds. So they haven't had to think about mass audiences and mass communications and affecting mass behavior. I think that there's a cultural antipathy toward the mass market, a cultural alienation from television and other forms of mass communication.

"How many groups do you know, who, when you ask them about themselves, will hand you a video?" Fenton adds in frustration. "For young people, videos and computers are the dominant form of communication, and it's not like that's a new phenomenon."

Many on the left blame their communication breakdown on the vast sums of money behind right-wing media such as Rupert Murdoch's Fox News or Rush Limbaugh's widely syndicated radio show. But the right wing has always had huge amounts of money and powerful media allies, like Henry Luce and William Randolph Hearst. In ages past, the left wing trumped reactionary media ownership with charismatic and creative populist messages.

Bill Clinton had personal charisma, but he used it more for defense against the right wing than for the advancement of progressive issues or for party building. Otherwise, the image of the Democratic Party on the national stage for the last few decades has been as dull as dishwater. Jack Newfield once asked me rhetorically, "How did we get these fucking zombies as our candidates? If you put Mondale, Dukakis, and Gore next to each other, they couldn't utter an interesting sentence between the three of them." In 2004, John Kerry, whose life story was genuinely fascinating, apparently took zombie instruction and came across as only marginally more interesting.

A big part of the problem for Democrats is that they keep narrowing the spectrum of political debate, fearful of alienating anyone. In 2000, Democratic pollster Stan Greenberg urged Democrats to run a campaign stressing moral and religious values, because the Monica Lewinsky scandal had "again associated Democrats with sixties-style irresponsibility." This argument ignored poll after poll showing that most Americans were not as offended as Washington pols and pundits by Clinton's sexual misconduct.

In 2002, the experts hired by Democratic politicians told them to focus on the need for affordable prescription drugs. This is certainly a morally and politically viable issue. But it is not the only such issue. Prescription drugs are particularly important to older voters and less important to younger ones. The mavens didn't see any need for Democrats to have an issue that mattered to young people. The same mavens told Democrats not to criticize President Bush after September 11. This certainly made moral and political sense for the first month or two. But the Washington geniuses extended their noncriticism of Bush for fourteen months, until the 2002 election. There was no fierce scrutiny of the systemic breakdowns that allowed the September 11 attack to happen, nor criticisms, nor calls for resignation of any senior or junior staff in any security agency, nor any vocal Democratic demands for greater funding of security for harbors, train stations, and so on. Most notably, there was barely criticism of Bush's radical shift in American foreign policy. The conventional-wisdom police insisted that "serious" contenders for the presidential nomination support Bush's war resolution against Iraq—and John Kerry (and John Edwards) dutifully did so, thus setting the stage for the charge of "flip-flopper," when Kerry inevitably realized that Bush's policy was not right.

A vicious cycle was created. Bush gained popularity as a figurehead after a national tragedy. Democrats didn't criticize him for fourteen months. Bush, unchallenged, remained popular, and he used that popularity to defeat Democrats. Democrats, fearful of looking weak, supported Bush on Iraq, thereby enabling him to win reelection as a wartime president.

It's not just the loss of younger voters that should concern Democrats, it's the loss of youthful energy and innovation—the loss of teen spirit, embodied in a popular culture that almost inevitably is created by the young and then spreads to the rest of the population.

Given the intricacies of public policy, it seems trivial to some of my political friends that I spend so much time and energy worrying about "packaging" instead of "substance." But in a democracy, politics without communication is like the proverbial tree falling in the forest without a witness. The unseen and unheard message might as well not exist.

During most of American history, liberals and progressives understood how to communicate with average people through popular culture. The legendary American radical Emma Goldman once said, "I don't want to be a part of any revolution I can't dance to."

Harriet Beecher Stowe's melodramatic popular novel *Uncle Tom's Cabin* was one of the catalysts that galvanized Northern white support for opposition to slavery. Lincoln, upon meeting the diminutive novelist, is supposed to have said, "So you're the little lady who started the big war."

Upton Sinclair's muckraking novels helped launch reforms of factory conditions. Woody Guthrie's music was intertwined with the growth of American labor unions.

Franklin Delano Roosevelt, the architect of modern liberalism, calmed American fears after the Great Depression and sold his New Deal program through his mastery of a relatively new medium, the radio, with his fireside chats. John Kennedy was elected in large part because of his mastery of another relatively new medium of popular culture, television, and his popularity soared as a result of his casual, youthful energy, his sense of fashion, and his relaxed and witty televised press conferences.

Martin Luther King Jr. was a master of media strategy as well as the most compelling orator of the second half of the twentieth century. King knew exactly how Bull Conner's police dogs attacking children in Alabama would play on television and prick the conscience of mainstream America. At the March on Washington in 1963, King's famous "I Have a Dream" speech followed performances by Mahalia Jackson, Bob Dylan, and Joan Baez.

It is impossible to imagine the civil rights movement, the labor

movement, the protests against the war in Vietnam, the environmental movement, the women's movement, and the struggle for
gay and lesbian rights without the powerful catalysts provided by
the energy and inspiration of the young and their popular culture.
The Democratic Party and the left will either heed that message or
find themselves doomed to more decades of cultural victories and
political defeats.

"If you remember the sixties," rock icon David Crosby said only half
jokingly, "you weren't there." Crosby was in part alluding to drugs,
but his remark also captures the intensely personal way that Americans experienced the kaleidoscopic and tumultuous events of the
sixties. It is hard to find any facet of contemporary politics and culture that does not in some way reflect that decade. Yet no single
version of that rich, contradictory, and sometimes incoherent era
can ever feel fully authentic to most of us who were there.

Ironically, many who claim to remember the era clearly and
well—and this includes most Washington politicians and pundits—
don't seem to remember it at all. What they remember, or pretend
to remember, is a cartoon of the sixties.

Chronologically, I am defining the sixties as the decade that began with President John F. Kennedy's assassination on November
22, 1963, and ended in 1974 with the resignation of President
Nixon.

Subjectivity aside, there is no doubt that the following changes
were achieved or powerfully set in motion during that period:

- The civil rights movement stirred the conscience of millions and
  spurred legislation that put the force of law behind black demands for equal treatment in schools, employment, housing, and
  public accommodations, at least cracking open the doors of the
  American Dream for millions of African Americans.

- The women's movement inspired new legislation and fought for the enforcement of existing laws forbidding discrimination on the basis of gender in the workplace and in other key areas of society.
- Widespread availability of birth control pills and legal access to abortions gave women much more choice about when and if they bore children, making it much less difficult for them to pursue careers and enter professions, and introducing an era of freer sexuality.
- Court decisions virtually eliminated government censorship of the arts, and books and movies that used frank language and explicit images to portray life realistically were embraced by most Americans.
- The war in Vietnam spurred hundreds of thousands of Americans, most of them young, to become active in a massive peace movement that ultimately made Vietnam the nation's most unpopular war and forced politicians to end it.
- Gay activists, long limited in influence to relatively small bohemian subcultures, brought gay men and women openly into mainstream American life.

In the world of popular music, "the sixties" is definitely a positive reference, a time when creativity exploded and profits soared. Rock music, stimulated by the explosion of FM radio and multitrack recording technology, produced the soundtrack to many sixties lives. We still feel the influence deeply: Modern recording artists sample or emulate Jimi Hendrix, Sly Stone, the Beatles, and the Motown sound. Until the death in 1995 of Jerry Garcia, the Grateful Dead was the most popular touring band in America.

Today, classic rock radio stations draw millions of listeners and remain immensely profitable by playing the music of the sixties. In national polls, that quintessential sixties happening, the Woodstock

Festival, shows up along with the moon walk as the most significant event of the era.

In the political world, however, the phrase "the sixties" is used almost exclusively as a negative. The prevailing political images of the sixties are of the "hippie" protesters at the 1968 Democratic Convention and the disastrous George McGovern presidential campaign of 1972. Conventional wisdom has it that sixties protesters ruined the 1968 convention on the outside and the 1972 convention on the inside—too many women, blacks, gays, longhairs, and showbiz types turned off moderate voters and gave the federal government to Republicans. The Democratic presidential vote declined from 61 percent in 1964 to 44 percent in 1968 to 40 percent in 1972.

Virtually all of today's Democratic political figures entered politics in the wake of those losses and of the Watergate scandal. Former president Bill Clinton and presidential aspirants Al Gore and Richard Gephardt, among others, were first elected to political office in 1976. John Kerry's career was a pure reflection of the times, as he became both a Vietnam War hero *and* a war protester.

The myth that these Democrats and their media allies thrust upon us today is that their party was able to regain parity only when it embraced traditional politics and rejected the idealistic fervor of the sixties. The myth ignores the potent role in the Democratic presidential victories of 1976, 1992, and 1996 played by the pro-choice movement, the women's movement, the environmental movement, the civil rights movement, and minority voter registration spurred by Jesse Jackson's presidential runs. And it closes its eyes to the staid, conventional, un-sixties personae of Democratic candidates like Walter Mondale and Michael Dukakis. But because the myth reinforces the cultural prejudices and the political authority of powerful Democratic politicians and their allies in the media elite, it prevails.

"The sixties still haunts politics," CNN political editor William Schneider told me one summer afternoon in 2001. "I used to call it the thirty-year war, but at the rate things are going it could be the forty-year war. Most of politics today, in one way or another, is a reaction to the sixties. Republicans and conservatives explicitly offer themselves as a contrast to the sixties."

That's true. Ronald Reagan made his national reputation as governor of California in great part for cracking down on campus peace demonstrators. Marilyn Quayle reminded the 1996 Republican Convention that "not everybody dropped out and took drugs in the 1960s." George W. Bush cited *The Dream and the Nightmare*, Myron Magnet's excoriation of "the sixties culture," as a key inspiration for his successful 2000 campaign.

But many Democrats also seem to show revulsion for the culture of the sixties. As a result, those millions of voters who supported the civil rights and antiwar movements, and who embraced the profound cultural changes associated with the sixties, feel far more distant from Democrats than movement conservatives do from Republicans.

To me, and to many other so-called baby boomers, the sixties stirred the collective American psyche and soul in ways that defy conventional political analysis and that included a spiritual dimension, a search for unconventional and nonmaterialistic kinds of freedom that inspired millions of people—and clearly turned off millions of others.

The movie that best depicts the period is *Easy Rider*, which embraces the mind-expanding potential of psychedelia but harshly condemns mind-numbing hard drugs. Not coincidentally, *Easy Rider* was the first Hollywood film to use rock music successfully as shorthand for emotions. Its soundtrack featured then-current songs like Steppenwolf's "Born To Be Wild" and the Band's "The Weight" as metaphors for the quest for freedom.

Easy Rider captures something crucial in an exchange between the longhaired hippie Billy (Dennis Hopper, who also directed) and the shorthaired lawyer George (Jack Nicholson):

BILLY: People think we're gonna slit their throat or something. They're scared of us.

GEORGE: Oh no. They not scared of you, they're scared of what you represent to them.

BILLY: All we represent to them, man, is someone who needs a haircut.

GEORGE: What you represent to them is freedom.

BILLY: What the hell's wrong with that? Freedom is what it's all about.

GEORGE: That's what it's all about, but talking about it and being it—that's two different things. I mean, it's real hard to be free when you're bought and sold in the marketplace. 'Course, don't go telling anyone they're not free cause then they're gonna get real busy killing and maiming to prove to you that they are free. They talk and talk and talk about individual freedom but when they see a free individual, that's gonna scare 'em.

Sadly, since at least the mid-1980s, the Democrats and the left seem to be the ones who have been running scared. Meanwhile, the Republicans and the right win most of the races.

Tom Hayden, one of the few authentic sixties protest leaders to have entered electoral politics, says, "The Democrats who got elected to office in the seventies were catering to a market of protest voters, but they themselves were not a part of either the civil rights movement or the antiwar movement in any significant way, with rare exceptions such as [Georgia congressman] John Lewis. You've got a lot of careerists who never inhaled the sixties so, of course, they have no perspective on what it was all about."

In Washington, it is an article of faith that Bill Clinton is a "sixties" guy. CNN's Schneider looked at me like I'd lost touch with reality when I even questioned the notion. "He was the first president who grew up in the sixties, he smoked pot, he avoided military service in Vietnam," the affable pundit reminded me.

To me, it is mind-boggling that Bill Clinton is considered a symbol of the sixties. I can't imagine him sitting around a campfire sharing a joint and talking about freedom with Billy in *Easy Rider,* nor hanging out with the Yippies of Paul Krassner. He was not at Woodstock, nor at any American antiwar rallies. His musical hero is Elvis Presley, not Dylan or Hendrix. He plays the saxophone, not the guitar. His erotic posture resembles that of the macho fifties "rat pack" that entranced his hero John Kennedy, not the sexual liberation of the sixties. Clinton is a brilliant type-A careerist, driven to escape the poverty of his upbringing and always focused on conventional achievement, in many ways more influenced by the culture of the fifties than the sixties.

While conservatives thought Clinton was being disingenuous when he said he had smoked marijuana once but "did not inhale," I along with many former hippies feared that Clinton was telling the truth. As *New York Times* columnist Frank Rich says, "Calling Bill Clinton a sixties person is like calling Dick Clark the voice of rock and roll."

The 2000 Democratic ticket was overtly anti-sixties. When Al Gore named cultural reactionary Joseph Lieberman as his running mate in the 2000 election, one of my friends protested to liberal Democratic senator Barbara Boxer. She snapped, "Don't get stuck in the sixties." John Kerry was not as sanctimonious as Gore and Lieberman were during their campaign, but he barely mentioned his protest of the Vietnam War in his 2004 campaign, preferring to endlessly emphasize his heroics as a soldier. Thus, he took heat from

Vietnam vets who resented his protest, but he derived none of the moral authority from the courageous and visionary choices he had made and their relevance to the Iraq War. He may have lost some support if he had opposed the war in Iraq from the beginning and linked it more directly to his opposition to the war in Vietnam. But he would not have been called a flip-flopper.

Attacks on popular culture and in particular the lyrics of popular music by Lieberman and other Democrats, including Tipper Gore and her censorious coterie (the late Frank Zappa called them "the Mothers of Prevention"), were the original inspiration for this book. Tom Hayden explains this ultimately self-destructive syndrome by saying, "It's like a rite of passage to prove that the sixties is totally out of your system. It's like a drug test, as if they're saying, 'I'm clean. I have attacked those lyrics.'"

But is the denunciation of the sixties really necessary, or even productive? Immediately after the 2000 election in which both parties implicitly ran against "the sixties," Capitol Records released a collection of number-one singles by the Beatles, a band once excoriated for all the supposed sins of the sixties, from long hair, wild clothing, and loose living, to experimentation with mind-altering substances, drug references in their songs, and even allegedly slandering the name of Jesus Christ.

The Beatles' *One* collection sold 10 million copies and was easily America's best-selling album—some thirty years after the Beatles had broken up, long past the time when most Americans supposedly had become completely turned off by the sixties—at least, according to the tone-deaf mavens of American politics.

Of course, the continuing popularity of the Beatles and other bands of the sixties does not mean that everyone who bought the *One* album also bought John Lennon's egalitarian political ideals or George Harrison's meditative spirituality. But for many millions of baby boomers who were there, and millions of younger people who wish they had been, the sixties was a good time, a time of hope, idealism, exuberant youthful rebellion, and sheer fun. Countless national advertisers try to hook into those good vibrations to sell products to people who want to feel young and hip, co-opting even politically edgy songs like Lennon's "Revolution" (Nike) and, perhaps most astonishingly, Creedence Clearwater Revival's scathingly bitter antiwar anthem, "Fortunate Son" (Wrangler).

It should go without saying that there were plenty of negative aspects of the sixties, including drug abuse and senseless radical violence. The popularity of sixties culture indicates that a large portion of the public views the positive elements and constructive changes of the sixties as having been more significant in their memory. It seems perverse that the Democratic Party and the left in general shy away from using the same favorable public feelings about the sixties to promote progressive ideas, while advertisers have no qualms about using those collective emotions to sell running shoes.

CHAPTER 1

The Sixties

The Cartoon vs. the Realities

*There's this saying, "May you live in interesting times." I always
thought—"Hey, that's great. It could be my mantra."*

*But then I learned it was a Chinese curse. Well, maybe it's a curse to
the ruling class. But to people who would rebel against the ruling class,
living in interesting times is a blessing, not a curse.*

—Paul Krassner, editor of the *Realist* and cofounder of the Yippies

I N 1963, WHEN I WAS THIRTEEN and the Beatles' recordings made their first invasion of the United States, I was already in love with the sixties, even if the decade was just
beginning to define itself. I had few friends and lived vicariously
through the media. My biggest source of inspiration was *Mad* magazine, whose sarcastic and sometimes outrageous parodies of pop
culture and politics fed the restless imaginations of teenage baby
boomers across America, but I also loved the gleaming, inspirational image of youthful President John F. Kennedy. I bought books
containing his speeches and taped photos of him above my bed.
When President Kennedy was assassinated, my parents, my brother,
and I were devastated, and we watched television coverage obses-

sively for days in a deep emotional connection with the tragedy and with the rest of the country.

My younger brother Peter and I grew up in a liberal household. Our father Victor was a textile executive and our mother Mimi was a poet and protégé of William Carlos Williams. My parents had both worked on the Henry Wallace campaign in 1948 and our household was always filled with talk of current events. When our youngest sister, Rachel, was born in 1963, the civil rights movement was crusading through the American South.

Our family enthusiastically followed the efforts of Martin Luther King Jr.'s Southern Christian Leadership Conference (SCLC) and other groups fighting racial segregation. I particularly admired the Freedom Rides organized by the Congress of Racial Equality (CORE), with blacks and whites risking their lives by traveling together on buses through the most segregated parts of the South.

I also reveled in the triumphs of a brash young boxer named Cassius Clay. One day, early in 1964, a junior high school friend named David Simon told us he had seen Clay on the subway and had gotten an autograph. We looked over his shoulder and saw a name we'd never heard before: Muhammad Ali. We thought David had been duped by an imposter and called him "simple Simon" for a few days, until we read in the newspaper that Clay had indeed become a Muslim and changed his name. My adulation of Ali only increased as the years went by, particularly in the light of his idealistic opposition to the Vietnam War and his extraordinary comebacks.

In the summer of 1965, between tenth and eleventh grades, I attended a weeklong Quaker workshop in nonviolence. At that point, the burgeoning Black Power movement and the rising tide of street demonstrations against the war in Vietnam were creating a schism on the left between people who trusted the traditional political structure to produce change, and people, most of them young, who impatiently pushed for more radical action.

Sitting around a campfire, I heard one of the older teenagers play and sing a song with the following opening verse:

> I cried when they shot Medgar Evers, the tears ran down my spine
> I cried when they shot President Kennedy, he was like a brother of mine
> But Malcolm X got what was coming, he got what was coming this time
> So love me, love me, love me, I'm a Liberal.

The subsequent verses of "Love Me, I'm a Liberal," written by Phil Ochs, continued to draw the distinction between mushy, middle-of-the-road liberals and committed, leftist radicals.

The sadly debased word "liberal" originally referred to the anti-Communist left as epitomized by Eleanor Roosevelt, people committed to equal rights for minorities and women and to government help for those left out of free-market success. But by the mid-1960s, self-described liberals were the leading proponents of the Vietnam War. The distinction between liberals and radicals was crucial, and I thought—and still think—that Ochs nailed it. I discovered that music could mirror my own feelings and magically make me feel more powerful and less alone.

By the late sixties and early seventies, the word "radical" had been equally debased by violent fringe groups like the Weatherman. Remaining uncomfortable with the Vietnam-era connotations of "liberal," many on the democratic left switched to the word "progressive," which is what I currently call myself, although it seems like a bit of a mouthful.

I saved my allowance money to buy Ochs's two albums, *I Ain't Marching Anymore*, and *All the News That's Fit To Sing*.

Later in the summer of 1965 I volunteered in the ultimately unsuccessful mayoral campaign of New York congressman William

Fitts Ryan, a passionate left-wing Democrat who outspokenly opposed the Vietnam War, rare at that point for an elected official. For me, a high point of the campaign was the afternoon I sat in a sound truck next to James Farmer, the leader of CORE, whose booming bass voice had inspired millions in his television appearances talking about the Freedom Rides. The memory of sitting next to and talking to such a great man would get me through many dark, angst-ridden periods of my teenage life, particularly because Farmer had been so accessible and friendly. At his suggestion, he and I actually took turns on the microphone exhorting listeners to vote for Ryan.

Later that same year I went to Washington for a peace march and was transported when SDS leader Carl Oglesby spoke of how Lyndon Johnson's cold warriors "broke my liberal heart." I became an ardent fan of the counterculture, although at that point mostly through the media. I listened fervently to New York's free-form listener-supported radio station, WBAI-FM, and loved the trenchant wit of Abbie Hoffman and Paul Krassner on the all-night "Radio Unnamable," hosted by Bob Fass. I devoured books by James Baldwin, Rachel Carson, Michael Harrington, and Marshall McLuhan, and I grabbed copies of Krassner's fearlessly radical satirical journal, the *Realist*, and any other underground newspaper I could get my hands on.

I didn't agree with everything I read or heard. Some of the more radical and apocalyptic leftist rhetoric, even then, grated on my sense of proportion and view of reality. I loved the idea of trying to break through the materialistic, narrow-minded, Cold War status quo. But I thought John Lennon was right on the mark when he sang to radicals in his song "Revolution": "But when you talk about destruction, don't you know that you can count me out."

Music had always provided an emotional connection to the world in my house. My parents loved folk music and my childhood years were filled with Pete Seeger, Odetta, and Burl Ives. Then came the folk revival of the early 1960s, with musicians like Peter, Paul and Mary, Judy Collins, and Joan Baez setting a standard of political credibility that would influence musicians for generations to come, and my own work as well.

In my earlier teen years, I also developed a love for classical music, but Beethoven and Bach and all the rest were put on hold when I started eleventh grade and passionately embraced rock and roll.

More than thirty years later, I can vividly remember my record collection from that time. The first Beatles album I bought was *Rubber Soul*. The first Stones album was *The Rolling Stones Now*. I cherished the Lovin' Spoonful, Muddy Waters, Mississippi John Hurt, Howlin' Wolf, Junior Wells, Tim Hardin, Simon and Garfunkel, the Holy Modal Rounders, Arlo Guthrie, Dave Van Ronk, the Fugs, Tom Rush, Judy Collins, Joan Baez, the Young Rascals, Country Joe and the Fish, Blue Cheer, the Velvet Underground, Tom Paxton, Big Brother and the Holding Company, Donovan, Cream, Steppenwolf, Jefferson Airplane, everything by the Beatles, everything by the Rolling Stones, everything by Jimi Hendrix, everything by Phil Ochs, and, most especially, everything by Bob Dylan.

I still recall the afternoon during eleventh grade when an older kid named Paul Mintz pulled me aside in a school corridor to play Dylan's "Ballad of a Thin Man" on his portable record player. I was transported when I heard Dylan sing the chorus line, "Because something is happening here, but you don't know what it is, do you, Mr. Jones?" Mintz and I weren't friends, he was just so excited about the song he had to play it for somebody that very instant. Like a lot of young Americans, I was to spend a significant amount of energy over the next decade trying to ensure that I was nothing like the clueless Mr. Jones.

Over the next several years, a close and deep awareness of these rock albums became a cultural code for many baby boomers. A teenager could go to someone else's house and immediately feel a sense of kinship from looking at the record collection piled on the floor. I always thought it was an auspicious sign if there were blues albums alongside the rock and roll. And I could bond immediately with a stranger who quoted key Dylan lyrics intelligently.

The carefully detailed political position papers that radical groups labored over so strenuously paled in comparison to the visceral power of songs that made manifest shared political beliefs, songs like Dylan's "Only a Pawn in Their Game," about the murder of civil rights leader Medgar Evers, and Buffalo Springfield's "For What It's Worth," which described the ominous police presence at a protest march in Hollywood.

Rhythm and blues, gospel, and other kinds of black music had been intertwined with the civil rights movement since the late fifties. No one personifies the musical artist as activist more than Harry Belafonte, who in the fifties had been one of the biggest pop stars in the world as the result of such hits as "Jamaica Farewell," and that staple of sports arenas, "Banana Boat Song (Day-O)." Belafonte was also one of Martin Luther King Jr.'s closest advisors.

Belafonte recalls that on the night of Dr. King's historic march from Selma to Montgomery he asked for a concentration of artists in Selma to "lift the spirit of the troops." Mike Nichols, Elaine May, Billy Eckstine, Leonard Bernstein, and Sammy Davis Jr., among others, joined Belafonte for the event, which took place on the grounds of St. Jude's Catholic School, "the only place in Selma we could rely on to be safe." Belafonte told me, "Because the ground was rain soaked we made a stage out of eighty empty coffins. Artists stood and sang, and Dr. King gave a speech about the importance of culture—people were tired and wet as they waited for the push into Montgomery the next morning."

Aretha Franklin and others worked with Belafonte to support Dr King all over the country. At the 1963 March on Washington it was Belafonte who organized the entertainment that helped draw the crowd for King's "I Have a Dream" speech.

Because of the international contacts Belafonte had made in his travels as a performer, he was able to expand Dr. King's network at a crucial time when money was needed to keep the organization going and the first wave of American donors was tapped out as the result of unrefunded bail money. Many of Dr. King's advisors counseled against taking the civil rights struggle out of the country, including King's influential father, Martin Luther King Sr. "Daddy King was upset," Belafonte recalls. "The argument was that it was a mistake to put our dirty laundry out in public." Dr. King ultimately took Belafonte's advice and authorized the singer to stage an event at the American Church in Paris. When the U.S. State Department pressured the church to withdraw sponsorship, Belafonte flew to Europe and organized a private event with help from European actors Peter O'Toole, Simone Signoret, Yves Montand, and Melina Mercouri, as well as leaders of the French labor movement. The result was a sold-out event at the Palais du Sport, the city's biggest arena. Shortly thereafter he organized a similar event in Sweden with the king of Sweden as the event's chair. "That was before he got the Nobel Prize," says Belafonte. "It helped set him up for the prize. Artists did that."

These events not only raised money and raised the spirits of the "troops," they also raised the visibility of the civil rights movement, so that the moral message could be seen and heard by millions of whites who hadn't been paying attention. "We struggled to get attention in the civil rights movement," I was told by the Reverend Jesse Jackson. "When Harry brought down Tony Bennett and Marlon Brando and other entertainers, that's [when] the coverage of demonstrations started getting on the news."

At the same time, less overtly political artists such as Ray Charles appealed to Middle America and humanized the black experience to a depth previously unknown by many whites.

"People say that art is a reflection of reality, but the R&B of the late 1950s and early 1960s was really pushing society," Georgia congressman and civil rights hero John Lewis told NPR. "It was like a headlight, not a taillight, with the rest of society trying to catch up."

Black music crossed over to the young white audience, with the greatest impetus coming from Detroit's black-owned Motown Records. Under the leadership of Berry Gordy, Motown launched the careers of the Supremes, Smokey Robinson and the Miracles, and the Temptations, who turned out Top 40 hits and made repeated appearances on national TV shows such as *American Bandstand* and *The Ed Sullivan Show*. Berry Gordy was criticized by some political leaders for not involving his artists more overtly in civil rights marches. However, Motown released recordings of Martin Luther King's speeches and was the label that effectively integrated American musical culture.

Later in the sixties, many R&B artists became more politically outspoken, including Curtis Mayfield ("People Get Ready") and, most notably, Marvin Gaye, who wrote the compelling antiwar song "What's Goin' On" in honor of his brother's return from Vietnam.

Experimentation with psychedelic drugs was woven into the fabric of dozens of songs, like the Jefferson Airplane's "White Rabbit" and Jimi Hendrix's "Purple Haze." Later, George Harrison's discovery of meditation as a more profound alternative to drugs inspired me and millions of other rock fans. It is hard to imagine the subsequent birth of the New Age movement without the influence of rock musicians such as Harrison, John McLaughlin, and Carlos Santana.

Foreshadowing schisms that would haunt the political left for decades to come, many lefty folk music fans felt betrayed by Bob

Dylan's 1965 switch from acoustic folk to electric rock music, and his radical change from linear political anthems like "The Times They Are A-Changin'" to impressionistic and surreal personal songs such as "Like a Rolling Stone." I was young enough that I discovered and embraced his first half-dozen albums, folk and rock, political and personal, all at the same time. To me, the purists who didn't like the electric Dylan were left-wing versions of Mr. Jones.

During 1965–67, while I was in eleventh and twelfth grades, I was much more of a spectator than a participant in the sixties culture, but the would-be hippies I hung out with at the progressive Fieldston School in New York were an interesting and intense bunch. Among my best friends were Peter Kinoy and his sister Joanne, who were the children of noted civil rights lawyer Arthur Kinoy—his clients included Martin Luther King Jr. and Adam Clayton Powell. My best friend, Joel Goodman, was the nephew of counterculture icon Paul Goodman, whose book *Growing Up Absurd* was ubiquitous on college campuses. Joel and his older sister Rachel had recruited me to join them in protesting air-raid drills in 1962. Although we got into trouble, we noticed that the school stopped having the drills the following year.

Another friend was Gil Heron, later to become famous as the brilliant political songwriter and jazz/R&B/poetry artist Gil Scott-Heron. Even in high school, Gil had an uncanny ability to express himself and would come into class with intricate autobiographical short stories that dwarfed anything the rest of us could write, and he played the piano seemingly effortlessly while the rest of us were agonizing over our lessons. Another high school friend, Susan Solomon, married the drummer of Country Joe and the Fish, "Chicken" Hirsh. (Susan later married journalist Paul Goldberger.)

Much of the controversy about rap and rock music over the years has focused on the way teenagers process song lyrics. I certainly knew as a teenager that songs could carry powerful messages, but I can say definitively that my friends and I never took lyrics literally. The Rolling Stones' great song "Satisfaction," for example, would lead you to believe that Mick Jagger was not getting laid. Yet my friends and I assumed quite the opposite. We felt he was expressing a feeling from his past and telling his male fans that it was okay to be lonely and frustrated when you're young. If a rock god like Mick could have once felt that way, we could deal with our (hopefully) temporary lack of satisfaction as well.

More to the point, we understood lyrics impressionistically and metaphorically. I didn't know any daughters of royalty like the character in the Stones' "Play with Fire," and I certainly had no idea what the culture of "Knightsbridge" was. But I loved being able to sing along with the chorus, "Don't play with me cause you're playing with fire." His projection of strength compensated for my feeling of weakness.

On the other hand, I always was uncomfortable with Jagger's anti-female lyrics (we didn't know the word "misogynistic" in those days) in songs such as "Stupid Girl" and "Under My Thumb." I just tuned them out or skipped over them so I could focus on the songs I loved. I think teenagers, then and now, can appreciate the work of an artist without buying the whole package.

Deeply felt songs also give young people vivid insights into lives far different from theirs. I loved Woody Guthrie's song "Hard Travelin'" and Big Bill Broonzy's blues classic "If You're Black Get Back." As a comfortably middle-class white kid, I had nothing in common with the poverty and prejudice reflected in those songs, but through the alchemy of art, an emotional connection was made. I assume that today's middle-class kids, white and black, connect with the emotions of ghetto-inspired hip-hop in the same personal way.

Listeners interpret songs very subjectively. During the film *In the Name of the Father*, the Irish protagonist (played by Daniel Day-

Lewis) plays Bob Dylan's "Like a Rolling Stone" on the jukebox. As with many of Dylan's lyrics, the literal meaning of the words is a torrent of venom, in this case clearly aimed at a woman, a former lover. Yet the Lewis character's joy in the song is utterly unconnected to feelings about women—or to anger. The chorus, "How does it feel!!?" drives him to pump his arms in exhilaration. Somehow the fact that Bob Dylan can scream above his pain gives us the courage to feel we can overcome our own and rejoice in that recognition.

Even at this most political of times, explicit "message" songs like those of Phil Ochs or the early Bob Dylan were the exception. Poetic and musical expressions of angst were more common. A friend of mine interviewed that most politically earnest of sixties artists, Joan Baez, for his school newspaper, and she talked about how much she loved the Rolling Stones' angry impressionistic rant "19th Nervous Breakdown."

We all felt that the rock artists we followed were different from other people exposed in the mass media. Rockers, we imagined, were a lot like us. In San Francisco, local hippies freely mingled with the Grateful Dead and the Jefferson Airplane. My own brush with hippie immortality came one Saturday afternoon in high school. A few friends and I were sitting in sunny Central Park feeling very "summer of love" and playing a silly kissing game, when Joan Baez herself walked over with a boyfriend and hung out with us.

Her famous long brown hair had recently been cut to shoulder length, but that did nothing to diminish her stunning beauty, and fame had not spoiled her unpretentious nonchalance. She was not on a star trip, and it was strictly first names only. We were all simply enjoying a spring day together in the new world of the sixties.

I got a chaste kiss on the cheek from the queen of folk music before she sauntered away. My friends and I were all way too cool to make much of a big deal about it, but we shared quick delighted glances.

My academic career was a huge disappointment to me and my parents. I dropped out of the University of California in Berkeley after a single week in the fall of 1967. In the Bay Area, where I continued to live for a while after I dropped out, I befriended a group of Vietnam vets who had become druggies in Vietnam and had great connections for every sort of illegal substance. (One of the lies implicit in the cartoon version of the sixties is that hippies hated the guys who fought in Vietnam, which couldn't have been further from the truth. It was the politicians we blamed.) I had started smoking pot in my junior year of high school, begun taking LSD in earnest in my senior year, and in Berkeley and Oakland I did just about every other drug that existed at the time.

The first time I went to Winterland was also the first time I saw Janis Joplin perform, with her band Big Brother and the Holding Company. As I watched Joplin's passionate performance, a young woman in a diaphanous white dress with flowers in her long blond hair came walking through the audience and handed me a white tablet from a stash of free samples. It was "White Lightning" LSD, manufactured by the notorious Bay Area chemist Owsley, who had borrowed a marketing technique from the mainstream.

For a brief period, outward symbols such as long hair on males, the lack of brassieres on women, the peace sign and symbol, and energizing injections of hippie slang into meaningful conversation created a genuine sense of community. And then, it seemed, it was over almost before it had begun.

Quickly, the fashions and language became absorbed by the mainstream media, and charlatans, from cult con artists getting rich off converts to the murderer Charles Manson, exploited the very sense of trust that the outward symbols conveyed. Various forces, including the invasion of hard drugs and the inevitable process of aging, obliterated much of the complexity, vision, and sense of community that had inspired millions of young people.

The outward trappings of hippiedom quickly became just part of the cartoon, a caricature of pot-smoking airheads wearing bell-bottom trousers and love beads and using words like "man" and "dig" in place of coherent sentences. As the Vietnam era grew uglier in the late 1960s, particularly in the wake of the King and Robert Kennedy assassinations, the mainstream media focused on the tiny coterie of radicals who engaged in violence.

Films and novels about the period have generally failed to capture the communal spirit and the lively diversity that endures in the memories of many of us who were there. One of the few things that survived with its soul intact is the period's music.

To walk around the Bay Area in 1967–68 was to hear the same songs broadcast on the "underground" (but commercial) radio station KMPX-FM pouring out of every store and apartment. Rock music was a soundtrack for the lives of millions of people across America, and it proved a heartier cultural artifact than fashion, slang, or rhetoric. The power of the music has endured, especially the more obscure album cuts that haven't been overused as source music in movies or for TV commercials.

Many of us saw a glimmer of hope for a better world, and hearing the music brings back that feeling, not just for baby boomers but for younger people eager to recapture something they have read and heard about. I know I am not the only one who plays old records behind closed doors to get myself re-energized for the battles of day-to-day life.

For young people in the sixties, the feeling of connectedness and freedom was real and unforgettable, but for me and many others, a reliance on drugs began to sour the spirit of the times. One afternoon in the early spring of 1967, I went to the San Francisco airport to fly home and visit my parents. I was barefoot, as I often was in those days, and I was informed by the authorities that I could not board a plane without shoes. With the heady confidence of the era I looked around the airport and my eyes fell upon a young man with longish light brown hair who had that "sixties" look.

It turned out that he had just landed and was on his way home. After hearing my dilemma, he promptly offered me his shoes and gave me his address so I could mail them back. My exhilaration at having been protected by the hippie universe soon turned to mortification when I lost his address. I suspect that millions of such spaced-out incidents shortened the communal spirit of the sixties, and I still regret my inadvertent betrayal.

Nine months after having moved to Northern California, and six weeks before my eighteenth birthday, I was arrested in Berkeley on assorted possession charges after having asked policemen for directions while I was virtually nodding out on Seconals.

Back in New York, after the expensive lawyer my parents hired got me released into their custody, I attended group therapy sessions that convinced me that my attraction to drugs was self-destructive. Still inspired by rock and roll, I listened carefully to George Harrison's songs and began a long devotion to meditation and Eastern spirituality as an alternative to drugs.

Despite my new straightness, I had no interest in going back to college, which still felt alien to the rhythms beating in my head. I had an extremely high number in the selective service lottery, which meant I would never be drafted. In the fall of 1968, through an ad in the New York Times, I got a clerical job at Billboard, the music business trade magazine. It turned out that my job was in what was called the "chart department." Prior to my first day on the job I had no idea that there were "charts" showing which records had sold the best the previous week.

The first week that I called stores for information, one of the singles on the checklist was "Piece of My Heart" by Janis Joplin and Big Brother. I inserted several extra checkmarks next to the song. I liked to tell myself that the single went Top Ten because of my secret help.

I was transported the first time I saw an actual issue of *Billboard*, filled with color advertisements for albums, some by my favorite rock bands and some by country and western, R&B, or pop artists I'd never heard of. It hadn't previously occurred to me that rock and roll was part of a business. The idea that the business was big enough to justify putting out a thick color magazine blew my mind. (There were actually three weekly music trades at that time, the others being *Cashbox* and *Record World*.)

I quickly learned the names of all of the record companies and discovered that getting radio stations to play the records was the most important route to a hit. This, too, was news. My main sources for learning about new rock musicians had been my friends and the music sections of the *Village Voice* and *Rolling Stone*.

Radio stations around the country used the *Billboard* charts to choose which records to play, and many stores stocked records based on them. So the charts had a huge effect on sales. One afternoon, James Brown himself called to check the chart position on "Say It Loud, I'm Black and I'm Proud." It was number twenty with a bullet (moving up) on the pop chart that week.

What Brown really wanted to know was how well his song was doing with white "pop" audiences. It was already number one on the R&B charts.

Although black musicians were the prime force behind the creation of rock and roll, and Motown had made huge strides in merging pop and R&B, there were still a lot of racial barriers in the music business. There would not be a black president of a pop label until the 1980s. A few black musicians such as Jimi Hendrix and Sly Stone had substantial white audiences, but rock would remain dominated by white musicians until the late nineties, when rap conquered the predominantly white-male rock audience.

Every week at *Billboard*, the staff would listen to all of the new singles that were submitted for review and rate their hit potential. One of my assignments each week was to call the influential tip sheet editor Bill Gavin with the list of our predictions. Gavin was shocked when I told him we had picked "Give Peace a Chance" by the Plastic Ono Band as a future Top 20 hit.

"You're kidding," he said. "There are hardly any instruments on it, no one knows the name Plastic Ono Band, and as far as we can make out there is some bad language. Radio stations aren't going to play it."

Biting my lip and speaking as tactfully as I could, I explained that as important as radio was, the underground and rock press were also very influential. Beatles fans knew that it was a John Lennon record. His fans would accept the unorthodox production and the song was clearly about ending the war in Vietnam, a compelling topic to many young record buyers.

Gavin was correct that the powerful Top 40 radio stations, for the most part, wouldn't play "Give Peace a Chance." And I was right that it didn't matter. The single indeed went to the *Billboard* Top 20 and became one of Lennon's most famous records. And by then, in cities across America, innovative stations like WBCN in Boston were hiring young, hip DJs and letting them choose longer and less-publicized songs from albums by artists like Dylan and the Beatles. Within a few years, these album-oriented rock stations came to rival Top 40 stations for market dominance.

One of the fascinating things about working on the charts was that it seemed as if all of America were present. This was 1968, a year in which the country was famously divided on political and cultural issues. Yet through the prism of the record business, one could see pro-military country records, antiwar rock records, Christian music, R&B, classical, and jazz all coexisting. For the music business, America was one big record store.

I soon discovered that there was a job at record companies called "promo man" (they were all men in 1968). These guys, made semi-famous in 1965 when the Rolling Stones sang snidely about an "Under-Assistant West Coast Promo Man," didn't look anything like hippies. The older ones wore expensive suits and carried themselves like gangsters, and the younger ones had self-consciously styled longish hair and weird, pseudo-hip clothes that seemed to exist solely for their profession.

Shortly before Christmas 1968, Lew Selener, a promo man from Capitol Records, paid our department a visit. Lew, probably in his early thirties at the time, seemed far too old to me to "get" rock and roll, but there he was, sporting an early version of the blow-dried haircut, wearing an all-white jumpsuit, and handing me a free copy of the just-released and much-coveted Beatles *White Album*. I think my jaw literally dropped. A free Beatles album, exactly on the release date! Clearly, being in the music business wasn't a normal job. Thirty-three years later I still marvel at my good luck in stumbling into it.

Despite my joy at getting free records, I was too much of a hippie to fit into the promo world. I discovered that another section of the *Billboard* office housed music journalists, people who not only got free records and free tickets to concerts but actually got paid to review them. There was one writer on staff, Ed Ochs, who liked rock music and was reputed to have actually met the members of Steppenwolf.

The older editors avoided rock concerts in favor of nightclub performances, where they could get free drinks and dinner, and before long they assigned me to cover the rock shows that Ochs couldn't get to, including some at the Fillmore East auditorium and at rock clubs such as Unganos and Steve Paul's The Scene. One evening, while walking down the stairs at a club called Salvation, I

actually passed Jimi Hendrix, who was walking up the same stair-
case. "Hi," I mumbled. "Hi," he replied.

I felt as if I had stepped through the looking glass.

There have been countless arguments—and even books written—
about when innocence was lost in rock and roll. I can tell you for
certain that by the time I started at *Billboard* in 1968, rock music
was a business.

The communal group the Diggers had staged "The Death of
Hippie" in San Francisco in 1967 to blame the mass media for de-
stroying the intimacy of experimental culture in Haight-Ashbury.
Some rock purists went back a year and pointed a finger at the
Monterey Pop Festival, when Columbia Records president Clive
Davis signed Janis Joplin, and Mo Ostin of Warner Brothers signed
Jimi Hendrix. Others blamed Dylan and Joplin's manager, Albert
Grossman, for introducing high-pressure, big-bucks bargaining into
sixties rock, or Columbia Records for running much ridiculed print
ads headlined, "The Man Can't Bust Our Music." Some even went
back to the fifties and blamed Elvis's manager, the huckster Colonel
Tom Parker.

My own theory is that there was never pure innocence in rock
and roll. It was always about money and only sometimes about art.
John Lennon used to tell the early, poverty-stricken Beatles they
were going to the "toppermost of the poppermost." Jimi Hendrix
himself had the idea of playing guitar with his teeth to get attention. A volatile brew of art, spirituality, and commerce is built into
the genetic code of pop music and always has been, and the con-
tradictions exist not only in the guts of the business but in the
hearts of the audience and the souls of the artists as well.

Ten months after my first day at *Billboard*, I went to the 1969
Woodstock Festival in a limo commandeered by press agent Jane
Friedman. No one else on the magazine's staff had any interest in
going. Barely nineteen, I had a hotel room nearby and a backstage

pass to the climax of sixties rock. I wrote a long, starry-eyed review of Woodstock, and *Billboard* ran it on the front page. Although I was drug-free and gainfully employed, I was still deeply inspired by the communal spirit of the audience. Even though I was able to go backstage and gawk at Joe Cocker and Joan Baez, I was much more interested in roaming through the vast, unruly audience, exchanging smiles and cosmic one-liners with my fellow hippies.

While a lot of the counterculture had been developed as a result of shared enemies—parents, police, the government, people who just didn't like long hair—the spirit at Woodstock had almost nothing to do with any sense of antagonism toward the straight world. The townspeople, cops, and other "straights" were, in fact, quite pleasant and considerate to the invading horde of freaks, and the hippies, for the most part, were genuinely full of love and good feeling for the world outside, as well as for each other. We felt a sense of community in our musical tastes, clothes, and culture, but not to the exclusion of the rest of the world. The feeling is captured beautifully in Michael Wadleigh's feature film, *Woodstock*.

The spirit of mutual love and freedom emanating from upstate New York via TV news was just the sort of evidence of a cultural upheaval that terrified the Nixon administration and other parts of the political establishment, who fought back bitterly in that period.

Vice President Spiro T. Agnew became the first major national political figure of the period to attack rock and roll, castigating the Beatles for the allegedly pro-drug content of the lyrics to songs such as "Lucy in the Sky with Diamonds" and "With a Little Help from My Friends." The FBI, which had targeted all antiwar and civil rights groups under its now notorious COINTELPRO program, relentlessly investigated John Lennon, and the government attempted to deport him.

Paul Krassner reflects, "People who were rebelling were rebelling not just politically but spiritually and economically. They shared automobiles. They used a lot of candles instead of electricity. They didn't have insurance policies. They were becoming more tribal. They made their own clothing. They didn't get addicted to cosmetics. They got interested in Eastern religions of liberation rather than Western religions of control. They were a threat and I still would love to see whatever files there are. How the think tanks extrapolated the hippie lifestyle."

But not all of the destructive forces that attacked the counterculture came from establishment opposition. A few months after Woodstock, an ill-conceived deal with the Hells Angels to provide security for a rock festival in Altamont, California, headlined by the Rolling Stones, led to the stabbing death of a fan. By then, illegal drug use had degenerated from the daring experimentation of intellectuals such as Timothy Leary and Ken Kesey into widespread abuse of amphetamines, barbiturates, heroin, and that old standby, alcohol. Jimi Hendrix, Janis Joplin, and Jim Morrison all would soon kill themselves with drugs, all at the age of twenty-seven. Millions of less famous young people developed drug and alcohol problems.

The Black Panthers, whose organization began with legitimate complaints about police attitudes toward blacks in Oakland, California, and several of whose members were killed by police in various cities under suspicious circumstances, soon degenerated into a drug-dealing thuggish culture. And the Weatherman, a radical offshoot of the Students for a Democratic Society, were always a fringe group with a tiny following, but their violent actions darkened the image of the predominantly nonviolent antiwar movement.

"Their very name gave them away," Paul Krassner recalls, still amazed after all these years by the obtuseness of their choice. "They were trying to co-opt rock fans so they named themselves after a Dylan lyric—but they obviously never listened to the song. They took lyrics that said you don't need leaders and used it to declare *themselves* the leaders." (Dylan's "Subterranean Homesick Blues," which contains the line, "You don't need a weatherman to know which way the wind blows," later admonishes, "Don't follow leaders.")

Not long after returning from Woodstock, I switched to a competing trade magazine, *Record World*, where I wrote a weekly column. I met many rock critics of the time at an endless series of press parties and concerts. One of my first columns praised a concert by the MC-5, a raucous, politically left-wing Detroit band that I had seen in Queens. I soon got a phone call from Danny Fields, who had signed the band to a recording contract at Elektra and then had taken them with him to Atlantic Records. He had coined the phrase "company freak" to describe his role at Elektra as the liaison between the traditional executives and artists like the Doors and Judy Collins. Danny was later to discover and manage the Ramones.

Danny introduced me to Gloria Stavers, editor of *16 Magazine*, who had been one of Lenny Bruce's lovers and close friends with Jim Morrison. I also met Australian journalist Lillian Roxon, who had just written the *Rock Encyclopedia*, and club owner Steve Paul. These four elders—Danny, Gloria, Lillian, and Steve—became my mentors, as they did for other young New York rock writers, including Dave Marsh, Lisa Robinson, Nick Tosches, Richard Meltzer, Lenny Kaye, and Lester Bangs.

Because of Danny's blessing, I was welcomed in the back room of Max's Kansas City, a restaurant with a music stage upstairs. Max's was run by the curmudgeonly Mickey Ruskin and was originally a hangout for New York artists, many of whom paid their bar bills with paintings. Max's proximity to Andy Warhol's studio, the Factory, helped make it the nighttime home for an assortment of drag queens, poets, actors, and uptown celebrities looking for an edge.

The music people who were part of the Max's scene were mostly cynical, bitter, and possessed of an acute and ironic sense of the zeitgeist. Alice Cooper, David Bowie, Janis Joplin, Leonard Cohen, and many others spent hours trading one-liners with the backroom crowd. Max's was my entry point into the New York seventies rock scene, and it was there that I developed friendships with Patti Smith, members of the New York Dolls, and others.

The rock writer from our clique besides myself who would enter the high-octane commercial music business was Boston's Jon Landau. At the time, he was the most respected *Rolling Stone* writer and was soon promoted to editor of its highly influential record-review section. He later became the personal manager for Bruce Springsteen and Shania Twain, among others.

I wrote sporadically for *Rolling Stone*, the *Village Voice*, and *Crawdaddy*. During those years, I was one of about fifty New York writers who would go to editors and publishers and explain that we "understood" the new rock music because we had long hair and were the right age. Although I was a relatively low-level rock writer, I was nonetheless invited to significant events, like Bill Graham's legendary Thanksgiving dinners at the Fillmore East, where the guests sat at long tables on the Fillmore stage next to Graham favorites like members of the Jefferson Airplane.

I was still emotionally connected to aspects of the political agenda of the counterculture. In May 1970 I joined yet another antiwar march on Washington with Danny Fields. Danny knew writer Stu Werbin, one of the organizers of the event, so we were welcomed into the fenced-off backstage area. This was before the era of slickly produced plastic laminated backstage passes. If you got backstage, you stayed there.

I was astonished to see my hero Phil Ochs, who had walked out into the crowd, trying to convince one of the young antiwar-movement security guards to let him back into the stage area. I rushed over and yelled at the guard that Ochs was part of the program. The guard acquiesced immediately, since I was on the right side of the fence and had conviction in my voice. Ochs waved appreciatively.

It was to be my only face-to-face encounter with my hero.

In retrospect, I realize that the confrontation between Ochs—with his populist instincts and his expansive nature—and the insecure security guard, binding himself with ill-defined rules of turf and an arbitrary pecking order, was an ominous symbol of a sad but stubborn fact: Political activists don't always respect or understand artists, even politically committed artists. And the resulting failure to communicate has haunted progressive American politics since the sixties.

CHAPTER 2

The Sixties II

Culture vs. Politics

During the past few years, I have straddled the line between "the move-ment," and "the community," between "the left," and "the hip," between the world of "the street," and the world of "the media." I have doubts I can go on balancing these forces in my head much longer.
—Abbie Hoffman in *Woodstock Nation*, 1970

LONG AFTER BOB DYLAN went electric and the openly political songs of Phil Ochs and Tom Paxton were superseded by psychedelic rock, politically charged music could still ride high on the rock charts. In November 1969, the Jefferson Airplane released their most fiercely political album, *Volunteers*. ("Up against the wall, motherfucker!" they screamed at reactionaries in the song "Volunteers.")

The "supergroup" Crosby, Stills, Nash and Young created a pow-erful and hugely successful anthem and eulogy with "Ohio," re-leased within weeks of the killing of student antiwar protesters at Kent State University in 1970. The governor of Ohio vainly tried to ban airplay of the song in his state, claiming more violence would result from lyrics such as the dirge-like refrain, "Four dead in Ohio."

Graham Nash had a solo hit in 1971 with "Chicago," about the Chicago Eight conspiracy trial of Abbie Hoffman, Jerry Rubin, and other leaders of protests at the 1968 Democratic Convention. ("Is your brother bound and gagged?" Nash angrily asked, referring to the judge's actual treatment of defiant defendant Bobby Seale of the Black Panthers.)

Still, gulfs between left-of-center politics and the increasingly popular alternative culture kept yawning open. The political left had mixed feelings about the counterculture from the beginning, and those doubts and tensions led to the cultural/political fragmentation that drives me crazy today.

The person who most successfully walked the tightrope between the doctrinaire political left and the chaotic, exploding baby boomer culture was Abbie Hoffman, who had a brilliant sense of how to use the mass media. But even Abbie occasionally stumbled, most famously at the Woodstock Festival. Tripping on acid, he made the mistake of grabbing the microphone during a set by the defiantly antiestablishment British rock band the Who.

Hoffman began lecturing the crowd about the imprisonment of John Sinclair, and guitarist Pete Townshend literally kicked him off the stage. Years later, in a *Rolling Stone* interview, Townshend said that he felt in retrospect that Hoffman had been right to try to focus the crowd on a political agenda, but another opportunity for détente had been lost.

The conflict goes back practically to the beginnings of the sixties counterculture. An early battle came in the San Francisco Bay Area in the fall of 1966, while I was still in high school back in New York reading the *Realist* and listening to Bob Dylan. Thirty-six years later I discussed what happened with three of my elders: Allen Ginsberg, Paul Krassner, and Berkeley leftist Michael Lerner.

Ginsberg, Timothy Leary, the Diggers, and others planned a "be-in" in Golden Gate Park to celebrate the burgeoning counterculture. The phrase "be-in" echoed "sit-in" and "teach-in," con-frontational tactics used by civil rights and antiwar groups. But the full name of the event—"Gathering of the Tribes for a Human Be-In"—hardly suggested a confrontation.

Assuming that any large coming-together of longhairs had a po-litical subtext, a group of Berkeley political radicals, including Lerner, his roommate Jerry Rubin, and a friend named Stew Al-bert, set up a meeting with the San Francisco hippies. Also at the meeting were members of the Jefferson Airplane and Country Joe and the Fish.

One of Lerner's political cohorts asked the hippies, "What are the demands going to be?" The response was laughter. "Demands" were made at demonstrations—this was going to be a be-in, a gath-ering. Michael Lerner still burned with frustration as he recalled what he sees to this day as a missed opportunity:

"Jerry Rubin, Stew Albert, and I were hoping to build a mutually respectful alliance between the counterculture and the political an-tiwar movement . . . with the hopes of creating a be-in like our teach-ins, including not only politics but also the spirit of the coun-terculture. We were perfectly prepared to have music be the major part of the day, but we also wanted to have political content artic-ulated and taught. The musicians and their friends acted as though we were crazy to want that. They said, 'Hey, man, this is a gather-ing of the tribes.' And we said, 'Well, our tribe likes to communi-cate not only with music but also with words.' But . . . the countercultural people could not imagine any sharing of the space. It was to be music and nothing else."

In fact, both the Jefferson Airplane and Country Joe were in-tensely political in other contexts. I don't think the rock and hippie culture ever wanted to control political debate. They simply insisted on not being dictated to by lefty politicians at what were essentially musical and cultural events. They were not going to toe a party

line, or have the poetic spirit of cultural events transformed into
political rallies.

The Human Be In drew 20,000 people, a huge number for a
counterculture festival at the time, and featured music by the Airplane, the Grateful Dead, and the Quicksilver Messenger Service,
and poetry from Allen Ginsberg, Gary Snyder, and Lenore Kandel.
Krassner recalls, "Ed Sanders and his sense of theater greatly propelled such events."

Jerry Rubin was one of the few political radicals who spoke. In *A
Long Strange Trip*, a history of the Grateful Dead, Dennis McNally
says that Jerry Garcia was completely turned off by the anger in Rubin's speech. From that point on, the Dead were studiously apoliti-
cal in their songs, although they would perform at many benefit
concerts for progressive causes over the years.

One year later, Hoffman, Rubin, Krassner, and a few others
formed the so-called Youth International Party—the Yippies. The
immediate goal was to inject some creative countercultural fervor
and a pointed sense of the absurd into the deadly serious protests
planned by left-wing political groups for the 1968 Democratic National Convention in Chicago. Jerry Rubin, formerly a conventional
left-wing politician who had actually run for mayor of Berkeley, had
become a self-appointed spokesman for the very hippie culture he
had once thought lacked seriousness.

In the aftermath of the madness of the 1968 convention, both
inside the hall and outside in the streets, many liberal Democrats
blamed the Yippies for creating the sense that the party was unable
to control the chaos in its midst. And that sense of chaos, they
maintained, led to Richard Nixon's narrow victory over Democratic candidate Hubert Humphrey.

After Chicago, Rubin and especially Hoffman became the best-
known opponents of the Vietnam War. With the timing of a Las
Vegas stand-up comic and an intuitive understanding of mass me-

dia unrivaled at the time, Hoffman was completely at home in the hippie culture. He was among the Yippies who created media theater with a sharp political edge through events such as throwing dollar bills onto the floor of the New York Stock Exchange.

In 1970, A.J. Weberman convinced various New York political radicals including, sad to say, Abbie Hoffman to picket Bob Dylan's house on MacDougal Street in Greenwich Village on the occasion of Dylan's thirtieth birthday. The pickets demanded that Dylan resume writing "political" songs instead of "personal" ones like those on his then-current album *Nashville Skyline*. Dylan was in Israel at the time and his creative dynamic proceeded according to his own internal rhythms, presumably unaffected by the protesters, who looked like idiots to the very constituency they wanted to "educate." Ultimately, the radical left pushed the culture away, not the other way around. Hoffman later expressed regret for the Dylan picketing.

Hoffman wistfully hoped that the trial of the Chicago Eight would open a dialogue between hippies and radicals, and he arranged for Judy Collins and Allen Ginsberg to testify.

Rubin and Hoffman understood television better than anyone on the left. "You can't be a revolutionary today without a TV set," Rubin wrote in his book *Do It*. "It's as important as a gun. I never understand the radical who comes on TV in a suit and tie. Turn off the sound and he could be mayor. The words may be radical but . . . television is a nonverbal instrument. The way to understand TV is to shut off the sound. No one remembers any words they hear; the mind is a Technicolor movie of images, not words."

For all of the foibles and limitations of the Yippies—and at times the loose-knit organization seemed little more than a PR umbrella for the activities of its founders—they were unique among their peers in figuring out how to actually communicate with and move a mass constituency. Their efforts were a major factor in bringing hundreds of thousands of Americans into the streets to oppose the Vietnam War, a level of protest against a war Americans were fighting unheard of in our history.

By 1971, at the advanced age of twenty-one, I was already slightly older than the core audience for rock music. As managing editor of *Circus* magazine, I decided to embrace the next generation by being the first editor to put the newly popular Grand Funk Railroad and Alice Cooper on the cover. A few of the more intellectual critics excoriated me for the Grand Funk cover, but I was convinced that to remain relevant we had to stay open-minded about what younger kids liked. This philosophy formed the basis of the rest of my career, and has also informed much of my criticism of the political left.

Aging is apparently not a problem for the best rock critics, as writers such as Robert Christgau, Jon Pareles, and Robert Hilburn have proven with their brilliant, up-to-date writing over the past thirty years. I, however, had another problem that doomed my career as a journalist. I hate to criticize musicians. As someone who had never learned to play the guitar, I tended to put musicians on a pedestal and felt guilty when I gave them too hard a time. At *Billboard* I had reviewed a concert by the Rascals and included a line dismissive of the guitar playing of Gene Cornish, while lauding the band's star vocalists Eddie Brigati and Felix Cavaliere. I was mortified when Cornish called me and complained.

I was in my early twenties and mainly interested in having a good time. I went through four jobs over the course of eighteen months, including one with Albert Grossman's music publishing company. I idolized Grossman, who worked with great artists and combined his status as a wealthy businessman with a knowing embrace of hippie culture. I got closer to him in later years, but this time around I had only a few brief audiences with him. One day, though, Janis Joplin came into the office and I got to shake hands with her. "I work here," I said nervously. "So do I," she wearily replied.

I found a cabinet in Grossman's office with pristine copies of the legendary and then-unreleased "basement tapes" of Dylan and the Band and made copies for a few of my friends, including Patti Smith, who was then a clerk at Scribner's bookstore. Copies of the basement tapes had already started circulating, but they were hard enough to get that they still had some cachet.

Patti reciprocated by stealing me a copy of the *I Ching*. Soon thereafter I was able to get Patti a job at a minor publication called *Rock* magazine, which is where she was first published, before launching her extraordinary career as a poet and rock singer.

Finally cutting the cord with rock journalism, I got a job as director of publicity for a collection of labels called the Famous Music Group. The highlight of my time at Famous was publicizing an album by the band Detroit. It starred Mitch Ryder, a great singer and an authentic rock and roll madman best known for his performance of "Devil with a Blue Dress On."

Detroit's manager was John Sinclair, who had been the leader of the White Panthers, a radical left-wing group in Michigan around which the MC-5 developed. In late 1969, Sinclair had been arrested for possession of two marijuana cigarettes and given a ten-year jail sentence. The injustice spawned a protest movement and a concert and rally in late 1971. Allen Ginsberg read, and John Lennon and Yoko Ono wrote and performed a song that began, "It ain't fair, John Sinclair, ten for two for smoking air."

Four days later, helped by the publicity, Sinclair was released. Fresh out of jail, Sinclair took awhile to come to grips with the rapid mainstream assimilation of previously underground symbols. He naïvely told me he was optimistic that America would change radically because so many more people now had long hair.

Other Famous Music releases I worked on included Melanie's

biggest hit, "Brand New Key," and Billy Joel's first album, *Cold Spring Harbor*, but my primary contribution to innovative rock culture during this period was to introduce our head of A&R (Artists and Repertoire) Marty Thau to the seminal music of the New York Dolls. Marty went on to become their manager and a significant figure in early New York punk rock music.

At this stage of my life, I was ill-suited for the corporate world. Constantly restless and reckless, I was shown the door at Famous Music after a year. I occasionally sold a freelance piece to the *Village Voice* or *Rolling Stone*, but I was unemployed for several months and really depressed.

Then Gloria Stavers turned me on to a radio lecture by Baba Ram Dass, and later introduced me to him. Ram Dass, who had previously been Richard Alpert, Tim Leary's LSD cohort, had turned to Eastern spirituality. Through him I met a nonsectarian yogini named Hilda Charlton. I began attending her weekly meditations, which, among their many virtues, focused me more seriously on work.

In 1973, I was hired by Lee Solters, the venerable Broadway press agent whose clients included Frank Sinatra, Barbra Streisand, and the Ringling Brothers, Barnum and Bailey Circus. My job was to be the longhaired guy who could communicate with rock bands and the writers who covered them.

Solters taught me a crucial lesson in PR. I had thought that my job was to use relationships with writers to get coverage for our clients. He correctly explained that this approach limited the results: How many favors could a writer do for even his closest friend? The key, he explained, was to give the writers a good story.

One of the first clients I was assigned was jazz saxophonist Stan Getz, who was between records and had an engagement coming up at the Rainbow Grille. Getz was a shy man who would rather play Ping-Pong than discuss PR angles. I told Lee that there just wasn't anything interesting about the guy except that he had a birthday coming up. Pulling a classic PR chestnut out of his hat, Lee told me to contrive a birthday party for him. We got a few of his friends to agree to come, and one afternoon at the Rainbow Grille Stan Getz's birthday was observed by jazz legends Zoot Sims and Dizzy Gillespie; Louis Armstrong's widow, Lucille; Stan, his wife, his high school band teacher, me . . . and four TV news cameras! The lesson—create a good story and you don't need a favor—has helped me ever since, and has important relevance to politics as well as music.

I was able to convince Steve Paul to give us his clients Johnny Winter and the Edgar Winter Group. And I got a huge break when Led Zeppelin became a client of Solters.

Lee knew they were big, but he hated their music, so he had me accompany him to Paris, where he signed them. The group's stars, singer Robert Plant and guitarist Jimmy Page, were fascinated by the American hippie era and liked that I was a little younger than them and had long hair but could still communicate with people in suits. Working with Led Zeppelin would be the turning point in my career.

By 1973, the conventional wisdom on George McGovern's landslide defeat by Nixon the year before had been set in concrete—McGovern lost because of the sixties, including the highly visible support he got from feminists, left-liberal movie stars, and even Yippies.

It's easy to forget that the Democrats staged a stunningly inept campaign, beginning with the fiasco over vice presidential candidate Thomas Eagleton, who hastily withdrew from the ticket after it had been revealed that he had received electroshock therapy for depression, not the greatest way to launch a campaign. Of course, McGovern was running against a still relatively popular incumbent. And the Nixon campaign, we learned later, wasn't playing by the rules. The Watergate scandal, which brought Nixon down less than two years later, originated in a burglary of McGovern's campaign manager's office.

In any event, as CNN's William Schneider has told me more than once, the Democrats have never gotten over their misinterpretation of McGovern's defeat. Schneider recently reminded me of the Nixon campaign's caricature of McGovern's platform: "Acid, amnesty, and abortion." Yet a year after that election, abortion became legal, a decision supported by a majority of the American people, and a few years after that President Carter granted amnesty to Vietnam draft evaders, a move applauded by most Americans. And the earnest George McGovern, a decorated Air Force pilot, the son of a Methodist minister, was about as far from an acidhead as you could get. So what explains the intensity of the mainstream Democrats' reaction against "the sixties"?

"The sixties," explains Tom Hayden, "didn't produce any lasting figures or institutions to carry the banner, to carry the flame, and to keep the soul of the sixties alive. It was too anarchistic for that." Into the vacuum, Hayden says, stepped "Democrats who got involved with politics in the early seventies and had no background at all in the civil rights movement or the Vietnam protest movement.

"There was a quest for power by the people who came out of the sixties but were not of the sixties," he told me. "They opened the door to the black middle class. And to women. And they withdrew from the embarrassing exposure in Vietnam. They gave the eighteen-year-old the vote. So they created a niche for working within a reformed system. Which gave people who had been on the outside a lot of mileage for a while . . . It led to McGovern, it led to Carter, it led to environmental laws being passed in the eighties. But these Democrats ran out of steam because there was no longer a culture behind them."

The new Democrats were scared of sixties culture, even though much of it had been embraced by a wide cross section of American society. And conservatives helped widen the gulf by intimidating Democrats into distancing themselves from a huge chunk of their natural base. Millions of people who were inspired by the nexus of politics and culture in the sixties, members of the so-called Woodstock Generation, people like me, would increasingly find themselves without a political home.

CHAPTER 3

The Real Seventies Show

Those memories come back to haunt me,
They haunt me like a curse.
Is a dream a lie if it don't come true,
Or is it something worse?
—Bruce Springsteen, "The River"

T HE VIETNAM WAR officially ended in 1973. In August of 1974, Richard Nixon was driven from office by the Watergate scandal. The sixties were over.

Nixon was replaced in the White House by Vice President Gerald Ford. As a Republican congressman and speaker of the House, Ford had been a true-blue conservative, supporting Barry Goldwater and urging the impeachment of Chief Justice Earl Warren, a perennial right-wing target. Ford had ascended to the vice presidency in 1973 after the archenemy of sixties pop culture, Spiro Agnew, resigned as a result of his own scandal due to alleged financial improprieties during his time as governor of Maryland.

However, in his half term as president, Ford was an affable moderate, and his administration was culturally neutral. Ford's son Jack and daughter Susan liked rock and roll. When I read in *People* magazine that Susan Ford's favorite band was Led Zeppelin, I contacted White House photographer David Kennerly, who was also a friend of the Ford family, to see if the Fords wanted Zeppelin to visit. The visit never worked out, but the fact that I could have a normal conversation about such a thing with someone in a Republican administration was a radical change from the embattled atmosphere between the White House and the world of popular culture during the Johnson and Nixon administrations.

Most significant, Betty Ford was like a sea change from the previous First Ladies, Pat Nixon and Lady Bird Johnson. Betty Ford would talk openly about her own past drug abuse and made it clear that she had not lectured her kids about avoiding premarital sex.

Some of the dreams of the sixties were coming true. In 1973, the Supreme Court legalized abortion in the *Roe v. Wade* decision, and another Supreme Court decision aimed at rolling back free speech had unintended consequences. Warren Burger, Nixon's replacement for Earl Warren as chief justice, wrote the majority opinion in the *Miller* decision, which held that "obscene" speech had no First Amendment protection. But the ruling allowed local "contemporary community standards" to be one of the tests of prosecutable obscenity.

The *Miller* decision was an invitation for local prosecutors to roll back liberal court decisions that went back to the mid-1950s and had opened the door to widespread use of profane and obscene language and frank sexuality.

In 1956, newly appointed Supreme Court Justice William J. Brennan had written in the *Roth* pornography case that literature, art, and ideas "having even the slightest redeeming social importance—unorthodox ideas, controversial ideas, even ideas hateful to the prevailing climate of public opinion" were protected by the First Amendment.

Allen Ginsberg's "Howl" provided the first major test of the new standard. The "Howl" obscenity trial in 1957 produced this classic exchange between metaphorically challenged prosecutor Ralph McIntosh and literary critic Mark Schorer:

MCINTOSH: You understand what "angelheaded hipsters burning for the ancient heavenly connection to the starry dynamo in the machinery of night" means?

SCHORER: Sir, you can't translate poetry into prose. That's why it's poetry.

MCINTOSH: In other words, you don't have to understand the words.

SCHORER: You don't understand the individual words taken out of their context. You can no more translate it back into logical prose English than you can say what a surrealistic painting means in words because it's *not* prose. I can't possibly translate, nor, I am sure, can anyone in this room translate the opening part of this poem into rational prose.

Judge Clayton Horn, who taught a Bible class in Sunday school, dismissed the case. He cited Brennan's doctrine, writing that, "Unless the book is entirely lacking in 'social importance' it cannot be held obscene." Ginsberg had used words like "fuck," "cock," "ass," and "cunt," Horn stated, because "he believed that his portrayal required them as being in character . . . An author should be real in treating his subject and be allowed to express his thoughts and ideas in his own words."

Allen Ginsberg was one of the few heroes of the Beat Generation of the fifties who remained a significant figure in the counterculture, not just into the sixties but until his death in 1997. In his last years, Ginsberg told me of a maddening conversation he had in the mid-nineties with Federal Communications Commissioner James Quello, who might have benefited from going back and reading Judge Horn's decision.

"'Howl' is a very good poem," said Quello. "If only you could change a few of the words, I wouldn't have any objection to it being broadcast."

Despite Chief Justice Burger's worst intentions, local prosecutors across the country reacted to the *Miller* decision by apparently deciding that voters in their communities didn't want a rollback in free speech. The effect was to lock in a level of legal free speech in the arts that would have been unthinkable even a decade earlier.

The loosening of restrictions on profanity also received unlikely and inadvertent help from President Nixon. The Watergate-related release of Nixon's taped White House conversations showed that behind closed doors the president had cursed incessantly, so much so that almost every sentence in the edited mainstream press version of the transcripts seemed to contain the phrase "expletive deleted."

The seventies climate of freedom and plain speaking produced a golden age in American movies as directors such as Martin Scorsese, Robert Altman, Hal Ashby, Michael Cimino, and Francis Ford Coppola reinvented the motion picture with more realistic portrayals of sex and violence. Their works were quickly accepted by worldwide audiences.

The war in Vietnam was reimagined via Ashby's *Coming Home*, Cimino's *The Deer Hunter*, and Coppola's *Apocalypse Now*. All three films, and others to come, focused on the humanity and pain of veterans and led to greater empathy and understanding between the vets, their families, and the American people, particularly those who had opposed the war. More populist entertainment also embraced free speech, as tough guys Clint Eastwood and Charles Bronson, among others, appeared in hit movies featuring new levels of violence, profanity, and sexual frankness.

In comedy, the brilliant social satirist Richard Pryor and hundreds of comedy club followers used the freedom Lenny Bruce had fought and died for—Bruce's all-consuming legal battles left him broke and in despair, contributing to his death in 1966, but shortly afterward a federal court decision on one of his appeals extended First Amendment rights to the performing arts.

On television, *Saturday Night Live* debuted in 1975 and began a tradition of satirizing American presidents, starting with Chevy Chase's slapstick version of Gerald Ford constantly slipping and falling down. Ford's press secretary Ron Nessen, embracing the zeitgeist, appeared on the show as a guest host.

The most important cultural catalyst of the seventies was TV producer Norman Lear. His *All in the Family* and *Maude* took sixties civil rights and feminist ideas and popularized them for tens of millions of people who had never attended a teach-in. During most of the seventies, *All in the Family* was the most-watched TV show in the United States, and *Maude* was regularly in the top ten.

Democrats were resurgent in Congress in 1974, winning a huge majority with "Watergate baby" candidates. Although, as Tom Hayden pointed out, these Democrats were for the most part beneficiaries of the feminist, civil rights, environmental, and antiwar movements, rather than participants, they were elected in a climate where such movements were part of the Democratic coalition, and a number of antidiscrimination and environmental laws were soon passed.

In 1976, Jimmy Carter, the governor of Georgia, emerged as a surprise winner in several Democratic primaries, defeating such Washington stalwarts as Hubert Humphrey, Henry "Scoop" Jackson, and George McGovern. Carter shrewdly positioned himself as a political outsider and made conscious efforts to reach out to the counterculture. One of Carter's earliest supporters in the media was Hunter S. Thompson, "gonzo" writer for *Rolling Stone*, who reported approvingly that Carter's standard stump speech included a Bob Dylan quote: "He not busy being born is busy dying."

Twenty years later, when both Bill Clinton and Al Gore used the same Dylan quote, it had the hollow ring of a well-worn cliché. But in 1976 it was unheard of and exciting for a presidential candidate to quote Dylan. Carter corresponded with Thompson and gave him access to his campaign at a time when conventional Democratic campaign managers considered *Rolling Stone* irrelevant compared to "serious" journalism. Carter and his advisors knew the magazine reached a huge audience of younger voters.

Short of money in the early stages of the primaries, Governor Carter turned to the rock and roll business in Georgia, specifically to Phil Walden, owner and president of Capricorn Records, which at the time was riding high with the Southern rock of the Allman Brothers and other bands. Walden had been Otis Redding's manager and was passionate about civil rights. He saw Carter as the paradigm of an enlightened Southerner. When I managed the Allman Brothers in the late 1980s, they proudly told me of their role in getting Carter to the White House.

I had wondered whether or not the Allmans exaggerated their early value to Carter until the mid-nineties, when, as president of Mercury Records, I made a deal with Phil Walden to distribute his Capricorn label, and he arranged for Jimmy and Rosalynn Carter to have dinner with my wife Rosemary and me.

"I never could have gotten elected if it weren't for Phil Walden," the former president recalled with pride. "The concerts that the Capricorn artists did for us in the early primaries kept us going. Otherwise we would have been completely out of money." Twenty years later Carter's eyes still lit up when he talked about the Allman Brothers, remembering with delight not just their help in raising money and attracting supporters, but their extraordinary Southern blues-rock musical chemistry.

The term "yuppie" was coined by the media sometime in the eighties, apparently an acronym of young, upwardly mobile, and professional. The word became a catchall to describe former hippies who rechanneled all their energy into making money and living elegantly hip lives.

Yippie cofounder Jerry Rubin tried to institutionalize the phenomenon by staging "salons" at which ambitious people could "network." Rubin sought me out to participate in music-business salons. I found Rubin a lovable rogue but never could relate to his endeavors, which seemed contrived. I didn't think you had to deny your political beliefs to be able to focus on a career, so while I enjoyed Rubin's occasional company, I stayed away from his events.

The 1983 film *The Big Chill*, written and directed by Lawrence Kasdan, captured (and helped mold) conventional wisdom about so-called yuppies. *The Big Chill* is a very well-written and acted ensemble comedy/drama about seven college friends from the sixties who are reunited fifteen years later for the funeral of a friend who has committed suicide. The movie leans heavily on music as shorthand for a sense of community. Motown songs are played repeatedly, and the Kevin Kline character boasts that he only listens to music from the sixties. In a crucial early scene, the JoBeth Williams character plays the Rolling Stones' "You Can't Always Get What You Want" on a church organ, evoking smiles of recognition and sixties camaraderie from the other main characters.

The Big Chill became a big hit and helped establish a cartoon version of yuppies with its extremely cynical take on sixties activists. Sam, a former campus radical leader played by Tom Berenger, now made millions as an actor starring in a cheesy TV action show, and most of the other characters had drifted far from the political commitment of their college days.

I actually wish that some radical activists from the sixties had become TV stars, but most of them entered academia and remained committed to causes like civil rights and feminism, largely out of the glare of publicity. Few of them actually turned into yuppies.

I never fit the yuppie stereotype of caring about the vintage of wine or the provenance of cheese, nor did I change my political views, but I did focus my energy on my career after I began working for Lee Solters. My focus became crystallized when I started representing Led Zeppelin.

They were about to become the biggest rock band in the world, and I eagerly threw myself into their tours, starting in 1973. Led Zeppelin's live shows were the most intense of their time, highlighting lead singer Robert Plant's screeching high vocals, guitar hero Jimmy Page's Hendrix-like pyrotechnics, and virtuoso drummer John Bonham, who did the loudest, longest drum solos in rock and roll, and who became the role model for several generations of hard rock drummers. In their recordings, Led Zeppelin would alternate sexually blatant hard-rock shouts with sensitive, impressionistic, mystical numbers like "Stairway to Heaven," which for over twenty years has been the most requested song on rock radio stations around the world.

Like Grand Funk, Zeppelin was disdained by snobbish rock critics for whom all creativity had stopped in 1969. To publicize the band, I followed the Solters formula of finding good stories; for example, issuing press releases that stressed Led Zeppelin's impressive statistical accomplishments—they had even broken some Beatles attendance records. Eschewing *Rolling Stone*, I made sure the band did interviews with the less trendy and thus more receptive music writers from daily newspapers around the country.

In LA, I hooked them up with a fifteen-year-old journalistic prodigy that the *LA Times* had begun using, Cameron Crowe. I was in a suite with Cameron and Zeppelin singer Robert Plant at the Ambassador Hotel in Chicago when Robert said to him, "I am a golden god," which Cameron later ascribed to a character in his wonderful cinematic memoir of the early seventies, *Almost Famous*.

The next year, Zeppelin hired me as vice president of their

record label, Swan Song. Peter Grant, Led Zeppelin's manager, was a hulking Cockney 300-pound ex-wrestler, but he was also one of the great geniuses of the music business at that time. Coarse, profane, and physically intimidating, Peter cared only about keeping his clients happy and successful. When Peter started as a manager, concert promoters got 50 percent of the gross profits of a show. Peter invented the concept of the "90/10 deal," with the artist keeping 90 percent. Many of the most successful British managers and performers of the time, including Queen and the Rolling Stones, would ask Peter for advice on how to deal with promoters and record companies.

One evening, Peter Grant took me aside during a Zeppelin stadium concert and excitedly pointed to cars streaming down a freeway, zooming off into the night oblivious to the concert. "In here," said Peter, "50,000 people are having the time of their lives, and out there those people in their cars don't have any idea what's going on here." I told that story later to Stephen Davis, who wrote the brilliant and definitive (albeit "unauthorized") Led Zeppelin biography, the best-selling *Hammer of the Gods*. Stephen misinterpreted the story, taking Peter's gesture as a command for me to make Zeppelin famous to all those "straight" people.

In fact, Peter was not separating the world into *us* and *them* in any judgmental sense—he was not waving a flag in a culture war—he was marveling at the disparity of cultures coexisting in one geographical spot, dazzled by the diversity of human enthusiasms and the sheer bigness of America. Even 50,000 concert fans were a subculture.

The Swan Song job required me to travel all over the United States. Whereas movies are promoted via massive advertising campaigns and press junkets organized by a central office in Los Angeles, most records are promoted in a decentralized manner defined by the radius of a radio station's signal. Zeppelin fans were as intense and plentiful in Salt Lake City or Tampa or Detroit as they were in New York or Los Angeles. Direct experience with so much of the country came in handy years later, when people in Washington accused those of us in the music business of being "elitists." We were quite the opposite, and could demonstrate it.

In addition to the power of artists, I also learned about the power of the public. Our first release on Swan Song was by a Scottish singer named Maggie Bell. At the peak of my PR abilities and with Zeppelin in my back pocket, I got her enormous press coverage, including features in both *Time* and *Newsweek*, unheard of for a new artist. We also got her on the music TV shows of the time, and Atlantic Records (Swan Song's partner and distributor) made sure that important radio stations played her music. Peter Grant used his favors in the concert business to showcase her in front of ideal rock audiences. The public didn't buy it.

The next artist we put out, Bad Company, exploded instantly because of their hit song "Can't Get Enough of Your Love." Same business team, same kind of promotion, radically different results. Bad Company's debut album went to number one.

The third group we released was actually Led Zeppelin's favorite, The Pretty Things. Zeppelin personally introduced them to the rock press at several parties, and they too got all the promotional clout of a major label. Their records bombed.

Many of my rock critic friends were experiencing the same sense of limitation. The New York Dolls and MC-5 could not have been more beloved by critics but had limited public appeal. "The Dolls were the best band any of us had ever seen," said music journalist Dave Marsh, "and when they didn't conquer the world, it was very confusing."

It wasn't that critics were always wrong. Another press favorite, David Bowie, became a huge phenomenon. But the lesson was clear, and I had to internalize it quickly: The public itself created stars. The music professionals and the artists could lengthen or shorten the odds, but the business was ultimately driven by an elusive connection between artists and their music and millions of people whose names they would never know. It was great to fight for music I loved, but I realized that to be successful meant also respecting the mysteries of the marketplace.

I left Swan Song in 1976. I wanted to be a manager like Peter Grant, but clients were hard to come by, and the one I was most involved with, Mink Deville, was a critical darling but didn't generate much money. I was, however, in demand as a publicist, so I started Danny Goldberg Inc., a PR firm that represented KISS, Electric Light Orchestra (ELO), and Todd Rundgren, among others.

One of my clients was Bearsville Records, owned by Paul Fishkin and my ex-boss Albert Grossman. Albert recommended me as a PR person for a new film Bob Dylan was working on. A few weeks later I entered my idol's house in Malibu and together we watched the full length of his legendary four-and-a-half-hour surreal autobiographical documentary *Renaldo and Clara*. Dylan commented on it as it went by on the editing machine.

Sitting next to Dylan that afternoon, listening to him free-associate about movies, obscure folk singers, the music press, and his own mythology, satisfied some deep yearning I'd been harboring since high school. Soon thereafter, Dylan decided he didn't want a press agent for the project after all, but my inner teenager has been forever grateful for the time spent with him.

Of course, an afternoon with Bob Dylan was not the usual run of business. I spent a lot of my time contriving photo-ops, combining clients with other celebrities. For instance, although the Electric Light Orchestra was led by a shy genius named Jeff Lynne who would have been happy with no publicity, ELO's manager Don Arden was of the British tough-guy school, and he coveted the limelight. I satisfied Don by staging a party at the disco Regine's following an ELO concert and got former heavyweight champion Joe Frazier to attend.

When a photo from the Regine's party ran in *Billboard*, I was assured several more months of fees, but I had a sinking feeling that I'd become a schlock cliché. One writer for a New York newspaper who liked to drink more than he liked to write would put just about anything in his column as long as I wrote it out in his style word for word. I was afraid that doing PR was making me a little cynical. Thus, I was excited when I was drawn into political activism by one of my clients, John Hall, who had written songs for Janis Joplin and Bonnie Raitt and whose group Orleans had a couple of big hits, "Still the One" and "Dance with Me."

Not long after his first daughter was born, Hall read that a nuclear power plant was going to be constructed near his home in Saugerties, New York. John had been a physics major in college and was worried about the health consequences of the plant. He was convinced that cancer risks were greatly increased by nuclear power and had become an antinuclear activist.

John asked me to arrange a press conference with him, Bonnie Raitt, James Taylor, and Carly Simon to announce that a group of musicians were coming out for safe energy. At the time, Carly Simon was the biggest name of the four because of her recent gigantic hit "You're So Vain." Aided by political PR expert David Fenton, we were preparing the musicians for questions before opening the doors to the media when Carly announced that her manager, Arlene Rothberg, didn't want her to participate.

James Taylor, then married to Carly, sat impassively, his gorgeous blue eyes staring into space as if focused a thousand miles away. Bonnie simply got up and walked out of the room. John Hall, the least famous of the group he had assembled, looked at me with panic in his eyes.

I think my activist career began at that exact moment. I had spent a large part of the previous five years ass-kissing artists and managers to get them to trust me as a publicist. Conventional careerism called for me to accept Carly's course reversal and make the best of it. But I had been so energized by John Hall's explanation of the environmental hazards of nuclear power that I felt transported back to my high school persona. This was civil rights and Vietnam all over again! I asked Carly for Arlene's phone number.

Arlene told me that Carly had a long-standing policy of not participating in political events. She had turned down several requests from her feminist friends for press conferences. I snapped back that Carly had given permission for her name to be on the media pitch and explained that there were a dozen reporters outside, several of them with camera crews.

"If she doesn't do this," I said, "the story is going to be about Carly pulling out, and that will cause a lot more questions than if she participates." Arlene gruffly threw out an olive branch, agreeing that Carly would answer questions but not make an opening statement.

At the press conference, a member of my staff directed the first question at Carly and she proceeded to describe the cancer-causing dangers of radiation, the questionable safety features of most plants, and the difficulty of safely storing nuclear waste for long periods of time. Overall she gave the most powerful and coherent statement against nuclear power of the day. Her eloquence provided the sound bite that ran on TV and a key quote for the newspapers.

The next year, after the Three Mile Island nuclear accident, the issue became big news. John and several other artists and activists created Musicians United for Safe Energy (MUSE) and began planning several concerts at Madison Square Garden to benefit antinuclear and environmental groups. John, remembering my passion at the press conference, asked if I wanted to participate, and I suggested making a musical documentary film.

Jackson Browne was first among equals in the MUSE organization. Although I had absolutely no background in making films of
any kind, Jackson bought into my notion that only a movie would
maximize the audience for the political ideas underlying the MUSE
concerts.

Having just released the multi-platinum album *Running on Empty*,
Jackson was at his peak in popularity. He had combined his timely
and insightful lyrics with the zeitgeist of California rock music.
With the cheekbones of a model and what Bonnie Raitt called
"rock and roll's most perfect hair," Jackson was a powerful combination of poet and pinup.

I met Jackson for the first time at his Hollywood home and was
immediately disarmed by his unpretentiousness. The $500,000 ad-
vance we got for recording rights to the upcoming concerts was
plowed into the costs of filming the shows. Only Jackson's steadfast
endorsement of the movie fended off the anxious concerns of the
political activists, who feared their grassroots grants from MUSE
might go up in smoke if we didn't get an adequate return on the
movie.

Jackson's one major request was that we include Native American leader John Trudell, who was organizing a protest of planned
uranium mining in the Black Hills of South Dakota, sacred to Native Americans. With a small documentary crew, I flew to South
Dakota for the march the following week. Trudell was indeed a
mesmerizing speaker, as was the then-teenage Winona LaDuke—
two decades later, she would become Ralph Nader's running mate
in the 2000 presidential election.

Jackson joined Trudell on a fifty-mile walk through the Black
Hills. I, however, had already turned yellow from a case of hepati-
tis and begged off. I returned to LA, where I now had a home, to
recuperate.

Graham Nash, like John Hall, had developed an intense interest in banning nuclear power because it came close to home. Nuclear waste was slated to be stored on the Farralon Islands near where Graham lived in Northern California, and he had written a song called "Barrels of Pain" about the potential devastation such waste could cause. Graham was and is one of the clearest-thinking, most pragmatic artists I have ever met, and he reunited the fractured Crosby, Stills & Nash for the MUSE concerts.

Bonnie Raitt, who joked that she was the "token woman" on many benefit concerts, was the other artist deeply involved in MUSE's creation and administration. The definitive female blues singer and guitarist of her generation, Bonnie had a bawdy sense of humor, a razor-sharp intellect, and a deep political commitment grounded in her upbringing as a Quaker. Her father, singer John Raitt, had been an important Broadway star in the 1950s and had encouraged his children to support the civil rights and peace movements. Bonnie was integrally involved with every aspect of MUSE.

The most prominent of the activists involved in MUSE was Sam Lovejoy, who had attracted national attention for toppling a tower of a proposed nuclear power site in his native Massachusetts. Lovejoy represented himself at trial and emerged as a Jimmy Stewart–like hero, pleading self-defense on behalf of his community and using the trial as a platform to lay out the health hazards of radiation from nuclear power plants. He was acquitted.

Also on the MUSE board was Howard Kohn, who had written the *Rolling Stone* articles bringing into full light the struggles of Karen Silkwood to alert her Oklahoma community to safety hazards in the nuclear power plant where she worked. She died in a mysterious car accident. The hit film *Silkwood*, with Meryl Streep in the title role, was based on Kohn's articles.

Tom Hayden showed up at a few meetings but stayed pretty much in the background. Journalist Harvey Wasserman, who over the years has consistently written the most coherent analyses of the nuclear power issue, was on the board, as was Tom Campbell, an ex–union organizer who acted as a trusted liaison between Bonnie and Jackson and various grassroots groups. He helped supervise physical production, and twenty years later he was still organizing benefits on behalf of those artists and others.

But it was Jackson Browne whose energy drove the events. It is very rare for an established star to take the emotional risks of conflict and rejection that a conventional concert producer regularly deals with. I will never forget watching him on the phone pleading with Joni Mitchell to join the concerts. Jackson had the vision that her song "Shadow and Light" would add a unique, creative layer to the concerts, and spent the better part of an hour vainly trying to persuade her. Jackson was more successful in recruiting the Doobie Brothers to headline the first two evenings, with Bruce Springsteen and Jackson himself headlining the other nights.

In September of 1979, five nights of concerts packed Madison Square Garden, and a post-concert rally in Battery Park, beneath the Twin Towers of the World Trade Center, drew 250,000 people. Performers included Jackson, Bonnie, John Hall, Crosby, Stills & Nash, Springsteen and the E Street Band, James Taylor, the Doobie Brothers, Jesse Colin Young, Gil Scott-Heron, Peter Tosh, Tom Petty and the Heartbreakers, and many others. Roughly a million dollars was raised.

The activists in MUSE had wanted to make sure that there was a political element to the film, so they had teamed me up with Barbara Kopple. She had won a best documentary Oscar for her 1977 film on coal mine workers, *Harlan County, U.S.A.* Oscar-winning cinematographer Haskell Wexler, best known for *Medium Cool*, a harrowing quasi-documentary about protests at the 1968 Democratic Convention, also joined the team.

At the concerts, Kopple and Wexler shot backstage footage for the documentary. The performances themselves were filmed by a group of camera people assembled by New York writer and film-maker David Silver. Barbara introduced me to her friend, former Paramount film executive Julian Schlossberg, who agreed to co-produce the film, which was a godsend since Julian brought film-making experience and talent that the rest of us lacked.

It soon became clear that Kopple and Wexler, backed by some of the activists, wanted to make a traditional political documen-tary with a little rock music in the background. To me, this was an echo of the controversy around the be-in in the sixties—culturally tone-deaf political activists were undermining their own cause. The purpose of the movie was to reach people who weren't already activists.

Ironically, Julian Schlossberg ended up siding with me. To us, a rock and roll–driven movie was preferable politically. We could reach a million rock fans who hadn't been able to go to the con-certs. And we could create a document that would live on, and might be seen by another million or so on TV. Moreover, a concert film could make back the $500,000 we had invested, and then some. A pure documentary almost certainly would not.

Jackson, Graham, and Bonnie agreed to do the film our way. Barbara Kopple and Haskell Wexler quit. Julian and I became codirectors as well as the coproducers of No Nukes. (We ended up giving Anthony Potenza, the film's editor, a codirector credit as well.)

To sell the movie to a film distributor, we edited together around forty minutes of musical performances. Jackson Browne was fa-mously slow in finishing and delivering his albums, and his producer Greg Ladanyi was appalled when I explained that he only had two days to mix Jackson's songs. Ladanyi looked at Jackson with raised eyebrows, expecting the auteur to explode, but Jackson's political activist persona trumped his inner perfectionist, and he told Ladanyi to meet our deadlines.

But the biggest star in terms of selling the movie was Bruce Springsteen. He was just beginning his long and well-deserved run as a superstar and there existed, at the time, very little film footage of his extraordinarily dynamic stage performances. Bruce came to see our forty-minute presentation, which included two of his songs. A few hours later, Bruce's manager, Jon Landau, called to say that Bruce had some ideas about the movie he wanted to discuss over dinner at Patsy's Italian restaurant.

Although I would find in later encounters with Bruce that he is among the most articulate of men, I had a hard time figuring out what he wanted at first. He was downbeat about what he felt was a prosaic collection of performances, mostly oldies. I think he was trying to be polite and thus he obliquely suggested, "It should be more like the movie *Mean Streets*."

I nodded earnestly but had no idea what he was talking about. *Mean Streets* was a drama, this was a documentary. Over the course of the dinner I figured out that he was trying to say that he wanted the "drama" of a potent message, not just a series of well-performed songs. I assured him that after we sold the film it was our intention to make the final product around 20 percent political.

After much pleading on my part, we were permitted to use Bruce's name in the sales pitch to studios with the proviso that he would get to see a final version before he decided which songs we could use. Bruce was particularly worried that his version of the Gary U.S. Bonds rock and roll classic "Quarter to Three," which he liked to use as an audience-rousing encore, was too trivial for a political documentary. From our point of view, the theatrics and physical energy of "Quarter to Three" were the highlight of the movie and we were desperate to keep it.

Armed with this tenuous commitment, Julian shopped the film to various studio heads. Terry Semel at Warner Brothers bought it for $1 million, low even by 1980 standards, but enough to finish the film and to return the $500,000 record advance to MUSE so that the grassroots grants could once again be given out.

We shot interviews with Jackson Browne and Graham Nash, who were articulate about their reasons for doing the concerts, but the movie still didn't have enough teeth. We added the overtly political songs "We Almost Lost Detroit" by my old high school pal Gil Scott-Heron, Graham's "Barrels of Pain," Hall's antinuclear anthem "Power," and Jackson's prophetic "Before the Deluge."

Julian Schlossberg was friends with Elaine May, a genius whose many talents include the ability to "fix" troubled movies. Usually paid opulent sums by the likes of Warren Beatty for her insights, Elaine worked without pay, as Julian and I and all of the performers had. She created a movie within the movie that included a conversation with nuclear scientist Dr. John Gofman, historical footage from TV networks, and a brief clip of Trudell's speech in South Dakota, fulfilling my early promise to Jackson. We ended with shots of the huge rally in Battery Park, including excerpts of speeches from Ralph Nader, Jane Fonda, and Gray Panther leader Maggie Kuhn, and ended with John Hall's stirring "Power" and Jesse Colin Young's sixties anthem "Get Together."

When Bruce saw the now-politicized version of the movie, he hugged me approvingly and promptly gave his permission to include any of his songs that we wanted. Even though Bruce himself never uttered a political word in the movie, his motivation was to get a message out. Once his stage gymnastics were put in that context, he embraced the film, and his performance was the galvanizing highlight and got the lion's share of attention from the press.

No Nukes was released in July 1980, less than ten months after the concerts. It played for only a few weeks in theaters, but it has been shown almost every year since on PBS or VH-1 and has had a long life in home video. Twenty years later, after the September 11 attack on the World Trade Center, some of the issues raised by MUSE, including the safety hazards of nuclear power plants and the value of energy conservation and alternatives to oil, had renewed salience.

In subsequent years, as Springsteen became one of the world's biggest rock stars, he always supported grassroots groups and has periodically aligned himself with political positions; for example, by recording the Edwin Starr antiwar song "War" in the mid-eighties, when the Reagan administration was making aggressive moves in Central America. His 1995 album *The Ghost of Tom Joad* is filled with romantic political idealism, and in 1999 Springsteen wrote the song "51 Shots" to protest the police killing of Amadou Diallo in New York in 1999.

In 2002 Springsteen released *The Rising*, which was filled with eloquent references to September 11, but this particular body of work is more about grief, recovery, heroism, compassion, and universal humanity than about any particular political point of view. In 2004, twenty-five years after the No Nukes concerts, Bruce made a powerful and emphatic plunge into electoral politics in support of John Kerry.

Bonnie, Jackson, John Hall, Crosby, Stills & Nash, Jesse Colin Young, James Taylor, and many of the other MUSE artists have continued to raise money for progressive groups and hand out literature at their concerts. The MUSE artists have proven over the course of a quarter-century that they are indeed the worthy successors to Woody Guthrie, Pete Seeger, and Joan Baez.

Of course, not all rock stars are like Bonnie Raitt and Jackson Browne. In the summer of 1980, I was at a party making small talk with California governor Jerry Brown about *No Nukes* when Mick Jagger walked up and said, "I think nuclear power is a bullshit issue." "Why?" said Brown, always ready for a tussle. "It's just a bullshit issue, that's all," giggled Jagger, and walked away.

That November, Jimmy Carter lost the presidency to Ronald Reagan. At least some of the blame for his defeat has to fall on the

Washington liberal elite, politicians, and pundits who were uncomfortable with Carter's populist tendencies and wrote and spoke of him with ill-disguised scorn.

Carter should have hung on to his egalitarianism. Instead, the candidate who had said he could not have won the Democratic nomination without the Allman Brothers, the president who had invited Willie Nelson to the White House, seemed to blink under the haughty stares of the Washington snobs. He tried to refashion himself as a traditional Democrat, going so far as to tone down symbolic gestures such as carrying his own garment bag, and wound up with a blurred image. This allowed the media wizard Reagan to masquerade as an outsider, even though his policies were aimed at protecting and reinforcing the wealth and power of the superrich.

As the Reagan era dawned, very few graduates of the sixties movements actually became conservatives, contrary to the popular myth. But in the face of the maddening similarity of messages coming from the two parties, and the virtual disappearance of left-wing ideas from mass media discourse, many simply retreated from politics altogether.

CHAPTER 4

The Early Eighties

Ronald Reagan and the New Hollywood Left

*Politics is just like show business. You have a hell of an opening, coast for
a while, and then have a hell of a close.*
—Ronald Reagan, 1966, as quoted in Paul Slansky's book *The
Clothes Have No Emperor*

B Y 1980, I was finally able to succeed in the music business
as something other than a publicist. I formed Modern
Records with my friend Paul Fishkin and Fleetwood Mac
star Stevie Nicks. Modern's primary purpose was to produce and release Stevie's solo albums.

Although she had little interest in politics, Stevie was very much
influenced by hippie culture. She had a romantic notion of the relationship between her inner voice and her art, and she felt very
close to her fans. Many of Stevie's female fans imitated her long,
fluffy hairstyle and wore shawls like the ones she twirled around onstage. Backstage, she would spend as much time with fans as she
would with the music and media heavies.

Because of Fleetwood Mac's immense popularity (their then-
current album *Rumours* was number one for a record thirty-nine

weeks), Stevie was exposed to music professionals far more power-ful than I. The key to our arrangement was my intense emotional commitment to her as an artist. The entourage around Fleetwood Mac treated her as a "chick singer" rather than as a major talent and a superstar, which is how I saw her. Stevie's first album for us, the quadruple-platinum *Bella Donna*, became the number one seller in the United States in 1981, and her solo career was launched.

I had moved my primary residence and office to Los Angeles when I started working with Stevie Nicks. In the wake of Ronald Reagan's 1980 victory over Jimmy Carter, I started getting calls from liberal politicians and public interest groups asking for help with publicity and fundraising. It was as if the amorphous connec-tions between music, hippie culture, and politics that were symbol-ized by the Woodstock Festival were finally coalescing for me a decade and a half later.

Entertainment and politics were coming together in a dynamic way in Hollywood in the eighties. Jane Fonda and Tom Hayden had frequent salons in their Santa Monica home, attracting a new gen-eration of entertainers to political activism. Warren Beatty, Barbra Streisand, and Paul Newman supported liberal candidates for office. Songwriter Marilyn Bergman and others, including Barbara Corday, Susan Grode, Pat Lee, film producer Paula Weinstein, Fonda, and Streisand, formed the Hollywood Women's Political Committee.

Stanley Sheinbaum, who was married to movie mogul Harry Warner's daughter Betty, was a major force in the progressive com-munity. Stanley was a member of the University of California Board of Regents and publisher of *New Perspectives Quarterly*. He had been active in the McGovern campaign and frequently collaborated with entertainment figures on liberal causes, playing a significant behind-the-scenes role in virtually every Southern California progressive initiative of the time. He and Betty hosted dozens of American and international intellectual and political leaders in their Brentwood home. Stanley would become my primary mentor in entering the activist world.

As I became more involved with Hollywood liberals and progressives in the 1980s, pundits, left-wing activists, and politicians—perhaps irked by the sharp questions some of us posed—would ask me what on earth show business had to do with the serious, complex issues of politics.

I always invoked Ronald Reagan.

For conservatives, Reagan was a galvanizing force, but his ability to get a large majority of Americans behind him had a lot to do with his ability to speak to nonconservatives who liked his accessibility, even if they disagreed with him about such issues as abortion. Reagan's mass appeal was directly related to his background as an actor, and he enthusiastically used all of the tools of public relations that more conventional politicians resisted. Reagan shaped perceptions and gave them concreteness. Millions of working-class whites might already have been thinking their personal economic problems were somehow related to the civil rights movement, but Reagan legitimized their worst feelings when he talked about mythical "welfare mothers with Cadillacs."

In press conferences, Reagan employed humor better than anyone since John F. Kennedy, and unlike any president before or since, Reagan used entertainment-business references to bond with a broad range of Americans. Referring to the Carter administration, Reagan said, "We were being led by a team of people with good intentions and bad ideas, people with all the common sense of Huey, Dewey, and Louie."

Campaigning at the Grand Ole Opry in Nashville, Reagan said, "The other side's promises are a little like Minnie Pearl's hat. They both have big price tags hanging from them." On a college campus, Reagan responded to cheers by saying, "If you ask me, as Robert Palmer has been singing recently, you are simply irresistible." Even on a very serious occasion like his 1986 State of the Union address, President Reagan quoted from the film *Back to the Future*: "Where we're going, we don't need roads."

First Lady Nancy Reagan kissed TV star Mr. T on the head at the White House and appeared as herself, preaching against drugs, in an episode of the sitcom *Diff'rent Strokes*. When Ron Reagan Jr., parodying a scene from the film *Risky Business*, danced in his underwear on *Saturday Night Live*, President Reagan said, "Like father, like son."

In 1983, President Reagan posed shirtless and pumping iron for a cover story in *Parade* magazine headlined, "Move Over Jane Fonda, Here Comes the Ronald Reagan Workout Plan." Reagan even tried to co-opt the Boss in 1984, saying in a campaign speech, "America's future . . . rests in a message of hope in the songs of a man so many young Americans admire, New Jersey's own Bruce Springsteen." Springsteen, a progressive Democrat, rebuffed Reagan the next day at a Pittsburgh concert: "The president was mentioning my name the other day and I kinda got to wondering what his favorite album must have been. I don't think it was the *Nebraska* album," referring to his recently released collection of songs about the dark side of the American soul.

Inspired by Reagan's success, many other conservatives, like young Georgia congressman Newt Gingrich, became highly attuned to popular culture and posed as rebels and outsiders. Conservative Republican representative John Kasich went so far as to talk enthusiastically about his love for the Grateful Dead, and he made his antitax libertarianism sound like a plan for personal growth instead of a scheme to make the rich richer.

In 1983, I sold my half of Modern to Atlantic Records and created Gold Mountain Entertainment. I was the executive producer of Bette Midler's *No Frills* album and supervised music and soundtrack albums for movies and television, most memorably the film *Dirty Dancing* and the TV series *Miami Vice*. But my primary focus was the management of musical artists. Gold Mountain clients included Belinda Carlisle from the Go-Gos, who had a number one song with "Heaven Is a Place on Earth," Alannah Myles, who reached the top of the charts with "Black Velvet," and Bonnie Raitt.

Bonnie was being dropped by her longtime label, Warner Brothers. But my partner Ron Stone and I were convinced her best years lay ahead. Happily for all of us, they did.

With my *No Nukes* partner Julian Schlossberg, I also started a small label called Gold Castle that made new recordings of some of my early-sixties folk music heroes: Joan Baez, Judy Collins, and Peter, Paul and Mary. They had all fought long and hard for such causes as civil rights and peace. All later agreed to appear in a series of concerts I organized to raise money to lobby Congress against aiding the right-wing Contras in Nicaragua.

Outside of the activist musicians, the two entertainment figures who would have the most impact on me were Norman Lear and Ed Asner.

Norman was at his peak of TV prestige in 1980, having come off the decade as producer of the hit TV series *All in the Family*, *Maude*, *The Jeffersons*, *One Day at a Time*, *Mary Hartman, Mary Hartman*, and so on. These series, unlike anything that had come before, dealt head-on from a liberal perspective with cultural issues such as feminism, gay rights, and race relations.

Following the 1980 election, Norman grew fascinated and appalled by the right-wing Christians who had become part of Reagan's electoral majority. They were building huge followings via cable TV and mass mailings. The most prominent was the Reverend Jerry Falwell, who called his organization the Moral Majority.

Norman recalls, "After a decade of producing TV shows I wanted to do something different and was developing a movie for Robin Williams and Richard Pryor about mail-order ministers. While I was doing research I started watching Falwell and Jimmy Swaggart and Jim Bakker, and I was stunned by the hatred and vitriol coming out of them. I actually heard a TV preacher once ask people to pray that a member of the Supreme Court would die. And I was frightened. I was frightened as an American, I was frightened as a Jewish man."

Norman created People for the American Way to counter conservative Christians who were trying to define patriotism solely through their beliefs. Twenty years later, Norman could remember in precise detail his approach: "I wrote the first TV spot, and it set the pattern for all of them. It was a guy not unlike Archie Bunker. He was sitting on a piece of heavy equipment in a factory yard with a hard hat on. And the camera moved in slowly on him as he talked about himself and his wife and his kids, saying that they have various political points of view and they all love each other and they fight all the time about these political points of view.

"'But now [he says] comes this group of ministers on the radio and the television and in the mail, right in my home, telling us we're good Christians or bad Christians depending on our political point of view.' He's saying, 'I would tell you my wife's the best Christian in this family and there's nobody that's going to disagree with that. But somehow these guys think I'm the best and I'm the one that's going to heaven because I agree with them. So we've been thinking, there's got to be something wrong when ministers tell you you're a good Christian or a bad Christian depending on your political point of view.'"

Norman, still burning with quiet, intense indignation after all these years, concludes: "And his last line was, 'That ain't the American way.'"

Through TV specials, mass mailings, countless op-ed submissions, and many TV appearances, People for the American Way launched an alternative vision of patriotism and morality, one that celebrated American traditions but opposed bigotry and narrow-mindedness, that saw tolerance and diversity as a part of the American dream, not as a contradiction to it. No political or academic figure affected American perception on this issue as much as Norman Lear.

Norman invited intellectuals, politicians, and other prominent people to his home to meet movie stars and other Hollywood figures. When I moved to Los Angeles, his assistant, Betsy Kenny, made sure I was on the guest list for these fascinating evenings, and I got to know many people I would later work with in Hollywood.

In 1981, Ed Asner, a brilliant actor who had starred in two top-rated TV series, *The Mary Tyler Moore Show* and *Lou Grant*, won the presidency of the Screen Actors Guild—the post that had launched Reagan's political career in the 1950s. A committed progressive, the avuncular Asner was a constant force from Hollywood evoking an alternate vision to Reagan's.

Ed got particularly involved in opposing the Reagan administration's unwavering support of the government of El Salvador while right-wing death squads from the Salvadoran military were torturing and killing people. Most notoriously, four American Maryknoll nuns who worked with the poor were murdered, followed by activist Catholic Archbishop Romero.

Officially, the United States backed the Salvadoran government uncritically because of its supposed strategic value in fighting the spread of communism in Central America. Asner lent his name to opposition groups. When *Lou Grant* was canceled in 1982, pickets appeared at CBS, and Asner himself was among those who blamed right-wing pressure on advertisers and the network for the cancellation.

That same year, Pam Lippe, who had helped organize the No

Nukes rally, introduced me to her new boss, Russ Hemenway, executive director of the National Committee for an Effective Congress. The NCEC had been formed by Eleanor Roosevelt and others in the early 1950s to encourage liberals to run for Congress and to support their campaigns.

Along with screenwriter/director Carl Gottlieb, we organized an HBO special called "Night of More Than a Dozen Stars" starring Asner, Robin Williams, Chevy Chase, and others, the proceeds of which went to NCEC. Hemenway, who continues to run NCEC in his late seventies, has a patrician accent reminiscent of the Roosevelts and yet has more populist inclinations than anyone in the current Democratic Party establishment.

In 1984, I teamed up with another No Nukes alumnus, stage manager Tim Sexton, to create voter registration spots aimed at young people. We approached MTV, which had launched a few years earlier and had quickly become the dominant national voice of pop and rock music.

After a polite reception from the MTV higher-ups, the idea was assigned to Judy McGrath, who at the time was in charge of in-house promotion, including the dazzling MTV network ID spots. Judy, who shared our political passion, embraced the idea and made sure our spots ran frequently. Over the years Judy has been the force for MTV's socially conscious programming even as she's risen in the hierarchy—eventually, she would become president of the network.

With MTV's imprimatur, it was easy to get cooperation from managers and artists. We made spots with a number of top stars of the time, including Huey Lewis, Cyndi Lauper, and KISS. Peter Wolf, who had just left the J. Geils Band, did a spot with Afrika Bambaataa, a pioneer in the then-new genre of rap. To address the issue of feeling of powerlessness among young people, I came up with the slogan "Feel the Power," and in homage to my hippie ideals I got the rights to use an excerpt of Jimi Hendrix's performance of the "Star-Spangled Banner" at Woodstock. These commercials were a precursor to the Rock the Vote campaigns that started several years later.

I was stunned when several local liberals implied that the spots might be counterproductive—Reagan had captured the imagination of many young people, so maybe it was better for Democrats if young people didn't vote. Democratic congressman Tom Harkin of Iowa, who was running for the Senate, didn't feel that way. "If I can't get the votes of young people I don't deserve to win," Harkin told us, his Midwestern twang evoking memories of Jimmy Stewart. Iowa had a particularly high concentration of cable TV homes, and he was glad that MTV had committed to run our spots. Despite the Reagan landslide in 1984, Harkin did win, and he always maintains that the MTV spots helped.

One day, influential Democratic lawyer Mickey Kantor asked Tim Sexton and me to meet with Congressman Al Gore Jr., who was running for his father's old Senate seat in Tennessee. Kantor had been a key advisor to Jerry Brown when he was governor of California. He was now a partner in the powerful law firm of Manatt, Phelps & Phillips. Kantor's biggest client, oil magnate Armand Hammer, had asked him to set up Hollywood meetings for Gore, an old friend and beneficiary. We met in the bar at the Beverly Hills Hotel.

I asked Gore about the so-called nuclear freeze proposal—basically, no more nuclear weapons would be made by either side. It was a hot issue with many on the left. We were concerned both about the amount of federal money being spent on nuclear weapons and about the danger of a war triggered by the arms race itself.

Gore's face then had the unlined perfection of a TV anchorman.

He earnestly responded, "Not long ago I had a nightmare in which I actually experienced what a nuclear war would be like. I was so shaken by it that when I woke up I promised myself that limiting the nuclear arms race would be the number one priority for the rest of my life." I found it somewhat unlikely that the congressman had actually had such a dream. It just seemed a bit too convenient. My own dreams have never been that literal. But I appreciated the sentiment and didn't want to insult Mickey Kantor, so I gave his campaign $250.

About that time, as Mikhail Gorbachev assumed power in the Soviet Union, opportunities opened up for Americans to communicate with Russians.

No one I know ever had the slightest enthusiasm for the Soviet regime. It is impossible for someone who loves free speech and the other guarantees of the Bill of Rights to identify with totalitarian regimes, and as a Jew I was appalled by the mistreatment of Soviet Jews. But many of us had long and fervently hoped for a break in the Cold War and were nervous about President Reagan's description of the Soviet Union as an "evil empire." And I, for one, was terrified of nuclear war.

I joined in various "person to person" exchanges, where American citizens could meet with Russians. I also went to meetings organized by 20th Century Fox production executive Claire Townsend with people from the media, as well as film stars like Sally Field, to discuss ways of lowering the temperature on the arms race. One memorable visitor was Dr. Helen Caldicott, the Australian who had organized Physicians for Social Responsibility, a group of thousands of doctors who opposed nuclear testing and proliferation.

In 1985, Bonnie Raitt asked me to accompany her to Russia. Raitt, Carlos Santana, James Taylor, and the Doobie Brothers had been invited to perform in Moscow near the end of the Cold War.

The Berlin Wall hadn't come down yet, but Mikhail Gorbachev had begun his "glasnost" program in the Soviet Union. American rock promoter Bill Graham had organized the first visit to Russia of American rock artists in many years.

The day before the show, we were given a tour of Red Square by a nervous Soviet guide. James Taylor asked to see the house that Leo Tolstoy had lived in, and we basked in the glow of the perfectly preserved nineteenth-century home of the literary and political genius. *San Francisco Chronicle* music critic Joel Selvin and I broke away from the group and found a small synagogue, where we prayed with a group of beleaguered Soviet Jews, most of whom probably left the country a few years later when Gorbachev opened up Jewish emigration.

The concert the next afternoon featured several government-sanctioned Soviet rock bands, and concert tickets had been distributed by the Communist Party. The venue for the event was a sports stadium that could have held 40,000 spectators. Soviet officials, however, limited the crowd to 10,000. They filled most of the grassy field, leaving the stands virtually empty.

We stood onstage in amazement as about 500 Soviet soldiers ran out onto the field to "protect" the stage from the audience, creating a vast space as a kind of no-man's-land. Graham had one of his famous temper tantrums and threatened to cancel the show. After an hour of fevered negotiations, the soldiers split the difference and let the audience come closer.

The day-long concert, middle-of-the-road rock even by eighties standards, went on under the watchful eyes of hundreds of armed Soviet soldiers. The paranoid Soviets had long banned the Beatles, KISS, and other Western rock musicians from polluting the minds of Soviet youth. Now they were acting as if James Taylor and the Doobie Brothers could spark another revolution. What, we kept asking one another, were they so afraid of?

Later that same year, I was invited to Central America on a trip that was organized by Margery Tabankin, who had run VISTA for President Carter and was executive director of the Washington-based Arca Foundation. Arca lobbies for liberal and progressive causes.

Many people I respected had become convinced that Reagan's policy in Central America was wrong-headed, supporting repressive elements in El Salvador and opposing a fledgling democracy in Nicaragua without considering the wishes and rights of the people of those regions. The Reagan administration had a knee-jerk bias in favor of any faction that was anti-Communist or opposed to Cuba.

Marge, an astute political analyst who was a true Washington insider without being trapped in Washington groupthink, decided that the only way to change the policy was to transform public opinion, because Democrats in Congress were not likely to oppose the Reagan administration unless the issue meant something to voters.

"You can't just rely on investigative reports and a few liberal congressmen," she explained. "You need other megaphones when you're up against an administration in power."

A number of groups were already organized on the issue. Some of them had a naïve sympathy for the Communist forces in the region, but most were veterans of the antiwar movement who saw eerie similarities between our Central American policy and our support years earlier for an unpopular, brutal anti-Communist regime in Vietnam.

A key to Marge's strategy of arousing public interest in the issue was getting celebrities and opinion makers, including political moderates, to visit El Salvador and Nicaragua. The group I was invited to join included several freshmen Democratic congressmen: Bart Gordon, who had taken over Gore's district in Tennessee, Jim Traficant of Ohio, and Albert Bustamante of Texas. Also with us were writers Rose Styron and Galway Kinnell, Carter administration State Department official John Holum, actors Mandy Patinkin and Peter Horton, and Robert Kennedy's oldest child, Kathleen Kennedy Townsend, who would later be elected lieutenant governor of Maryland.

At a meeting with El Salvadoran president José Napoleon Duarte, we kept asking questions about the murderers of the Mary Knoll nuns. I asked the president why he didn't arrest the military men strongly rumored to have been involved.

"Everything has to go at its own speed," Duarte said in perfect English. "It's like records. Some go around at seventy-eight, some at forty-five, and some more slowly at thirty-three." Several members of our group started giggling. "Forgive me, Mr. President," said Kathleen Townsend, "but the member of our delegation you are talking to is in the music business."

"Oh," replied Duarte, extending his arms toward me expansively, "then you know exactly what I am talking about," as if his nonsensical answer had responded to my question.

In Nicaragua, we met up with another American delegation that included Jackson Browne and his girlfriend at the time, actress Daryl Hannah, and Senators Harkin and John F. Kerry. Most of us from both groups were disappointed in the authoritarian attitude of the Sandinista officials. They were the sullen, humorless military leaders of a successful revolution who seemed to have little regard for freedom of speech and dissent and other rights associated with liberty and democracy.

Kathleen Townsend was very moved by a private meeting with Violetta Chamorro, the widow of a slain leader of the opposition. But we saw no justification for American intervention to overthrow the Sandinista government. The poor population, still reeling from the earthquake in Managua of several years earlier, seemed relieved to be out from under the yoke of the longtime dictator Somoza. An aggressive American presence could have led to a Vietnam-like nightmare, with the United States supporting unpopular anti-Communist puppets.

Another issue that captured the imagination of many in the entertainment world was South African apartheid. Bruce Springsteen's guitarist Steve Van Zandt returned from a visit to South Africa in 1984 and organized a benefit recording and music video of his angry anti-apartheid anthem "Sun City." My clients Peter Wolf and Bonnie Raitt joined Bruce Springsteen and dozens of others in the 1985 recording.

Six years later, black leader Nelson Mandela was released from prison in South Africa after twenty-seven years. I accompanied Bonnie Raitt on a trip to London for a concert with Peter Gabriel, U2, and many others in support of Mandela's African National Congress, which would become the country's ruling party. Mandela came backstage before the show and eloquently thanked the creative community for its long support of his cause.

While some on the left were using mass communications to advance causes, others had gone into academia and developed a kind of intolerance that soon became easily caricatured by the right as "political correctness." Some feminists spent their moral capital attacking what they defined as pornography in bizarre coalitions with right-wing Christians, who detested every other feminist agenda. Many campuses adopted codes of conduct banning so-called hate speech, and student groups booed and drowned out campus speakers whose positions they didn't agree with.

"There was a moment in the eighties when people on the left could have themselves opposed [these] undemocratic excesses," says former Berkeley radical Michael Lerner, who emerged from the Vietnam protest years as an academic, a rabbi, and the editor of the progressive Jewish periodical *Tikkun*. "Instead we all stayed silent and the right was able to coin the phrase and define so-called political correctness, which then became a tool for attacking legitimate concerns about prejudice and inequality."

On the national political stage, Democrats who had a feel for populist communication fell away one by one. Mario Cuomo chose not to run for president. Jesse Jackson could not overcome the resistance of Democratic insiders. And former California governor Jerry Brown, who had run for president in 1976 and 1980, was handily defeated in his 1984 run for the Senate by San Diego mayor Pete Wilson. Brown left the national stage for several years.

Jerry Brown had strong personal connections with pop culture. He dated Linda Ronstadt, and musical stars like the Eagles helped him raise money. Possessed of a contrarian mind and a deep intellectual curiosity about subjects ranging from metaphysics to pest control, Brown, during his two terms as governor, brought many bright and innovative people into state government who wouldn't otherwise have been there.

Ultimately, however, Brown seemed to overintellectualize politics to a degree that turned off many voters who might otherwise have supported him. And he tended to resist the simplification of issues (he would probably call it "oversimplification") required to lead and govern.

The one candidate in the best position to take on Reaganism in 1984—and the one most tuned to pop as well as political culture—was Gary Hart, Democratic senator from Colorado and the former head of George McGovern's presidential campaign. Years later, Hart described his 1984 rationale to me as follows:

"Those of us who were newer members of Congress or newer elected officials in the seventies and early eighties were trying to come up with a set of beliefs, or a set of principles, ideals, policies, and programs, that were true to our liberal heritage but were new in approach and method. Find new ways to redistribute wealth and take care of those at the bottom. And that's what the so-called Campaign of New Ideas was really all about."

Hart sees himself as a forerunner of Bill Clinton, but he also was a forerunner of nontraditional candidates like Ross Perot, Ralph Nader, and John McCain in the sense that he had an enormous impact very quickly because he was perceived as authentic by a mass audience.

Hart recalls, "If I had any talent at all in those days, I think it was not to talk down to people, not to simplify, but to talk up to them. I always found in Colorado and then across the country that the more you engage people in a serious dialogue and debate about the issues of the day, the more they respond to that. The more you treated them as adults—and I mean, here I'm talking about seventeen- and eighteen-year-olds as well as fifty-five-year-olds—the more they responded to that, because most politicians talk down to them."

Hart utilized the services of pollster/consultant Pat Cadell, who helped shape a campaign whose images included high-tech lettering in the graphics on his ads and photo-ops that conveyed youth and energy. The most famous one was of Hart throwing a large axe after winning the New Hampshire primary.

Because of his association with McGovern, Hart had a ready-made group of Hollywood supporters that included Warren Beatty, Shirley MacLaine, Robert Redford, and Jack Nicholson. Hart explains, "[They were] just emerging as the takeover generation in Hollywood in the mid-seventies in the same way my generation was doing it in politics. So I think there was very much a generational component." Musicians such as Carole King and Jimmy Buffett also supported Hart and helped give him a strong identity.

Unfortunately for Hart's media-savvy advisors, their candidate was, if anything, too sincere, too earnest, too reluctant to practice the kind of media manipulation that came so easily to Reagan and

later to Clinton. "I think I was different from most politicians," he
says. "I did read books. I was interested in a lot of other things; literature, history. I read a lot. The reason the press didn't get it was
because I didn't fit their idea of what a politician should be . . . The
key on the typewriter in those days was 'cool and aloof.' But it was
[my] basic shyness, really. I just never enjoyed the backslapping and
the working-the-room the way a Clinton did."

Hart had no strategy at all to deal with Democratic opponent
Walter Mondale's "Where's the beef?" attack on his campaign. "He
knew I couldn't put [my] new ideas on a bumper strip. And since
politics was increasingly in that bumper-strip mode, people like me
had difficulty."

The Democratic establishment's media allies chipped away at
Hart's personal integrity, labeling him "weird" because he'd shortened his name from Hartpence and listed his birthday a year later
than it actually was. (Four years later, of course, it was Hart's personal life that destroyed him as a national candidate when he got
caught up in a sex scandal.)

Despite Hart's liabilities, he won almost half of the primaries and
only lost at the convention because of Mondale's lock on the political insiders.

In retrospect, Hart now says he was wrong to have underesti-
mated the power of the stripped-down political communications
strategy of which Ronald Reagan was a master. "I bought the liberal line that Reagan was too dumb to be president. He was able to
reduce an entire political philosophy to four or five sentences. 'I'm
going to cut your taxes, strengthen the military, stand up to the Soviets, reduce the size of government.' And those were principles
that people could understand. And they were ready for it."

While all this was going on in party politics, the mid-eighties
brought an explosion of activism from the music business. In Eng-
land, Bob Geldof saw a news report on the famine in Ethiopia and

quickly organized British musicians to do a benefit recording of his song "Do They Know It's Christmas?" featuring members of U2 and Duran Duran. Michael Jackson and Lionel Richie followed with the massive "We Are the World" benefit, which featured Bruce Springsteen, Cyndi Lauper, and other stars. The next year came the Live Aid concerts, which raised tens of millions of dollars for famine victims.

Willie Nelson and John Mellencamp, moved by the plight of the American family farmer, organized Farm Aid. (Bonnie Raitt participated.) Shortly thereafter, Sting and U2 did a concert tour to raise money for Amnesty International. Popular culture was making enormous contributions to liberal and progressive causes, which were gaining increasing support across the country.

Meanwhile, the Democratic Party was backpedaling to the right. The party had no defining leader, and it was divided about the use of military force in what turned out to be the latter stages of the Cold War.

Al Gore was elected to the U.S. Senate in 1984, as Reagan won the presidency over Mondale in a landslide. Despite the "nightmare" of nuclear war he had told me about in Beverly Hills, Gore's campaign speeches in Tennessee proclaimed that America needed to learn the "right" lessons from Vietnam and be willing to intervene militarily when the situation called for it. In early 1985, Gore and a few other Democrats broke with the party's leadership and helped the Republicans gain a majority vote to fund the MX missile, a new nuclear weapons system. So much for Gore's "nightmare."

A few months later, Tipper Gore launched an organization called the Parents Music Resource Center. The PMRC, it seemed to me, threatened so much of what I had worked for and cared about.

CHAPTER 5

1985

The Parents Music Resource Center

This all started with Tipper Gore.
—Senator Joseph Lieberman, during his campaign as Democratic
candidate for vice president in 2000

I N AUGUST OF 1985, an opinion piece condemning "offensive" rock lyrics appeared in the *Newsweek* column "My Way."
The authors were Susan Baker, wife of Treasury Secretary James
Baker, and Tipper Gore, wife of the recently elected junior senator
from Tennessee.

Shortly thereafter, Tipper Gore and Susan Baker went on the
Phil Donahue Show to unveil an organization they called the Parents
Music Resource Center (PMRC), whose board included numerous
other wives of prominent politicians. *People* magazine responded
with a cover story asking, "Has Rock Gone Too Far?"

The PMRC disclaimed any desire for legislation or government
censorship but called on the record industry to create its own panel
that would assign ratings similar to those the film industry had established in the 1960s. Popular columnists like Mike Royko and
Ann Landers applauded the PMRC, and the group was backed by

the National PTA and the American Medical Association. Supporters cited a National Council of Churches study that purportedly showed a "direct causal relationship between violence in the media and aggressive behavior in society."

As far as I can tell, there have never been any studies of the effects of popular music on behavior, so I have to assume that these well-intentioned watchdogs were referring to studies of viewing television, a totally different experience.

The PMRC advocated a lyrics ratings system with categories of X for sexual explicitness, V for violence, D/A for drug or alcohol references, and O for occult content.

There was nothing new about conservatives going after rock music. Indeed, such attacks went back to the very early fifties, even before rock and roll was a well-defined genre. As Eric Nuzum's *Parental Advisory: Music Censorship in America* chronicles, radio stations, prompted by the FCC, banned Dottie O'Brien's "Four or Five Times" and Dean Martin's "Wham Bam, Thank You Ma'am" for being too sexually suggestive in 1951. In 1953, country singer Webb Pierce's "There Stands the Glass" was banned from radio because of supposedly pro-drinking lyrics. About the same time, the Boston Catholic Youth Organization began campaigning to stop airplay of "obscene" songs, and Congresswoman Ruth Thompson, a Republican from Michigan, introduced a bill to ban mailing of "pornographic records."

In 1955, Pat Boone began his career covering and sanitizing R&B hits, changing "drinkin' wine" to "drinkin' Coca-Cola" in T-Bone Walker's blues classic "Stormy Monday," and replacing "Boys don't you know what she do to me?" in Little Richard's "Tutti-Frutti" with "Pretty little Susie is the girl for me." The Juvenile Delinquency and Crime Commission of Houston, Texas banned thirty songs—almost all by black artists. The CBS network canceled *Alan Freed's Rock 'n' Roll Dance Party* after R&B singer Frankie Lyman danced with a white girl on the television show.

In 1956, ABC Radio banned Billie Holiday's version of Cole Porter's "Love for Sale" because of its allusions to prostitution. Most famously, in 1957 the top-rated *Ed Sullivan Show* insisted that Elvis Presley be televised above the waist so that America's teens could not see him swiveling his hips.

The attacks continued in the sixties. In one of the silliest antirock developments, Indiana governor Matthew Welsh vitriolically attacked the Kingsmen's classic party rocker "Louie Louie" for supposedly conveying obscene messages. A campaign was launched to ban the song. After a long study, including an investigation by the FBI, the FCC concluded that the words were unintelligible and thus not obscene.

In 1967, Doors singer Jim Morrison was arrested for lewd remarks in New Haven. In 1969, police in New York seized 30,000 copies of the John Lennon/Yoko Ono album *Two Virgins*, which had a nude photograph of them on the cover. Later that year the Catholic Diocese of Seattle ran an ad calling for prosecution of rock musicians and for bans of "rock festivals and their drug-sex-rock squalor culture."

In 1970, Vice President Spiro Agnew made his notorious attacks on supposed drug references in the Beatles' "Lucy in the Sky with Diamonds" and "A Little Help from My Friends." Over the next couple of years, prompted by Agnew, the FCC threatened to pull the licenses of stations that played songs that "glorify drugs," without supplying any criteria. In language that would be adopted by liberal politicians in the decades to come, conservative Republican senator James Buckley wrote a report linking rock to drug use and called for record companies to establish "self-regulation before government takes action."

In 1982, with MTV only a year old, Ronald Reagan's surgeon general, C. Everett Koop, said fans of rock video would probably have trouble "having satisfying relationships with the opposite sex" because they had been "raised with rock music that uses both pornography and violence."

So for thirty years, successive generations of young rock fans understood that conservatives were against them.

But the floodgates of liberal baby-boom resentment over the younger generation's culture were opened by Mrs. Albert Gore. In 1985, Tipper Gore was in her late thirties and was raising four children ranging in age from three to twelve. The wife of a Democratic senator, Tipper legitimized to many liberal baby boomers the snobbish, indeed arrogant, notion that their children were being exposed to music far less moral than the songs they'd grown up with.

The PMRC's list of songs with "offensive" lyrics included Madonna's "Like a Virgin," Prince's "Darling Nikki," which included the line about a girl "masturbating with a magazine," and Cyndi Lauper's "She Bop," with its sly double-entendre references to masturbation. The group also attacked heavy metal groups such as Motley Crüe and the rightfully obscure Wasp, whose single "Fuck Like a Beast" had a sleeve that showed a chainsaw between a man's legs. (I couldn't stand the Wasp record myself, and I often gave it as an example of a record I wouldn't want to be involved with but that should be strictly a personal decision in a free society.)

The summer of 1985 had been a slow time for my business. The Gold Mountain management company was just starting. Belinda Carlisle hadn't had her big hit yet. Bonnie Raitt was in between record deals. Nirvana would not come into my life for several years. Gold Mountain Records was struggling along with a brilliant but only moderately successful record from Bruce Cockburn called *Stealing Fire*.

I was thirty-five, and in a bit of a funk. The publicity about the PMRC pushed some button in me. The PMRC seemed to me to be attempting, at the height of Reagan's popularity, to repress popular culture, a culture that reflected an America very different from the one that ruled in Washington. The fact that it was a prominent Democrat's wife who was leading the charge of a bipartisan group made it even more dangerous.

For years, I had argued with friends outside of the music business who persisted in belittling each successive wave of teenage music. Given the incredible opportunities we baby boomers had been given to express ourselves culturally and politically, I was disturbed that so many people my age had so little empathy for younger generations.

To me, songs like Johnny Cash's sixties classic "Folsom Prison Blues," with its famous lyric "I shot a man in Reno just to watch him die," dramatized the absurdity of a rating system for lyrics. So did the violence and the intense sexuality of many classical operas. What criteria could be used?

Washington pressure on entertainers also had echoes of the dark side of the 1950s. Among my parents' best friends when I was growing up was the actor Howard Da Silva, who had been in more than forty movies before 1950. Blacklisted for alleged Communist affiliations—among his accusers, according to FBI files made public in 2002, was Ronald Reagan—he wasn't permitted to work in films again until the late sixties. Da Silva had a philosophical attitude about the blacklist and found ways to earn a living in theater. But he and my parents talked about dozens of talented people who were never able to regain their footing after having been deprived of work because of their political beliefs. Some committed suicide. Others turned on their old friends and "named names" to curry favor with Congressional committees. Any left-wing activity was deemed sympathetic to communism. In truth, there was never any security threat to the United States from anyone in the entertainment business, and by the late 1960s the blacklist was abandoned and discredited, but hundreds of careers had been ruined. I never forgot Da Silva and the blacklisting tragedy.

One of the biggest weapons the PMRC held was the popularity

of the film rating system. Film ratings, although criticized by many directors, had, at least, some objective criteria: nudity, sex, violence, gore, and obscene language. Song lyrics, which are often poetic and symbolic, have always been interpreted differently by different people. Many of the most popular lyrics are filled with sarcasm, irony, metaphor, and words used for their sound more than their literal meaning.

I opposed ratings for lyrics for the same reason that publishers would have fiercely resisted any attempt to "rate" their books, newspapers, or magazines. Besides, even for linear uses of language, the only concrete criterion for "rating" words that has ever been developed were the "seven dirty words" that the FCC for a while banned from broadcast. The majority of supposedly objectionable lyrics didn't even contain these words.

The record companies, then as now, were represented in Washington, D.C., by the Record Industry Association of America (RIAA). This was long before the era of the Internet and before extensive pirating of records put the RIAA in the spotlight. It was a sleepy organization that mainly addressed copyright legislation when it came up in Congress and was run by a retired record executive named Stan Gortikov, a sweet, affable man who was clearly blindsided by the attacks on lyrics from senators' wives. I and most people I knew in the business felt Gortikov's early responses were far too conciliatory.

The one voice opposing the Washington Wives, as they were quickly dubbed, was Frank Zappa, legendary rock singer, composer, producer, and cultural icon. Zappa was quotable but in a quirky way, calling the PMRC "a group of bored housewives" who wanted to "housebreak all composers and performers because of the lyrics of a few." While smart and gutsy, Zappa did not frame the issue in mainstream terms.

It seemed to me that this was an issue on which most Americans would disagree with the pundits and politicians. Attacks on art and entertainment reflected on the personal choices of millions of Americans. The real energy behind the attacks focused not on the themes or the lyrics but on the songs' supposedly lowbrow aesthetics. Critics were objecting to four-letter words, to coarse expression, to bad taste. But America was the home of "bad taste": Las Vegas, Burt Reynolds movies, soap operas, Evel Knievel, Liberace, and rock and roll (rap was not to emerge as mass culture for another year or two). The PMRC wasn't going after avant-garde poetry and art, they were going after the heart and soul of Middle America.

As I saw it, the whole culture that I was a part of was at risk. In my mind, there could be no Bruce Springsteen if heavy metal lyrics were repressed. And once censorship began, where would it end? You never knew when cheap shoot-'em-up Western movies would evolve into the majestic works of John Ford; the same musical genre that had inspired "Louie Louie" and "Splish Splash" had nourished the works of Bob Dylan and John Lennon. As it turned out, most of the artists who joined me in fighting back, like Don Henley of the Eagles, were not themselves under attack. It was as if the creative oxygen of every artist was intermixed, and any intimidation of one artist would narrow the field of "acceptable" content for all of them.

Marge Tabankin arranged for me to meet with Ira Glasser, executive director of the American Civil Liberties Union. He had taken over the post in 1978 and revitalized the ACLU during a time when many other progressive organizations declined in membership and influence, building it up to 300,000 members with affiliates in all fifty states.

A native of Brooklyn who still mourned the departure of the Dodgers, Glasser, then in his early fifties, was robust, dynamic, and well-muscled from regular playground basketball games. Unlike most ACLU staffers, Glasser himself is not a lawyer. He has a down-to-earth manner and can translate complex legal ideas into ordinary language. He turned out to be the perfect partner for me in the upcoming battles, and our first meeting led to a long friendship and working relationship.

I told him I wanted to create a committee called the Musical Majority, a takeoff on Falwell's Moral Majority. The name struck a spark with Glasser, as did the implication that most Americans didn't want regulation of popular music. He agreed on the spot that I could claim an affiliation with the ACLU.

I flew back to Los Angeles and starting making phone calls. Within a few days I had a list of supporters—personal managers, artists, radio programmers, and PR people, among others, including the leading music PR guys Mitchell Schneider and Howard Bloom.

Artists involved directly or indirectly via their representatives included Tina Turner, Cyndi Lauper, Don Johnson, Don Henley, Chicago, Prince, Lionel Ritchie, Dolly Parton, The Pointer Sisters, John Cougar Mellencamp, and members of the rock bands Duran Duran and KISS.

In the press release announcing our formation, I announced myself as chairman of the newly formed group and I gave the following portentous quotes: "With all due respect to the RIAA, I've talked to a cross section of some of the leading figures in our business and we're sick and tired of every extremist that wants to get their name in the papers using rock as a whipping boy. American music is one of the best goodwill ambassadors our country has. Anywhere you go in the world, people love American music. We empathize with parents who want their children to grow up in a better world and are concerned about outside influences. Labeling or rating records, however, will do nothing to remedy this problem but will cause greater problems, imposing an atmosphere of censorship on the creative community. It will interfere with a free marketplace. It will erode the First Amendment. It will damage two of the most wonderful American traditions: freedom of expression and music."

No record company executives would or could add their names because the companies were all divisions of bigger entities with strict corporate policies limiting executives' freedom to comment on controversial matters.

On September 13, 1985, a front-page story in *Variety* read:

MUSICAL MAJORITY FORMED TO COUNTER ATTEMPTS AT IMPOSING DISK WARNINGS

A major counter-offensive to attempts to impose "obscenity" ratings on recorded musical product has been launched, with the formation of the Musical Majority, a committee of artists, managers, publishers, publicists, and other industry figures.

Formation of the group comes in the wake of concessions by the Recording Industry Association of America representing all the major labels to demands made by the Parents Music Resource Center for detailed labeling/warnings on records and tapes.

"By marshalling the music community, Musical Majority hopes to reach out to the generations under 40 years of age which have grown up with rock music and thereby demonstrate that we define the majority in a positive way," Goldberg told *Daily Variety*.

The story, to my amazement, included all my quotes from the press releases and concluded with five paragraphs listing artists, programmers, agents, managers, PR people, and others in the music business who supported us. Either it was a slow news day or someone at *Variety* agreed with us.

The next day, I got calls from several TV shows and wire services. I had become a source for sound bites. I quickly developed a new interest—in being quoted and seen on TV. I suddenly had a whole new identity that made me more interesting to journalists, politicos, and artists. Publicity is an intoxicating drug, and based on my own experience, I never analyze the motivations of an advocate without taking into consideration the sheer attachment to visibility that co-exists with political conviction in even the purest heart.

On September 19, the Senate Commerce, Science and Transportation Committee, of which Al Gore was a member, held a hearing on rock lyrics. In my new role as a spokesman for free speech, I attended with Barry Lynn, then executive director of the Washington, D.C. ACLU.

The vast, stately hearing room, which had been used for some of the Watergate testimony, was intimidating. It was packed with several hundred spectators, most of them with press badges. In front was a long row of TV cameras, their bright lights darting off the massive crystal chandeliers, signaling a full-fledged media event.

I had hurriedly run off several hundred copies of our press release denouncing the hearings. Ira Glasser had given us a quote with the appropriate civil liberties gravitas:

"It is highly improper, and we think unconstitutional, for the Congress to be making an inquiry into the content of published material with a view toward classifying it or regulating that content by legislation, and legislation is the only reason to hold a hearing. What they are doing is using the threat of legislation to force voluntary compliance."

Anticipating the constitutional problems, Senator John Danforth, the Republican committee chairman, quickly made it clear that he contemplated no legislation. Instead, he said, the hearings were "providing a forum to air what is a real problem."

The primary spokesman for the PMRC was the Reverend Jeff Ling, who identified himself as a former rock musician. Ling quoted lines out of context from the songs of various metal bands. When he got to AC/DC, he reminded the committee that "one of their fans" was accused serial murderer Richard Ramirez.

But the TV cameras were there for the rock stars. After Frank Zappa called the proposed ratings system "the equivalent of treating dandruff by decapitation," Senator James Exon, a Nebraska Democrat, questioned again why there should be a hearing in the first place since no legislation was likely. I grunted encouragingly, but Barry Lynn cautioned that Exon was mercurial. Indeed, a few minutes later, Exon barked at the music people there, "Clean up your act."

We did not know why John Denver was called, and I was dreading that he might side with the PMRC. Instead, the earnest, apple-cheeked, middle-of-the-road balladeer became the most powerful witness against a ratings system.

Denver told the senators that his early-seventies song "Rocky Mountain High," a clearly inoffensive paean to nature and clean living, had been irrationally banned by several radio stations whose management had decided the song was about getting high on drugs. A few years later, several newspapers had refused to carry advertising for Denver's equally inoffensive film comedy *Oh God* because they thought it was blasphemous. Even the most innocuous entertainment can be misinterpreted, Denver said. That's why he did not want any organization, created by the record industry or anyone else, to have the power to interpret and label artistic work.

Senator Gore told Denver that he admired his music. He had said much the same thing to Zappa. Then he was confronted by Dee Snider, lead singer of Twisted Sister. Snider, with his frizzed-out hair and black tank top, looked like many parents' rock and roll nightmare, but he quickly identified himself as a father and a Christian who didn't smoke, drink, or do drugs.

As Gore began questioning Snider, the heavy metal rocker slyly interjected a question of his own. Was Gore going to say he admired Twisted Sister's music as well?

"No, I'm not," Gore replied sternly, and then asked Snider for the name of the group's fan club.

"SMF Friends of Twisted Sister," rasped Snider in his tough-sounding New York accent. Eyes gleaming with prosecutorial zeal, Gore asked Snider what the letters SMF stood for, and nodded self-righteously when Snider answered, with appropriate rock and roll panache, "Sick Mother Fucking." Looking satisfied at having unmasked a sinner, Gore sarcastically asked, "Is that a Christian group?" But Snider had the last word, snapping back, "Christianity has nothing to do with profanity."

Later, when the video of Twisted Sister's "We're Not Gonna Take It" was played as an example of the horrors teenagers were subjected to, I applauded, along with several musicians in the room. Danforth solemnly insisted that the audience maintain its decorum.

The song is a classic antiauthority anthem, and the video was the fantasy of a young teenage boy berated by a domineering father. The kid finally "can't take it anymore" and wreaks havoc. Demonizing such an inoffensive piece of teen kitsch (the music video contained no spillage of blood, no guns, no nudity, and no profanity) was the kind of overreaching that consistently hurt the PMRC.

Stan Gortikov did the best he could fielding questions from senators on behalf of the major record companies, but he seemed pretty ineffectual and almost apologetic in debate. The job of the Musical Majority, as I saw it, was keeping pressure on the record companies not to cave.

A week or so later, a PMRC staffer remarked in an interview that Bruce Springsteen's song "I'm on Fire" was too sexually suggestive to be appropriate for young children. "Even Bruce isn't clean," she said. We immediately placed the quote in our press kit. It was a lot easier to defend Bruce Springsteen than Motley Crüe.

Although no members of Congress were interested in opposing the PMRC, Los Angeles mayor Tom Bradley on September 30 held a press conference with me and a few other Musical Majority members. Bradley, who was in his second term as the first African American mayor of Los Angeles, had begun his long career in city government as a police officer. Well over six feet tall, with broad shoulders and an affable if somewhat impenetrable personality, Bradley seemed to me like a local antidote to President Reagan. He heartily welcomed us and made us feel that people in the music business had a defender. I did not realize at the time how rare such political support for the music business and for free speech would be.

Mayor Bradley spoke about what a good time he'd had at a Springsteen concert at the LA Forum a few nights earlier, and then asked, "What do Elvis Presley and Bruce Springsteen have in common? . . . Both have been targets of a small group of people who want to impose their standards on all American families. Fortunately, would-be censors have lost nearly every round against popular music.

"The people who have joined me today represent a multibillion-dollar industry that has been quick to respond to those in need," Bradley said, referring to the recent Live Aid and Farm Aid concerts. "Now they need our help to stop this crazy notion that by rating records we can somehow protect our children from the evils of the world."

Bradley emphasized, "We can and must protect children, but that is a role best filled by concerned parents, not by government. Parents must regulate what their children see, hear, and read, whether it is a movie, a record, or a book. If a small group of people are allowed to dictate what we can hear, how about what we read? If tens of thousands of records should be rated each year, why not a similar standard on books? The very idea is repugnant."

The speech delighted the small group of supporters I had brought to the press conference, including Kim Carnes, who was coming off a huge number one hit, "Bette Davis Eyes," Duran Duran's Andy Taylor, and most significant, Irving Azoff, then-president and CEO of MCA Music, a dominant company in the recording business. Azoff announced that MCA would not participate in any record-ratings scheme, effectively dooming any system that would include movie-style rankings.

One evening, Jimmy Iovine, who had produced the Stevie Nicks albums, invited me to one of his recording sessions for Bob Seger. I was a huge Seger fan and was thrilled to be there and hear the Detroit superstar deliver his trademark, scratchy-throated, soulful vocals. A few weeks later, Seger asked if he could come play me his new album.

Seger has "delivery anxiety," not uncommon among recording artists, and likes to play his records for sympathetic ears before giving them to the record company. The friendly, bearded Michigan rock pillar arrived at my rented Laurel Canyon house the next afternoon and played me *Like a Rock*, the title song of which would come to have a second life in innumerable TV commercials for Chevrolet trucks.

I particularly liked "American Storm," one of those rare rock songs with a direct message, in this case a scathing indictment of the cocaine abuse that had ravaged Seger's generation of rock musicians. "That's the best antidrug song I ever heard," I enthused. Seger looked at me sadly and said, "I don't think I'm gonna put it on the album. You know it's an antidrug song and I know it's an antidrug song, but what if the people who want to sticker records don't know it's an antidrug song, and then I won't be able to get my album into most of the stores."

Not long before, the equally commercial Midwestern rock band Styx had been attacked by a religious group who wrongly thought that an anti-cocaine song called "Snow Blind" encouraged drug use. I assured Bob that the attacks were not remotely likely to affect him. Seger, with his romantic, bittersweet references to "old-time rock and roll," was exactly the kind of rock star the Tipper Gores of the world were likely to embrace. Seger left the song on the album, and as I predicted, it created no controversy. However, the fact that a multimillionaire mainstream rocker like Seger would feel threatened by record labeling struck me as exactly the kind of hidden damage that could come from the attacks on rock music. If Bob Seger felt uncertain and inhibited and contemplated censoring himself, how would a powerless, broke, unsigned artist feel?

About that time, I was invited to debate Susan Baker on the Washington talk show *Panorama*. In the Washington TV studio I found my adversary intimidatingly well dressed, with impeccably coiffed hair, tasteful makeup, and breathtaking Southern charm.

I did not want to fit the rock and roll stereotype. Wearing a conservative pinstripe suit and couching my arguments in terms of preserving cherished American traditions, I empathized with all parents concerned about raising their kids but stressed the Musical Majority's main points:

1. Entertainment is not like soup. The ingredients can't be listed and judged in an objective fashion. Different people and different families have different views of appropriate language.

2. Parents in the fifties were worried about the exact same issues as parents in the eighties. Everyone knew that Elvis Presley wanted to be more to a girl than merely her Teddy Bear. The distinction between the songs of the two eras was cosmetic, on the surface, not substantive.

3. Even though many who were concerned about popular music in the eighties were moderates, it was inevitable that the politicization of culture would empower right-wing culture critics. This was already evident in the call for an "O" rating for occult lyrics, which seemed inspired by specific conservative Christian groups.

The fun of this argument for a longtime lefty like myself was that, for a change, we were defending the status quo instead of attacking it.

People magazine's "Has Rock Gone Too Far?" story, with its pro-PMRC slant, had generated 2,035 letters—the most in the twelve-year history of the magazine. In its November 4 issue, *People* noted that 90 percent of the mail had been critical of the magazine for seeming to support censorship. And Ann Landers, the Middle American icon of sensible adult advice, had gotten 20,000 letters opposing the linkage in her column of popular music with drug abuse and teen suicide.

People referred to the Musical Majority as "the most prominent counter-offensive" to the PMRC and ran a full-page photo of me and the seven supporters I was able to round up one Tuesday afternoon to rush over to my office. They included Alan Arkush, director of many of the *Fame* TV episodes, singer Michael Des Barres, R&B producer Ollie Brown, and Donny Osmond. Like John Denver, Osmond had extra value because of the inoffensive mass appeal of his oeuvre.

I thanked Osmond, who I assumed had run over merely at the direction of his voluble PR guy, Norman Winter, but it turned out that the singer was quite focused in his opposition to ratings. "We're Mormons," he said of his family, "and we were always under attack from one Christian group or another. I would never want people like that to have any say over what I do."

The "consensus" that was so clear in Washington truly didn't exist in the rest of the country. For me, the best part of the *People* magazine article was a quote from AC/DC's Angus Young, who to this day I've never met. He said, "People who want to strangle other people's rights are possessed by one of the worst devils around, the Satan in their souls, which is called intolerance. Rock and roll is about one simple thing, freedom. When someone tries to murder freedom, we're against it."

In November, San Antonio passed a law banning unaccompanied children under the age of fourteen from concerts or other theatrical presentations that "constitute obscene performances." The ordinance included a number of specific topics that were defined as "obscene to a child," ranging from "bestial sexual relations" to "vulgar or indecent reference to sexual intercourse, excretory functions of the body, or male or female genitals." The law was championed and signed by the mayor of San Antonio, Henry Cisneros, a rising star in the Democratic Party.

The law presumed that the Supreme Court standard for obscenity did not apply to minors. Kids under the age of fourteen were permitted at so-called obscene concerts if they were accompanied by a parent or legal guardian, but the prospect of young teens having to drag a parent to a hard rock show, and of parents having to document their relationship with their kids at the door, significantly dampened attendance at concerts by KISS, Motley Crüe, and AC/DC.

The leading promoter in San Antonio, Jack Orbin, enlisted the Texas ACLU to fight the law, which was eventually overturned. But the San Antonio law demonstrated the slippery slope laid down by the PMRC. Even though the group insisted that it opposed federal legislation, its stigmatizing of lyrics had led to local legislation. And San Antonio was the first of dozens of jurisdictions around the country that tried to throw legal roadblocks between teen entertainment and its fans.

The first week of November, the PMRC and the RIAA announced a compromise. There would be no ratings system, but each record company would place "parental advisory" stickers on albums it thought warranted them. I decided to declare victory while holding my nose. None of the artists who'd supported the Musical Majority wanted to fight against all of the big record companies, and neither, at that point, did I.

"On one hand, the PMRC backed down considerably from their original position," I told the *LA Times*. "On the other hand, I think it's a terrible mistake to have compromised with these people at all. It's like compromising with terrorists. These people are cultural terrorists and I'm worried that the industry will live to regret any agreement which lends credence to right-wing pressure elements operating in the guise of a parents organization."

Irving Azoff of MCA also tried to have it both ways: "I have no problems as long as judging what is explicit is left up to each record company," he said, and added slyly: "Then it would be fair to assume that any label which cares about the First Amendment could honor this agreement and not find any lyrics that were objectionable, couldn't they?" (As a practical matter, MCA would do the same thing as the other record companies—put stickers on albums with dirty words.)

Bob Merlis of Warner Brothers put his finger on the eternal issue of interpretation: "What we might view as oblique, the PMRC may see as explicit. They've put Madonna's current hit 'Dress You Up' on their Top Offenders list. Now, we can't figure out what evil thoughts they see here. I guess you can say that filth is in the ear of the beholder."

The week after the settlement, Frank Zappa released an album called *Frank Zappa Versus the Mothers of Prevention*. It included the song "Porn Wars," which featured excerpts of comments by Gore and other senators at the ratings hearings. A couple of weeks later, somewhat anticlimactically, I finally met Tipper Gore in person in San Francisco on a local TV talk show. Since the PMRC no longer had any demands, and was supposedly happy with the RIAA compromise, all we could do was rehash the arguments we had previously made. I once again cautioned that demonizing rock lyrics could be used to promote conservative agendas.

During a commercial break, Mrs. Gore turned to me with what

seemed like genuine bewilderment. "Why do you keep saying we're conservative?" she asked. "My husband and I are liberal Democrats." That led to a remarkably frank and interesting discussion of Democratic politics and of what I saw as the abandonment of a progressive agenda. I didn't back away from my position, but I found her very likable, surprisingly open, and vulnerable. It also became obvious that Tipper Gore loved being on TV as much as I did.

At this time, she was just one of hundreds of congressional wives. Rock lyrics had gotten Tipper on TV, and Tipper had gotten me on TV. Now that the compromise had been made, I assumed that Tipper would soon be out of my life, and that the controversy would quickly wither away. It didn't turn out that way.

CHAPTER 6

The Late Eighties

Ladies and gentlemen, the Reagan era is over.
—Presidential nominee Michael Dukakis at the 1988 Democratic
Convention in Atlanta

GOLD MOUNTAIN finally came into its own as a management company in 1987, when Bonnie Raitt won four Grammys, including album of the year for *Nick of Time*. That album eventually sold more than 4 million copies, and her next album, *Luck of the Draw*, sold more than 5 million, so Bonnie's so-called comeback was far more successful than her first time around. Unlike some artists of her generation, she never backed away from her strong political beliefs—indeed, her high political visibility and clearly sincere commitment to ideals shared by millions probably made her a bigger star.

Around the same time, two other Gold Mountain artists had significant success. Belinda Carlisle had a number one hit with "Heaven Is a Place on Earth," and Alannah Myles went to number one with "Black Velvet." We also got the opportunity to manage a couple of musical legends: the great rock and roll tenor Roy Orbison, who had not made a record in nineteen years, and the reunited

Allman Brothers Band.

The Allman Brothers Band, with its deep and vital Southern roots and its instrumental virtuosity, gave me some of the best evenings of music I have ever had. Dickie Betts's guitar improvisations merged blues, rock and roll, and jazz in a way no one else has ever done, and Gregg Allman's husky voice is a virtually perfect vehicle for the blues. The members of the band had a spiritual and intuitive connection with one another that came through passionately in their music, like the Grateful Dead at their best.

Gold Mountain also picked up Pat Benatar, with whom I worked closely, and I began managing record producer David Foster. Our first project together was Natalie Cole's *Unforgettable, With Love*, which went on to win multiple Grammys.

Many of the artists I worked with in the mid- and late eighties were recovering alcoholics and drug addicts. California attorney general John Van de Kamp approached me to produce antidrug public service TV spots with musical stars and provided a $25,000 grant, which Pepsi-Cola matched. With directors and most crews donating their services, we were able to produce around a dozen spots.

MTV agreed to broadcast them, as it had aired the voter registration spots several years earlier. Gene Simmons of KISS did a spot with monster makeup that later won a prestigious advertising award. Bon Jovi, then America's biggest rock band, let us shoot on the set of its music video for "Living on a Prayer," where we did a commercial that included the ambiguous line, "Drugs are not a part of my everyday life."

Michael Des Barres, my longtime client and friend, suggested calling the campaign Rock Against Drugs. Comedian Sam Kinison later took a shot at the name, cracking that it was like calling an organization "Christians Against Christ," but the vast majority of teens at MTV focus groups were comfortable with the spots, which were less preachy and more accessible than conventional antidrug commercials.

Politically, I became involved in early 1987 with Senator Gary Hart's campaign for the 1988 Democratic presidential nomination. Mike Medavoy, president of Orion Pictures, had been one of Hart's key campaign officials in 1984. In anticipation of the 1988 campaign, his wife Patricia put together numerous events at their Beverly Hills home to introduce Hollywood people to Hart.

A stunning blond beauty even by Hollywood standards, Patricia was an accessible and skillful organizer and schmoozer with a solid political background—she had previously worked in Washington as an aide to Senator Chris Dodd. Hart was delighted by the help, not only because of the funds raised but also because of the visibility the entertainment business could give him both nationally and locally— Los Angeles was the biggest population center in the key primary state of California.

One afternoon I sat at lunch with Barbra Streisand, director Paul Mazursky, and others from Hollywood and listened to Senator Hart hold forth on an array of domestic and international issues. I was inspired by Hart's courage in criticizing defense policy and in envisioning an end to the Cold War—attacking the defense establishment and the nuclear status quo had for some time been considered political suicide for national candidates. Hart had met with Soviet leader Mikhail Gorbachev and was convinced that a major de-escalation in the arms race could come soon. The senator articulated well-reasoned proposals for the reallocation of money the United States was spending on arms to domestic priorities.

It didn't hurt with our group that Hart also seemed extremely interested in art and entertainment. He talked to Mazursky about the role of movies in creating political mythology. "If you were ever portrayed in a film, who would you envision playing you? Clint Eastwood?" asked Mazursky.

Without a moment's pause, Hart shook his head and said, "Sam Shepard." For better or for worse, this was a subject to which Hart had clearly given some thought.

Streisand seemed particularly impressed by his views on foreign policy and agreed to support Hart, as did I. Almost immediately, I found myself in meetings with Hart's campaign staff, and for a few months I had the heady pleasure of contributing ideas and energy to a campaign for someone we all thought would be the next president.

The illusion came crashing down in May of 1987 when Hart was caught in a compromising situation with a young woman named Donna Rice. (As it happened, I had met Donna Rice several months earlier in Miami when Don Johnson was recording his first album and she was hanging around the studio, looking available.)

I found Hart to be very intelligent, thoughtful, and a great listener; he also had a sharp wit. Once in Denver, when I was in a group helping him prepare for a televised debate, one of his young aides asked him, "What do you say if Al Gore asks you if there's ever been a time when you disagreed with a position taken by the AFL-CIO?"

Hart stared into space for a moment and then said, "How about if I just say, 'Al—I don't like your smug face'?"

Years later, when I interviewed Hart for this book, I asked him about his relationship with Warren Beatty, who I heard him refer to as "the pro." Campaign staff had said that Hart sought Beatty's advice before television appearances. "I learned a lot from Warren about things like staging and public relations," Hart recalled. "But the most significant thing I'd say about Warren is that he is a real friend. When people think you might be president, everyone wants to be your friend, but over the years I have found that Warren has been completely consistent in a way, frankly, that most of my Washington friends have not."

I still feel that were it not for the Donna Rice scandal, Hart could have fashioned a Democratic victory over George Bush in 1988. He had some of the same notions about recasting the party's image as Bill Clinton four years later. Hart was a more committed progressive than Clinton, although, alas, he obviously was not as resourceful a politician. He has a piercing intellect that has never settled for conventional wisdom, and his departure from the national scene was a great loss. After the terrible acts of September 11, 2001, it was recalled that less than a year earlier, Hart and former Republican senator Warren Rudman had warned after a lengthy bipartisan study that America was perilously vulnerable to a major terrorist attack.

When Hart left the race, Patricia Medavoy helped create Show Coalition to keep people in the entertainment business informed about politics. I and many other Hart supporters joined, and we quickly arranged meetings with other Democratic candidates. But I was tiring of receptions where politicians traded their canned remarks for money and visibility. I didn't see what difference I could make this way.

I was rescued by my mentor Stanley Sheinbaum. Stanley was then in his late sixties, with a long gray beard that gave him the affect of an Old Testament patriarch. A well-established member of the Hollywood liberal elite, he had been appointed to the Board of Regents of the University of California by Governor Jerry Brown and was an influential critic of the university's nuclear research program. Stanley also published the *New Perspective Quarterly*, a well-respected political journal, and had intellectual and political contacts all over the world.

In the early 1970s, Stanley had become the principal fundraiser for the defense of Daniel Ellsberg in his trials for releasing the secret Pentagon Papers, which damned government policy in Vietnam. The experience left him with a lasting commitment to due process. Stanley then became chair of the American Civil Liberties Union Foundation of Southern California, whose significant supporters included such Hollywood luminaries as Burt Lancaster (one of Stanley's predecessors as chair), Sidney Poitier, Gregory Peck, and Barbra Streisand. With Executive Director Ramona Ripston and others in Stanley's orbit, they had helped transform a nearly bankrupt ACLU affiliate into the best funded and staffed in the nation.

I was surprised and delighted when Stanley suggested I become the new chair of the ACLU Foundation of Southern California: "If you're serious about doing things, there's nothing like it. You have a constituency of 25,000 members and it gets you into most of the issues you care about." He paused and peered shrewdly through his thick spectacles before he hooked me with, "Of course, it means that you're always gonna be a bit outside the political mainstream, but at least you'll stand for something."

Rosemary Carroll, my fiancée at the time, had a dim view of Hollywood meetings with politicians but was very enthusiastic about the ACLU, reinforcing my own instincts. I hastily accepted. My only bona fides, other than my battles with Tipper Gore, were Stanley and Ramona's belief in me. But the board had absolute belief in them, so in 1987 I became chair of the ACLU Foundation of Southern California.

Among the most committed ACLU board members were Alan and Marilyn Bergman, who had written many songs recorded by Barbra Streisand, including "The Way We Were." Marilyn was one of Barbra's most trusted advisors on political matters and had helped form the Hollywood Women's Political Committee a few years earlier. Alan and Marilyn were steeped in traditional songwriting—indeed, they are acknowledged to be masters of the form, having won many Oscars, Grammys, and other songwriting awards. They detested rock and roll and found rap barely deserving of being called music, but they never wavered in the ACLU's defense of free speech in those genres, any more than they wavered when the organization defended the rights of Nazis to march.

Much of the work of the Southern California ACLU involved the treatment of minorities and the powerless. The organization had successfully sued to get an Orange County schoolteacher's job back after he'd been fired for having AIDS. It helped monitor conditions in local jails and children's facilities, and handled more appeals of the death penalty than any other California organization.

The ACLU represented racial minorities who had grievances with the local police, hardly an insignificant matter in Los Angeles at that time. Police Chief Daryl Gates had a particularly bad relationship with the African American community. After more than a dozen black men (and no white ones) had been killed by LA policemen using choke holds, Gates denied that there was any racial prejudice in the application of the choke hold but speculated that the neck arteries of blacks were more sensitive to pressure than those of whites. The ACLU fought Gates and his increasingly notorious department through much of the eighties and early nineties.

After Gary Hart dropped out of the presidential race, Senator Al Gore started making overtures to Hollywood about his own recently announced candidacy for president, and one day I got a call from Mike Medavoy asking me to meet Gore at his house. "You're both friends of mine," said the avuncular Medavoy, "and you should be friends with each other."

We met in Medavoy's home on Coldwater Canyon Drive, a relatively modest place by mogul standards, but a sunny, comfortable Beverly Hills home with plenty of rooms to get lost in. After making us comfortable and offering drinks, Mike retreated to his study. If things went well, he'd get the credit; if they didn't, he didn't want either of us mad at him. Accompanying Gore was Peter Knight, then Gore's chief of staff and later the campaign chairman for the Clinton-Gore reelection effort in 1996. Mrs. Gore did not attend.

The senator looked uncomfortable. Elected officials do a lot of ass-kissing to get where they are, but it must have been particularly galling for him to be meeting with a mid-level rock manager to deal with his wife's "issue." Presumably, he'd been convinced that meeting with me would make him look like a mensch in the eyes of other possible Hollywood supporters. The strain of the effort showed.

"One thing I wanted to bring up, before we get into the other issues," he began, "is that you had said in an interview that I wasn't really for arms control because I voted for the MX missile." Gore was referring to a remark I made in the *Village Voice* in an article about Tipper. "There was a nuance there that you don't understand," he said in that stiff, professorial voice that years later would be fodder for late-night television comedians. "This was a bargaining chip to prevent an even bigger weapons system."

Gore spoke in a pained tone that suggested there were subtleties in government that mere mortals couldn't understand. I shrugged my shoulders. I was certainly not going to start arguing with him about nuclear weapons. Why he would care what a rock manager said about the subject in the *Village Voice* was beyond me.

Gore then addressed the "Tipper" issue. "She's very sincere about this," he said, "but she's not on some kind of crusade." Gore said he regretted the Senate hearing two years before and stressed that he envisioned no future hearings. "The point was to create awareness," he said.

We talked for about a half an hour, exchanging platitudes, then Gore said he had to go to the airport. He and Knight took me up on my offer to drive them there, and once we were in the car, and the awkwardness of the "meeting" was over, the conversation became more animated.

"Come on," I said, "don't you remember being a teenager and

laughing at Spiro Agnew when he said the Beatles were causing people to take drugs?"

Gore answered, "What about, 'I get high with a little help from my friends'?" He drew out the word "high."

I told him that I'd taken a lot of drugs in the sixties, but I also thought of "With a Little Help from My Friends" as a song about friendship. Gore laughed skeptically, but I was being serious. I launched into a monologue about the positive value of music and the mysteries of the subconscious as it related to music.

"I believe deeply in God," I said, about to connect the Beatles song with a positive spirituality.

"You do?" interrupted Gore, sounding amazed. I felt that it was Gore's single unguarded moment with me that afternoon, one that revealed the unvarnished truth of his assumptions about me and my world. It was as if he thought that someone in rock and roll, someone who would oppose his wife's noble efforts, couldn't possibly believe in the same God he did. His words hung in the air while we both realized that his revelation of genuine surprise was just too real for a friendly ride to the airport, and we resumed our light banter, staying away from the subject of Tipper Gore.

But Tipper remained a presence in my life and in the news.

Her *Raising PG Kids in an X-rated Society* would soon be published. I was mentioned in it inoffensively a couple of times, but I had serious problems with many other parts of the book. She repeated the PMRC habit of lumping mainstream artists with more extreme ones. I was particularly disturbed by an attack on pop singer Sheena Easton, whom I was comanaging at the time. The book also regurgitated propaganda linking rock with the occult that obviously had come from right-wing Christians like the Reverend Jeff Ling. I was surprised that the rhetoric wasn't more muted, coming from a senator's wife who hoped someday soon to be the First Lady.

In the back of *Raising PG Kids*, an appendix listed sympathetic organizations parents could contact. The list included Back in Control, an Orange County organization run by ex-parole officer Gregg Bodenhamer, who claimed to "de-program" teenagers from the evils of heavy metal music. I had debated Bodenhamer on *CBS Morning News* when he first started his organization and found him to be as hostile and humorless off-camera as on.

In a piece about the Tipper book for the *B'nai B'rith Messenger*, a long-established and respected LA Jewish weekly, journalist Phyllis Pollack revealed that Back in Control published a handbook listing the Jewish star as an "occult symbol." The piece, headlined "Presidential Candidate's Strange Ties," had this devastating lead: "Tipper Gore, wife of recently announced Democratic candidate Sen. Albert Gore of Tennessee, has ties with a Southern California group that claims the Star of David is a symbol of the devil."

Tipper Gore and the fruits of her campaign against rock and roll seemed to pop up everywhere in my life in those days. Our ACLU chapter was defending the punk rock group the Dead Kennedys in LA against obscenity charges—their album *Frankenchrist* included a poster by H.R. Giger that depicted rows of penises. Our lawyers eventually beat the charge, but the group spent so much time and money on the case that they and their independent record label, Alternative Tentacles, never really recovered. (The prosecutor in the Dead Kennedys case, incidentally, was City Attorney James Hahn, another Democrat and a future mayor of Los Angeles.)

For a story that appeared in *Musician* magazine, writer Charles M. Young asked Mrs. Gore about the case, in light of her repeated statements that she was opposed to government censorship. "I'm not going to defend or attack the Dead Kennedys," Tipper replied.

Like me, Young "found Tipper difficult to dislike on a personal level," but added, "There is something eerie about her as there is

with almost everyone connected with the national government . . . She might as well have been on Mars during the sixties."
Bizarrely, she told Young that the sixties was a time when there
was more music that "parents and children could enjoy together."
Young got no response when he pointed out that the most influential album of the 1967 "Summer of Love," *Sergeant Pepper's
Lonely Hearts Club Band*, included a song about a girl running
away from her parents, and the next most important album, *The
Doors*, featured "The End," a twelve-minute song about a son
killing his father.

In late October 1987, I joined other entertainment executives to
meet with Al and Tipper Gore over lunch at Universal Studios. Included in the group were Norman Lear; Irving Azoff of MCA;
Michael Mann, a film director who was also the executive producer
of *Miami Vice*, which was at the peak of its popularity; and several
lawyers from Manatt, Phelps & Phillips, including Gore's friend
Mickey Kantor. The only musician in attendance was singer/song-
writer Don Henley of the Eagles.

Tipper Gore quickly adopted a conciliatory tone, calling the
1985 Commerce Committee hearing "a mistake that sent the
wrong message." She said, "We sent the message that there's going
to be censorship and that's clearly not the case. I am not for government intervention. I am not for legislation." Her husband elab-
orated, saying that as a humble minority-party freshman senator he
had been in no position to stop the proceedings. "I did not ask for
the hearing," he said. "I was not in favor of the hearing." He suggested, much as he had a few months earlier in defending his vote
for the MX missile, that he had helped neutralize the Republicans,
who would have done something far more drastic if left to their
own devices.

He then defended his wife's crusade.

Even I, who detested the crusade, could feel some sympathy for a husband defending his wife. I could see clearly, as I had when we met privately, that he cared deeply for her—one of his most attractive qualities. My sympathy ended, however, as he recycled the notion that parents were "outraged about trends in popular culture." How could he speak for all parents?

I reiterated my belief that opposing legal censorship, as the Gores said they did, didn't deal with the chilling effect that came down when public officials (and their wives) jawboned the entertainment industry. And I objected to a typical catchall passage from Tipper's book in which she listed Sheena Easton with artists who sang about such subjects as "masturbation, intercourse, and sexual sadism." I indignantly asked why the sexually suggestive "Sugar Walls" was linked with sadism. I was not just defending my client but attacking the strong tendency of the book and the PMRC to make sweeping and generalized attacks that lumped eroticism with sadism and did not differentiate between pop romantics and the most in-your-face heavy metal acts.

Henley agreed. "'Sugar Walls' is the highest form of innuendo," he said. "Sometimes I write songs that have three or four different meanings. Who is qualified to interpret those lyrics? Who on a panel is going to say, 'This is what you meant'? And what if they're wrong?"

When the topic turned to television, Michael Mann made what I thought was the most interesting observation of the day: "It seems to me that there are three types of TV violence. There's cartoon violence, which is what we all grew up with where you see a bad guy getting killed very neatly with no blood. There are realistic depictions of violence, which is what we try to do on *Miami Vice*. And there's the kind of psychic violence of something like *The Cosby Show*, in which the audience is made to feel that every American family has a big nice house and a Cuisinart. What about the alienation that poor people feel [because] no one who looks like them or lives like them is ever on TV?"

Tipper Gore avoided the premise of the question, but did say she was sometimes disturbed by *Miami Vice* and gave a general exhortation for less TV violence.

Newspaper reports of the meeting mentioned Gore's attempts to distance himself from the Commerce Committee record-industry hearing. A staffer for Senator John Danforth, the Republican chairman of the committee, was outraged. He directed a reporter at *Daily Variety* to passages from the *Congressional Record* transcript of the hearing that showed Gore had been one of its primary advocates. The resulting detailed story was headlined, "Records Show Gore Backed Hearing."

The meeting at Universal is mentioned in several biographies of Al Gore as an example of the senator's waffling, of the apparent ease with which he shifted his principles to curry favor with financially useful show-business executives. Actually, I wish that Al and Tipper Gore *had* changed their position, but they didn't back off from their criticism of popular music in any meaningful way.

Three months later, in January of 1988, I debated Tipper Gore on the CNN show *Crossfire*. She and the show's cohosts, Tom Braden and Robert Novak, were in Washington, and I was televised remote from CNN's Hollywood studio. When asked by Novak if she and Senator Gore had "agreed to back off" attacks on "the record moguls," Tipper tried to have it both ways. She had not backed off from her concern about offensive lyrics, she said, but had wanted to meet with entertainment executives to set the record straight, because "inaccurate press reports" had described her as "representing censorship," which she had always opposed.

Novak turned to me and barked, with his trademark sneer, "Mr. Goldberg, you've been hounding Mrs. Gore for months."

I interrupted irately, "It's my business that has been hounded. I felt used as part of a presidential campaign.

"Let's face it, Mr. Novak," I continued, "the Gore strategy is the

Southern primaries. In the South there are a lot of fundamentalists. Fundamentalists often like people who attack rock music, and this was an opportunity to show those people that Mr. Gore may be attractive to people with those so-called moral beliefs."

In retrospect, I now see that I was wrong to identify Mrs. Gore's positions only with conservatives. She represented an elite Washington consensus that included many politicians and pundits who thought of themselves as liberals. But she was wrong to think that this elite perspective spoke for most Americans.

One of the musicians who was the most informed, focused, and committed on this issue was Don Henley, who as a member of the Eagles and as a solo artist has been one of the most successful rock musicians of all time. A graduate of the University of North Texas, Henley was viewed as an unofficial guru by many Southern California rock musicians. One night I had dinner with Stevie Nicks and Jackson Browne, and Stevie, typically passionate, blurted out, "You know, when I write my songs I'm really trying to please Don." Jackson, more self-contained, looked at her with understanding and quietly replied, "So am I."

In the years before he got married, Henley palled around with Warren Beatty and Jack Nicholson, and earned a reputation as a party animal second to none. In the recording studio, however, he was considered an exacting perfectionist who insisted that other musicians and colleagues live up to his high standards.

In the political realm, Henley was known for reading every piece of mail addressed to him and for writing voluminous memos and letters to those with whom he disagreed. I once sent him a note asking for help on an ACLU project. Henley returned the note with the grammar corrected, accompanied by a stern reminder that our political effectiveness would be undermined if we came across as less than literate. But Don Henley does not hesitate to step up to help a cause he believes in.

A week or two after the Gore luncheon, Henley and I confronted one of Gore's opponents for the nomination, Illinois senator Paul Simon, at a Show Coalition political event. Simon was running for the Democratic presidential nomination as an "old-fashioned liberal," while his wife Jeanne was listed as a member of the PMRC. We cornered Senator Simon and told him how offensive we thought the PMRC was, and how intimidating the attacks were to entertainment corporations. We were upset that his wife, using the prestige of his position, was adding to our woes. Simon, nattily dressed in a suit and his trademark bowtie, peered over his owlish glasses and listened with the trained politeness of a professional pol. His already pink face got a bit pinker as he denied any knowledge of the PMRC and recited his First Amendment bona fides. Henley smiled and asked, "So talk to the missus for us, will you?"

The next day, Jeanne Simon called me. "Paul was very upset with me," she said, and proceeded to explain how she had only the vaguest relationship with the PMRC and never participated in any of their planning. She had no idea that creative people were so upset and would resign forthwith. (If she did, she did it very quietly.)

Neither Gore nor Simon got far in the Democratic primaries, and Massachusetts governor Michael Dukakis went into the Democratic Convention in August with enough delegates to win the nomination. I attended the convention in Atlanta as part of a Hollywood contingent put together by California assemblyman Tom Hayden, who was then married to Jane Fonda. The group included Sarah Jessica Parker, Daphne Zuniga, Ally Sheedy, Alec Baldwin, Ed Asner, and Rob Lowe, among others.

The convention nominated Dukakis and Texas senator Lloyd Bentsen. The vice presidential nomination of the conservative Southerner Bentsen had blindsided the Reverend Jesse Jackson, who had hoped Dukakis would name him, or at least someone more to his political liking. Asked by a news reporter if he was angry at not having been told before the news was made public, Jackson said, "No. I am too controlled, too clear, too mature to be angry." The highlight of the final session was Jackson's eloquent and gracious speech, calling for the party to unite on "common ground" to defeat the Republicans.

After the last session, there was a party for our group at our hotel, the Hyatt, in an open area on the floor where all of our rooms were located. John F. Kennedy Jr. and some of his cousins had joined us. Inspired by Jackson, we looked ahead with hope to the fall.

As we were watching some TV postmortems, a law student who had helped organize a young Hollywood group rushed over to me and said excitedly, "Danny, you've got to come upstairs. The Gore party is one flight up and Tipper is drunk and coming on to Rob Lowe."

I protested that it would be rude for me to crash the Gore party. I had made disparaging comments about him to political writers throughout his presidential campaign. But the young man was insistent, so I agreed. It was a night of common ground, of celebration, and everyone was in a good mood. And I just had to see this.

We walked one flight upstairs to a suite that held around fifty people, most of whom seemed to be from Tennessee. Tipper was cheerfully chatting with Lowe, although certainly not coming on to him. (A few weeks later the tabloids would gleefully reveal that later that night Lowe slept with two underage girls who happened to have a video camera with them.)

After a few minutes, I was about to slip out when Tipper spotted me and shouted across the room, "Al, look, it's Danny Goldberg!"

The senator glanced at me quizzically. As people stared, nonplussed, Tipper zoomed over and kissed me on the cheek. "We're a little drunk," she giggled, "but what the heck. I told the kids, every once in a while you have to have a blowout."

I asked Tipper if it was really okay that I was here at the Tennessee party. "Of course," she said, echoing Jesse Jackson's speech
that night. "We have common ground." Then with a sarcasm I didn't
know she had, she said, "Anyway, I'm too mature to be angry."

She looked at me and said, this time in a tone of high school
boastfulness, "You know, Bea Bentsen is on the PMRC advisory
board," referring to the wife of Dukakis's running mate.

"Will you stop with this stuff?" I berated her good-naturedly, but
with a serious intent. "It doesn't do you any good. All you do with
the PMRC is alienate natural supporters."

She turned serious for a moment. "Tonight is not the time to talk
about it," she said, "but call me when you're coming to Washington." She proceeded to write out her home telephone number.

After several minutes of banter, an older woman tapped me on
the shoulder and asked, with a ladylike Southern drawl, "Mr. Goldberg, can I speak to you for a moment?"

It was Tipper's Tennessee aide-de-camp. She drew me aside and
said, "Tipper would really like to go to your party downstairs, and
she feels she might not be welcome there, and I wonder if you
would take her." I readily agreed. A few minutes later, Tom Hayden
rolled his eyes at me and said, "Now I've seen everything!" as I es-
corted Tipper into the Hollywood party.

Minutes later, Al Gore appeared, tieless and cheerful. He had
left the Tennessee delegation to themselves and was down among
the Hollywood folk as well, volubly schmoozing. For the moment,
the Gores had joined the party.

Over the next few months I entered a period my wife refers to as
"sucking up to Tipper." Shortly after the convention, with Mickey
Kantor and other LA politicos pressing me to give the Gores a
break, I wrote her that "many of my friends got a kick out of tales
that you and I found 'common ground.'" I suggested that she withdraw from the PMRC quietly, without ever criticizing it. Removing

that roadblock, I suggested, would make it easier for me and others in the music business to work with her on issues such as homelessness, which she had talked about with so much passion at the convention.

Tipper sent me a handwritten note saying, "It was fun to be with you in Atlanta," and then described her homeless project in detail. She had organized meetings of congressional wives to discuss the issue and invited knowledgeable people to speak. Homeless advocate Mitch Snyder had spoken so powerfully, she said, "that he had several people sobbing."

She ended with, "Thank you for your kindness, your suggestions. I'll think about them."

Michael Dukakis ran a dreadful campaign, one typified by a line from his convention speech: "This election is not about ideology, it's about competence." Democrats would never win that argument. The party's entire rationale is ideological—to use government to stand up for ordinary and underprivileged people against injustice, the inequities of the marketplace, or just plain bad luck. And Reagan had been quite competent at serving the interests of his supporters.

I watched the first Dukakis-Bush debate at the Medavoys's house with a crowd that included Gary Hart. At one point, the Massachusetts governor was asked by CNN's Bernie Shaw whether he would still be against the death penalty if his wife Kitty were murdered. Dukakis answered that he would be, in his pedantic, seemingly emotionless singsong voice. "I don't think the death penalty is a deterrent," he explained.

I had long opposed the death penalty, both personally and through my work with the ACLU, but I was distraught at the political ineptness of the answer. I had heard Mario Cuomo and others answer questions like that with feeling, beginning by saying they fully understood and empathized with the pain and the rage of the families of crime victims.

I got up from Mike and Patricia's soft sofa and paced into an adjoining room, where I encountered Gary Hart. His face seemed to be a mask of self-directed rage. I rolled my eyes in the direction of the TV set and Hart shook his head and quietly muttered, with bitter irony, "Unfortunately, Dukakis is right, the election *is* going to be about competence."

In that same debate, Bush noted that he was a proud member of the National Rifle Association. Dukakis, on the other hand, he said, was a "card-carrying member of the ACLU." His prosecutorial tone made it sound tantamount to being a member of the Communist Party. In the days that followed, Dukakis's membership in the ACLU was listed by the political media as part of his out-of-touch "liberal" pattern, along with his opposition to the death penalty and his support for a Massachusetts furlough program that spawned the infamous "Willie Horton" TV ad.

Dukakis's response to such attacks was to claim imperiously that they were diversions from the real issues. He never once explained why he was a member of the ACLU and why there was nothing wrong with that.

We at the ACLU had mixed feelings. The immediate result of the attack was a huge increase in ACLU memberships, as thousands of Americans who'd harbored vague feelings of support toward the organization formally became members. National director Ira Glasser quipped that if Bush lost the election he could find a job at the ACLU as membership director.

On the other hand, ACLU affiliates in small states in the South and Midwest, with staffs of two or three people, felt nervous and vulnerable after being, in effect, blacklisted by the vice president of the United States. In any event, it was in our nature to respond to attacks. I hastily contacted several celebrities and television directors to craft some public service announcements, on the theory that if we moved quickly enough we could make the news shows, even if we couldn't get stations to run them for free or raise the money to buy time.

It turned out that the national ACLU office in New York also wanted to create TV spots, and I was asked to fly to New York to see if we could have a unified campaign. Although there were hardly any specific policy or ideological differences between the national organization and that of Southern California, the geographical distance and freewheeling style of Los Angeles leaders had caused tension over the years. Ira Glasser and his staff produced some advertising types from the Chiat Day agency who informed me that celebrities were irrelevant on this issue.

Despite the fact that I admired Ira enormously, I was extremely irked by this patronizing and naïve position. The organization didn't have millions of dollars to buy time, and celebrities were the only way of getting a message out quickly.

Ramona Ripston and I decided to do our own spots in LA anyway. Michael Tucker and Jill Eikenberry, a husband-and-wife team who both appeared on the TV series LA Law, quickly put one together. For another, Barbra Streisand gave us a recording of her singing "America the Beautiful," which we played over a beautiful montage of patriotic images filmed by Louis Schwartzberg.

The spot that got most of the attention featured Burt Lancaster, the great actor who Ed Asner says showed everybody in Hollywood "how to be a liberal with balls." The Los Angeles ACLU staff had written copy for several different possible versions of the commercial, including quotes about the ACLU from ex-presidents Eisenhower and Kennedy. Lancaster, well into his seventies, was still a commanding presence, with a husky weightlifter's frame, a full head of white hair, and a booming, immediately recognizable voice.

As staffers tried to explain the versions to him, Lancaster called me over and said in an agitated voice, "I don't like any of these. I want to say, 'I'm a card-carrying member of the ACLU.' That's what I came here to say and after that, within the thirty seconds, I'll say some of the rest of this stuff." I quickly nodded in agreement, and Lancaster's instincts turned out to be absolutely right. He expanded the line to, "I have a confession to make: I'm a card-carrying member of the ACLU." Those forthright sentences from this famous man were prominent on the evening news. The spot was also broadcast on the *Today* show, and ACLU affiliates around the country asked to use it and our other celebrity spots for local fundraising.

The national ACLU ads made by the "experts" were never broadcast anywhere.

The Reagan administration's policies in Central America remained a contentious political issue in the late eighties, and one of great concern to many of us who had lived through the Vietnam era. A number of leading Democrats opposed aid to the Nicaraguan Contras. The administration's support for these killers was unappealing to a majority of voters, particularly after the Iran/Contra scandal came to light near the end of Reagan's second term.

Nonetheless, the presidency had enormous power, and the political influence of anti-Castro Cuban Americans deterred Democrats in Florida and a few other locales from opposing Contra aid. Marge Tabankin at the Arca Foundation had formed a group called Countdown '87 to put pressure on several dozen congressional swing votes on the issue of Contra aid.

Tabankin, whose self-deprecating, informal style masks a steel-trap mind for political tactics and a fierce unwavering commitment to progressive ideals, wanted to make Contra aid what pollsters called "a push issue." That means, she said, "a priority to voters that would affect their electoral decision instead of an issue way down on the list." This would be accomplished with TV commercials in the targeted districts. My role was to help raise money to pay for the fight. I organized benefit concerts in Washington, New York, and Los Angeles with performances by Don Henley, Bonnie Raitt, Judy Collins, Joan Baez, and Peter, Paul and Mary.

Contra aid was banned by a narrow vote in Congress.

Shortly after Bush won the election, I visited Washington. To my surprise, Tipper Gore not only took my phone call but invited me to her house for lunch. Having asked my office about my preference in food, Tipper cooked me some mixed vegetables and we ate and chatted in the Gore home in a woodsy section of Washington. The kids must have been in school, and as far as I could tell there were no servants.

Tipper had a piece of artwork from a Guns N' Roses album that flaunted a lurid drawing of a robot who seemingly had just attacked a scantily clad woman. "Do you really think this is okay?" she asked.

I replied, "I'm not really a big fan of comic book art, and I'm not a teenage boy . . . but if you're asking me whether or not I think this is dangerous in any way—no, I don't."

We proceeded to have a relaxed and friendly rehash of our previous discussions. I felt the warm glow of Washington-insider schmoozing, and understood a little better the force that made ideological opposites move closer together. I told her again I thought she should quit the PMRC and focus her energies elsewhere. I said that no discussion, no matter how friendly and cordial, would change my strong feelings about art and free speech, nor the deep opposition most people in my business and millions of fans felt toward attacks on popular culture.

A few weeks later, another article by Tipper Gore attacking the current deplorable state of popular music appeared in the op-ed section of the *Washington Post*. The piece singled out the Guns N' Roses album—which was already stickered with the exact kind of label she had advocated.

CHAPTER 7

Who Ruined the Democratic Party?

The Late-Eighties Version

Kurt: I love you and I love Axl! Why do I have to choose? I want to rock!
—Nirvana fan to Kurt Cobain, at a benefit concert to protect gay and lesbian rights

IN THE WAKE OF THE 1988 ELECTION, Democrats and progressives argued fiercely about how Michael Dukakis, once well ahead in the polls, had managed to snatch defeat from the jaws of victory. In my mind, and apparently in the minds of a majority of voters, Dukakis was a dry, emotionless candidate, steeped in policy jargon and academics, and he had a snobbish contempt for mass communication. He and his advisors ran a clumsy campaign and managed to convey the notion that this ambition-driven son of Greek immigrants was a typical Harvard East Coast elitist, a liberal snob.

The patrician Bush, a Yale graduate and former head of the ultra-Establishment CIA, was ably advised by his campaign manager, Lee Atwater, to cloak himself in populist symbols—this wealthy son and grandson of Northeastern privilege posed as a regular guy who loved nothing more than chewing pork rinds while listening to country music. And the Bush campaign invoked patriotism through such well-conceived media events as a visit to a flag factory, whereas Dukakis managed to look stupid standing up in a tank.

Some progressive Democrats decided it had been a mistake for the left to identify with social issues instead of the traditional class-oriented economic ones. These New Deal fundamentalists were forever trying to recreate the coalition that, according to legend, had been coalescing around Robert Kennedy at the time of his assassination in 1968.

As I mentioned briefly in the introduction, I was at a late-eighties conference on the future of the American left when fierce debate broke out on this topic. Richard Goodwin, whose illustrious career as a speechwriter and policy advisor included Kennedy's 1968 campaign, and Pat Cadell, Jimmy Carter's former pollster, both strongly advised us to avoid being "distracted" by divisive social issues such as freedom of choice.

Marge and I shook our heads in disbelief. We thought it was obvious that one reason President Reagan had so much credibility in knocking government programs was that people like Dukakis, Goodwin, and Cadell had failed to explain to working people why those programs were in their interest, relying instead on an arrogant sense of entitlement—their great intellects alone should be sufficient to secure the trust of the great unwashed. We felt that the left needed to develop a common touch, stay linked to popular social movements, and learn to use culture and the mass media to get its ideas across.

For instance, many members of Marge's HWPC were disturbed by attacks on the Catholic Church and banners calling for "Abortion on Demand" at demonstrations in Washington. Marge's influence among progressive groups extended well beyond her own organization, so she met with feminist leaders, and it was decided to emphasize "choice" instead of abortion. NARAL, the national abortion rights organization, recruited actress Holly Hunter as one of their spokespeople.

"We succeeded in changing the way the issue was framed, which made a lot of difference politically," Marge recalled. "A lot more people, especially women, are comfortable with the concept of choice, which is the legal reality of the policy debate. [Abortion] is just one of the possible choices."

Also, in protesting Vietnam and Watergate, the left had created a strong antigovernment style and had been unable to shift to *advocating* government programs that helped average Americans. Democrats would have lost by far greater majorities if it weren't for the so-called cultural issues. Large majorities supported stricter environmental regulation and opposed the religious right's crusade to make abortion illegal, two of the issues that economic leftists found trivial. Instead of blaming cultural forces on the left, I told the group, the economic left should embrace them.

A few months later I was asked to be part of an all-day conference on "discarded children" convened by Democratic congressmen John Lewis of Georgia, Tom Downey of New York, and George Miller of California.

George Miller and John Lewis are two of the people I admire most in politics. Lewis is a former leader of the seminal civil rights group SNCC, and he was brutally beaten in the course of fighting segregation. As a congressman he has been unusually passionate, guileless, and consistent. Miller, similarly, has won a reputation for uncompromising progressive beliefs, straight talk, and personal integrity. Over the course of several hours, they and several staffpeople spoke in eloquent and heart-wrenching detail about the many crises facing children in poverty.

Finally, Downey addressed the "communications people" and said to us, "We need you to get this issue on the cover of *Time* magazine. We can't get the attention of the public ourselves in a way that can make it a political priority. That's why we asked you here. That's what we need."

I chatted briefly with the other media advisors, who included Henry Hampton, producer of the brilliant PBS series on the civil rights movement, *Eyes on the Prize*, and the well-known political and media consultant Mandy Grunwald. We all had the same reaction.

I told the congressmen that the speakers had framed not one but numerous related issues. We had heard, among other things, about lack of full funding for Head Start, failure of public schools to teach poor kids to read, woefully inadequate education on nutrition for pregnant mothers, profound flaws in the foster care system, and the low quality of public day care programs. Each needed to be explained separately.

You can get the public to focus on one of these issues, but not on all of them at once. Which one, I asked, do you want on the cover of *Time*?

This is PR 101. Focus and repetition are the only ways to make an impact. Blurred, multiple messages cancel each other out and don't stick in people's minds.

The congressmen and the policy analysts were horrified. It was as if we were offering them a version of *Sophie's Choice*. How could they kill any of their babies? The meeting dwindled away into an unfocused muddle of frustration and resentment. Nothing came of it.

During the late eighties, I got to know Ron Brownstein, a political writer for the *Los Angeles Times*. Then in his mid-twenties, Ron was a journalistic prodigy, much younger than other writers covering politics, and he had an affable, disarming style and an incisive mind, both reminiscent of the young Cameron Crowe. Ron made the beat of Hollywood and politics his own. In 1990, he published his definitive book on the Washington–Los Angeles axis, *The Power and the Glitter*.

The early chapters of *The Power and the Glitter* contain the best work I have seen on the political activity of early film moguls like Louis B. Mayer and more recent ones like Lew Wasserman. The last third of the book covers the late 1980s, and Ron is particularly generous to me in his analysis.

But despite his affinity for Hollywood, and a well-balanced presentation of various points of view, Ron's personal take on the entertainment business and politics post-Dukakis reflects the jaundiced attitude of the Washington media and political establishment. For example, he mentions that in the 1986 elections, two Democratic candidates for the Senate, Harriett Woods in Missouri and Tom Daschle in South Dakota, were each attacked by Republican opponents for a connection to Jane Fonda. Fonda had made a donation to Woods and testified before a congressional subcommittee chaired by Daschle.

When Barbra Streisand hosted a Hollywood Women's Political Committee fundraiser at her home in Malibu, Woods decided to stay away and distance herself from Hollywood, while Daschle chose to attend. Woods made a point of criticizing Fonda's long-ago decision to travel to Hanoi during the Vietnam War and offered to donate Fonda's $2,000 contribution to a veterans charity. Daschle ran ads mocking his opponent for attacking him on such a flimsy basis.

Daschle was elected. Woods was defeated. She complained that the Fonda attacks "helped to keep me from mainstreaming myself," and Brownstein concludes that Woods lost because of an overidentification with Hollywood.

My conclusion is the opposite. Woods was defeated because she acted like the kind of politician who easily caves in to pressure, whereas Daschle, running in a politically more conservative state, was victorious because he came across as consistent, gutsy, and comfortable with himself.

Publications of the political elite enjoyed ridiculing show business activists. The *Washington Post*'s Jonathan Yardley wrote a diatribe belittling Barbra Streisand, and the *New Republic* referred to Barbra and other celebrity activists as "bubbleheads."

Hollywood certainly has its share of flaky dilettantes, but I have found Streisand, among others, to be extremely well read and thoughtful on the various issues we've discussed over the years. Her intensity can be overwhelming, but her intelligence and commitment cannot be reasonably questioned.

Similarly, Robert Redford is an effective, self-effacing, and tenacious environmentalist. Warren Beatty is intelligent and thoughtful and knowledgeable about the issues. Paul Newman has, quietly, been one of the biggest financial donors to the progressive *Nation* magazine, and millions of dollars of profits from Newman's Own line of foods have been donated to grassroots organizations working for progressive causes. To dismiss all politically active celebrities with glib or condescending phrases is neither intellectually serious nor politically effective.

In 1989, I married music business attorney Rosemary Carroll. Our wedding reception was held on Stanley Sheinbaum's front lawn. My management business, Gold Mountain, was continuing to thrive, but Rosemary was prodding me to get involved with the next generation of rock and roll, which at the time was called "alternative rock."

My opportunity came when the groundbreaking New York band Sonic Youth had a falling out with their manager just as they were delivering to Geffen Records their first major-label album, *Goo*. My colleague John Silva and I shepherded them through the system with no artistic compromises and a doubling of their sales.

Sonic Youth liked to introduce exciting new alternative bands as opening acts. Lead guitarist Thurston Moore raved to me about one, Nirvana, which had released an indie album on the Seattle la-

bel Sub Pop. We flew the band to Los Angeles and quickly signed
them. Silva had already seen Nirvana open for Sonic Youth in Europe. I had heard their record but did not actually see them until a
couple of weeks after they had become clients, when they opened
for Dinosaur Jr. at the Hollywood Palace. I drove home afterward in
a state of euphoria, knowing that I had seen one of the best bands
ever. I negotiated a record deal with Geffen. Nirvana became the
most important rock group of the 1990s.

Kurt Cobain, Nirvana's lead singer and songwriter, was one of
the few real geniuses I have ever known. Kurt always identified with
progressive causes, and his emotional connection with politics came
through the so-called social issues. As Nirvana's *Nevermind* was being released, soon to be the number one selling album in the world,
the band played a benefit in LA for the abortion rights group Rock
for Choice.

I have taken liberties with one of Kurt's most famous images by
using the phrase "teen spirit" as a metaphor for the political energy
of new generations. This is quite different from the way he originally used it in Nirvana's biggest song, "Smells Like Teen Spirit,"
which regularly shows up in rock magazine polls as the most popular song of the 1990s. Kurt originally used the phrase "teen spirit"
because it was the name of a deodorant. The song itself uses the
phrase sarcastically in a comment about assorted hypocrisies, including the shallowness of most teen entertainment.

Although he never wanted to flaunt it, Kurt had strong political
feelings about certain issues. In 1992, he and his wife, fellow rocker
Courtney Love, contributed to Jerry Brown's presidential campaign
after hearing him on the radio.

Kurt's lyrics are rich in metaphor and symbolism and laced with
irony. *Nevermind* includes "Polly," an anti-rape song that Kurt delivers in the voice of an obviously repulsive misogynist. Virtually
every reviewer and listener understood the song's harsh indictment

of abusive men, but one mentally disturbed fan in Colorado sang "Polly" while committing a rape. Kurt was devastated and sent financial help to the victim's family.

At the next MTV Awards, Kurt wanted to preview his new song "Rape Me," another strong, irony-laced feminist statement. MTV staffers got nervous and insisted that the band do a more familiar song. MTV president Judy McGrath later said one of her greatest regrets has been that she did not intervene and let the band do "Rape Me."

The biggest American band before Nirvana was Guns N' Roses, whose lead singer, Axl Rose, seemed to personify exactly the kind of macho rock and roll that Kurt was rebelling against. The week that *Nevermind* came out, Axl came backstage at a Nirvana concert. Kurt asked me to walk out of the dressing room close to him to help him avoid meeting Axl.

The next year, backstage at the MTV Awards, Kurt came over to Rosemary and me shaking his head in disgust after an unpleasant confrontation with Axl. Kurt's wife, Courtney Love, had been teasing Axl about his habit of dating models. Flanked by two burly security guards, Rose looked menacingly down at the slight five-foot-six-inch Kurt Cobain and yelled, "If you don't shut your woman up, I'm gonna slam you to the pavement!"

A week later, at the request of film director Gus Van Sant, whom Kurt greatly admired, Nirvana played at a benefit to help defeat an Oregon ballot proposition that essentially would have legalized discrimination against gays and lesbians. Kurt, who usually didn't talk much to audiences during concerts, told the Axl story. He said that prejudice against gays and contempt for women were part of the same sickness, and that the kind of rock culture he stood for had no room for it. Suddenly, a fan jumped up on the stage. Sensing that he was in no danger, Kurt waved away the security guards and let the kid take the microphone.

"Kurt," the teenager said, "I love you and I love Axl. Why do I have to choose? I just want to rock." I watched Kurt take in the boy's comments with the compassion that made him so special. Nonetheless, after giving the fan his say, Kurt reiterated his message. He didn't want fans who were bigots. To this day, I'm torn between sympathy for Kurt's point of view and the fan's.

On the next Nirvana album, an anthology of early works called *Incesticide*, Kurt wrote into his liner notes a message to his listeners that said he didn't want any fans who were antiwomen or antigay, to my knowledge the only time an artist discouraged anyone from being a fan.

Kurt was a unique and inspiring person and a brilliant artist. His suicide in 1994 haunts me every day.

In the aftermath of the disastrous 1988 election, I and many of my friends in LA focused on issues rather than candidates, although we discovered it was sometimes hard to separate the two.

The Southern California affiliate of the ACLU was growing, thanks to Ramona Ripston, and I stayed busy. We had an annual budget and case load greater than any other ACLU affiliate in the country. We put on two dinners a year honoring people we admired who supported us and our ideals. The numerous honorees included Sarah Jessica Parker, Jane Fonda, Barbra Streisand, Martin Scorsese, Joan Baez, Kirk Douglas, Congresswoman Maxine Waters, and former mayor Tom Bradley. Performers such as Bonnie Raitt, Elvis Costello, Billy Crystal, Warren Beatty, Tracy Chapman, and Jackson Browne appeared at the dinners. Meegan Ochs, daughter of Phil Ochs, did, and continues to do, a brilliant job of organizing these fundraisers.

Many in Hollywood focused on the environment. Norman Lear and his wife Lyn put together the Environmental Media Association of entertainment executives. EMA educated many TV and film producers about environmental hazards. Numerous shows adapted minor plot lines in which protagonists were earth-friendly, such as the TV character Murphy Brown, who was shown recycling trash and joining a car pool. Former Ted Kennedy aide Bonnie Reiss created the Earth Communications Office to organize celebrities around the environment. Barbra Streisand and Belinda Carlisle, among others, promoted environmental causes on their albums, and at Earth Day rallies in 1990, celebrities were ubiquitous.

The music business had its own environmental issue, the so-called long box, which had been created by record companies to placate music retailers when compact disc sales rapidly began replacing vinyl and cassettes over the course of the 1980s. The retailers didn't want to build new display cases and requested packages that fit the ones created for 12" x 12" vinyl albums. Gary Stewart, an executive at Rhino Records, then a small compilation label, become obsessed with the waste of paper that these boxes entailed. Like the situation we had with the Musical Majority, Gary had to create a coalition that didn't include major-label executives, since they were all bound by corporate policies. While still at Gold Mountain I became a member of his committee, and Don Henley and I did a press conference urging passage of a California bill that would restrict wasteful packaging on various consumer products, including the long box. Shortly thereafter the major labels capitulated and eliminated the long box, and music retail rapidly adjusted.

The spring of 1989, a Hollywood forum on the environment was assembled by the Hollywood Women's Political Committee and Show Coalition, the Patricia Medavoy political organization I had been involved with from the beginning. The featured speakers were to be two of the most environmentally active members of the U.S. Senate, Tim Wirth of Colorado and Al Gore of Tennessee.

Our group really didn't have anything to do with putting the program together. It flashed through my mind that it was weird for

Hollywood to legitimize Gore, given his and his wife's attacks on the music business. But Gore was a genuine environmentalist, so I bit my tongue. I joined in the unanimous vote to cosponsor the forum. We agreed to mail invitations to all of our members on our official stationery, which featured my name prominently—for no particular reason, I was at the top of a long list of founders.

Don Henley responded by firing off an irate letter castigating us for hosting Gore. I loved Henley and understood his point of view, but shrugged it off. However, the letter got around.

The event was held at a fabled Beverly Hills mansion owned by Interscope founder Ted Field, which had been built by silent screen comedian Harold Lloyd. Several hundred people attended. They had to pay close attention to the program after the public address system broke down.

On one of those perfect, clear, and balmy Southern California afternoons, Gore was particularly impressive. In the absence of amplification, Gore switched from his pedantic professorial voice to an old-fashioned stump shout, and his heartfelt passion for the environment came through with eloquence and authenticity.

After the speech, I walked over to Gore in one of the many foyers of the mansion and told him I thought he had been great and that it was obvious he had genuine passion for the issue. Gore turned and frowned at me and said, angrily, "I know what you did—how you tried to embarrass me."

Surprised, I snapped back, "Just because Don Henley was complaining about you doesn't mean I had anything to do with that. Everybody in the music business doesn't agree about everything all the time."

"That's bullshit!" Gore screamed at the top of his lungs. "You and your fucking group sent out that letter. You and your fucking group tried to embarrass me."

As Bob Burkett, Ted Field's political advisor, watched in horror,

I yelled back, "You don't know what the fuck you're talking about—look at the stationery!" I waved a sheet of Show Coalition stationery with my name on top. "I'm one of the people who was attacked by Henley for having you speak." He looked startled by this information, but nonetheless walked away in a huff. I would have preferred that Gore acknowledge his misconception of where the objection to him came from, but I think he was still furious at anyone who had criticized him in the past, and I actually appreciated the emotional honesty of his anger, which was a welcome contrast to the insincere affability of most politicians.

On August 3, 1990, our first child, Katie, was born. As Rosemary and I watched the TV news from her hospital room, we saw President Bush threatening war against Iraq, which had invaded Kuwait a few days earlier. At the time, although I understood the rationale of the war, I was opposed to it. As with Vietnam, my opposition was to the war, not to the Americans who were sent overseas by their government to fight. Gold Mountain clients would soon put out the preeminent antiwar song (and video) of the time, Lenny Kravitz's reworking of "Give Peace a Chance," and the best-known song supporting our troops, David Foster's "Voices That Care."

Kravitz, a management client, called me in mid-August extremely worried about the possibility of the conflict spreading into a world war, and I suggested that he call Yoko Ono and Sean Lennon about doing an updated version of John Lennon's Vietnam-era "Give Peace a Chance." A couple of days later, Lenny reported excitedly that Sean and he had written new lyrics and the project was happening.

Miles Mogelescu of Propaganda Films, one of the leading music video producers, shared the same political passion and agreed to produce a music video for cost. And Danny Schechter, who'd directed an antiapartheid "Sun City" video with Steve Van Zandt, agreed to do a "making of" documentary that would be sold on home video.

Lenny, Miles, and I called everyone we knew to join in the recording session. About a dozen stars agreed, including Bonnie Raitt. Our big score was rapper M.C. Hammer, who at the time had the highest-selling record of the year, which included the song, "U Can't Touch This." Hammer had been in the navy and went to great lengths to explain that he supported servicemen but opposed sending them to the Gulf to fight.

After the recording Lenny asked me to take him to Washington to learn more about the issue so he could speak knowledgeably in interviews. I was able to arrange time for us with Senators Bill Bradley and Ted Kennedy and with Jesse Jackson's foreign policy advisor, Bob Borosage.

MTV played the video in heavy rotation for a week, and Lenny and friends did a spirited version of "Give Peace a Chance" on *The Arsenio Hall Show*. Lenny became uncharacteristically tongue-tied when Hall asked him about his reasons for recording it. Happily, Tony Bennett was also a guest on the show, and he picked up the ball. Bennett turned out to be extremely knowledgeable, passionate about peace, and eloquent.

The next week, when the troops had finally been assembled in the desert and the war against Iraq actually started, the media pulled behind the war effort and the song pretty much died.

The song for the troops, "Voices That Care," was written by David Foster and his wife, Linda Thompson. Its main thrust was support for the young men and women risking their lives overseas for American foreign policy. I admired the song but had trouble with a line that championed the policy as well as the soldiers. I told Linda, the lyricist, that she could reach more people if the focus stayed on the troops. "Quincy Jones told me the same thing," said Linda, who proceeded to make the change.

David Foster had grown up in Canada and was an icon there. He had developed a close social friendship with Canadian prime minister Brian Mulroney, said to be one of President Bush's closest friends among world leaders. I asked David to get Mulroney's perspective on why Bush had launched the Gulf War. David reported back that the prime minister had "confidentially" told him, "George is really pissed off at Saddam Hussein."

David enlisted movie and television celebrities for a "Voices That Care" TV special, which was hosted by actor James Woods. A few months later, I sat with David at a USO luncheon honoring the people involved with "Voices That Care." The speakers were Colin Powell, chairman of the joint chiefs of staff, Secretary of Defense Richard Cheney, and President George Bush. To my knowledge, Lenny Kravitz was never acknowledged in any way by members of the peace movement. This contrast is typical of a pattern I have observed repeatedly. Conservatives cherish their supporters from the world of entertainment, while progressives often take theirs for granted, ignore them, or condescend to them.

In 1991, Oliver Stone's film *JFK* was released. Popular with the public and widely admired among film critics and the creative community in the film business, *JFK* was universally reviled by the political press, left and right. As a result of the barrage of criticism, the conventional wisdom about the film in Washington was that it was a woolly-headed collection of absurd conspiracy theories. To my mind the film is clearly a cinematic, impressionistic work about a major historical event, the facts of which are unlikely ever to be known. The contrast in the reaction of the public and that of liberal snobs in Washington to *JFK* is another milestone in the widening of the gap between the punditocracy and the tens of millions of ordinary people who were inspired by the film. Not being in the film business, I have never worked professionally with Oliver. In the world of progressive politics he has been one of the most generous and unpretentious contributors, always a soft touch for a good cause. He has been particularly supportive of the ACLU.

As a Jew, I have been unable to ignore the terrible decades-long conflict in the Middle East, and emotionally I have a great love for Israel. In 1987, I was asked by the CRB Foundation (set up by philanthropist Charles R. Bronfman) to try to put together a concert in the Negev Desert for the upcoming fortieth anniversary of the nation. The concert, which was to have both Israeli and Egyptian participation, was heavily supported by the Israeli left. Foreign Minister Shimon Peres and leaders of the Israeli group Peace Now came to Los Angeles to promote the concert, and I made several preparatory trips to Israel that only strengthened my emotional ties to the nation. Sadly, the beginning of the first Intifada ended the plans for the concert.

Two years later, the actor Richard Dreyfuss asked me to accompany him on his first trip to Israel. We had become friends through the ACLU, and Richard had developed a passion for the cause of peace in the Middle East.

As the star of Spielberg's immensely popular *Jaws* and *Close Encounters of the Third Kind*, and an Oscar winner for *The Goodbye Girl*, Richard was one of the most famous Jewish actors in the world, and he was able to meet with leaders on the highest level in every major faction of Israelis and Palestinians. We dined in the Knesset with Defense Minister Moshe Arens, met with influential rabbis, visited military facilities, and sat in the homes of Israeli peace activists as well as militant West Bank settlers. We also visited Palestinian refugee camps and spoke with several Palestinian leaders. Palestinian journalist Daoud Kuttab asked Richard when he thought Hollywood would depict a Palestinian as a hero. Richard tried to explain how such decisions are made at movie studios, which usually focus on offending the least number of people. Kuttab listened as Dreyfuss explained to him that only on rare occasions were Hollywood characters identified as Jewish despite the large number of Jews behind the scenes in the business, the orthodox theory being that ethnicity of any kind limits mass appeal. It was obvious from his mournful expression that Kuttab mistakenly thought Dreyfuss was being disingenuous. I was reminded once again of how much the Hollywood stamp of approval means to people around the world. With all of the efforts being made to convince the Muslim world that the United States respects them, some Muslim heroes in Hollywood films might create more goodwill than some of the more heavy-handed government-sponsored efforts have done.

I know there are no easy answers to this tragic and seemingly intractable conflict. I continue to identify with the so-called Israeli left and have been a member of the board of Americans for Peace Now for many years, but I part company from my friends on the American left when they uncritically glamorize the PLO or trivialize Israel's vulnerability.

I can offer at least a partial explanation for why some on the left feel the way they do, in terms of the theme of this book. In the early years of the nation, bonds between Israel and American progressives and young people were strengthened through popular culture, through books and movies like *Exodus*, and through support for the young nation by famous American entertainers. As Israel grew older, the American entertainers who vocally supported it grew older too, and moved from prime-time television to the veterans' wing of the dais at Friar's Club roasts.

At the same time, established American Jewish organizations grew more and more conservative, working up far more passion for attacking off-the-cuff remarks by the Reverend Jesse Jackson than for identifying with America's poor. And starting in the Reagan era, Israeli leaders bonded with American defense hawks and Christian conservatives and ignored the progressive political world. I don't see how it helps Israel that many younger American progressives perceive support of Israel as a right-wing cause. This need not have happened, and need not be.

* * *

Attacks on free speech continued to come from both the left and the right. Because of my ACLU position, Allen Ginsberg contacted me in 1990 to help with a lawsuit he and Boston civil liberties attorney Harvey Silverglate had filed against the FCC, a continuation of his decades-long battle against censorship of his poem "Howl."

Under Reagan, the FCC had created new limits on free speech for broadcasters. Radio stations previously had broad latitude on what they aired very late at night—a "safe harbor" when young children were extremely unlikely to be listening. The new doctrine prohibited "indecency" from being broadcast at any time. Indecency was not defined.

Pacifica noncommercial radio stations, like WBAI in New York and KPKF in Los Angeles, would air "Howl" once a year as a statement of free speech as well as artistic admiration. Now they stopped lest they be subject to crippling fines or possible loss of license.

I jumped at the chance to meet with Allen Ginsberg. Over croissants and coffee at a Santa Monica bistro, Allen reviewed in precise detail the long battle he had waged for artistic freedom and stressed how important it was for people to hear his poems, not just read them.

"My work is enhanced by hearing it," he said. "It takes on a different life as an oral work and not merely written."

We discussed a pending court case in which parents of a kid who committed suicide were suing the rock band Judas Priest, claiming that the band's lyrics "caused" the tragic act. I was deriding social scientists and prosecutors who said that music caused violent behavior.

Allen interrupted. "Don't ever say art has no effect," he said in a firm voice. "We spent a lot of effort on the idea that art *does* have an effect."

When Allen said "we," I felt a thrill. He was speaking for generations of visionary artists, for Walt Whitman and William Blake, for all-night impassioned brainstorming sessions with Jack Kerouac and William Burroughs, for the world in which Allen had been a pivotal influence since the 1950s. I quickly explained that I merely meant that art couldn't be held accountable for crime. Allen agreed. But the exchange underscored the subtlety of the underlying issues, as did his statement, "It's much better to fight these battles over art than over porn, you know." But Allen was no snob. Then in his mid-sixties, Allen was as up-to-date on rock and roll as any teenager.

In the FCC case, thirty years after the landmark court decision in favor of "Howl," Ginsberg and his allies were unsuccessful in using his most famous poem to further pry open the doors of government censorship.

Another free-speech battle over popular culture was triggered in 1989 when the rapper Professor Griff, a member of Public Enemy, made anti-Semitic remarks similar to some of Louis Farrakhan's. Under the leadership of the remarkable Chuck D., Public Enemy was the most politically conscious, thoughtful group that popular music had produced in many years. Chuck D. immediately denounced the remarks and asked Professor Griff to leave the group.

Bill Adler, a Jewish publicist for Public Enemy, arranged for Chuck D. to meet with Rabbi Abe Cooper of LA's Wiesenthal Center, which had created the "Museum of Tolerance" to educate the public about the Holocaust and the terrible costs of ethnic bigotry. Adler did not realize that despite the moral power of the museum, the organization behind it was culturally quite conservative, even by the centrist standards of the organized Jewish community.

Even though Chuck D. had not made the offensive statement and had gotten rid of the man who had, he was prepared to apologize on behalf of the group. Instead of accepting his apology, Rabbi Cooper insisted on more mea culpas and publicly chastised the rapper.

Later that year, Public Enemy released an album called *Fear of a*

Black Planet that featured Chuck D. rapping, "I asked the rab to get off the rag." The Wiesenthal Center and the Anti-Defamation League promptly branded the new song as anti-Semitic. I was nauseated by these attacks. Chuck D. clearly was criticizing a specific rabbi for refusing to accept a sincerely offered apology, not all rabbis or all Jews. I said so in an *LA Times* op-ed piece, which was the beginning of a long friendship with Chuck D. and Bill Adler.

On January 8, 1990, Tipper Gore weighed in with her own op-ed piece in the *Washington Post*. Headlined "Hate, Rape and Rap," it echoed Rabbi Cooper's criticisms of Public Enemy and also condemned the use of the words "bitch" and "nigger" by rapper Ice-T. "We must raise our voices in protest and put pressure on those who not only reflect this hatred but also package, polish, promote and market it," Mrs. Gore wrote. To me, this glib and mindless dismissal of Public Enemy showed that Tipper Gore was as snobbish and closed-minded as ever.

Such attacks inspired legislators across the country to try to limit access by minors to records and performances. In Missouri, Republican Jeanne Dixon introduced a bill requiring mandatory labeling of "offensive" records and limiting attendance to concerts to those over eighteen if "offensive" subjects were raised. Similar bills were introduced in Pennsylvania, Oklahoma, Arizona, Delaware, Florida, Alaska, Rhode Island, and Tennessee.

I revived the Musical Majority. In April of 1990, with the help of radio programming consultant Jeff Pollack and the ACLU of eastern Missouri, we organized a rally in St. Louis opposing the Dixon bill. The big local rock station, KSHE, cosponsored and broadcast the event, which featured Alannah Myles and the indefatigable Don Henley. Defeated Senate candidate Harriett Woods, who evidently had gotten over her aversion to the entertainment business, spoke at the rally. So did Missouri lieutenant governor Mel Carnahan, who thus became, to my knowledge, the first elected official since Los Angeles mayor Bradley to stand up for free speech in the music business.

Shortly afterward, the Missouri bill was killed in committee. By the end of April, most of the other bills were either defeated or withdrawn.

Later that year, the rapper Luke Skyywalker of 2 Live Crew was arrested after an adults-only performance in Broward County, Florida, that featured songs from the group's controversial new album, *As Nasty as They Wanna Be*. Republican libertarians responded to the arrest with more sensitivity to the First Amendment than did Democrats.

"These are adults," said Republican congressman Dana Rohrabacher of California. "This is a First Amendment question and the government should not be involved."

And Republican senator Connie Mack of Florida said, "Freedom is a precious and sometimes delicate issue. I'm sure many people find the lyrics reprehensible. And I agree. But words are words. Our Constitution protects our right to say what we feel . . . Once we begin selectively defining which words are acceptable, we enter a slippery slope where freedom is compromised. Sometimes the price of freedom is high. But no price is as high as the loss of freedom."

By contrast, the Democratic senator from Florida, Bob Graham, avoided the point by generalizing, "No freedom is unlimited. All freedom occurs in the context of freedom for others." He said he had not heard the record nor read its lyrics.

The actual arrest of a musician galvanized the music community. Bruce Springsteen gave Luke Skyywalker the rights to his song "Born in the USA" for a rap version called "Banned in the USA." Skyywalker was acquitted, with the help of the Florida ACLU.

In any event, 2 Live Crew was never considered a significant rap group, and deprived of controversy, their records quickly declined in sales.

In July, the Judas Priest trial took place in Reno, Nevada. The rock group had been sued by the parents of Raymond Belknap, an eighteen-year-old who killed himself with a sawed-off shotgun while listening to the heavy metal group's album *Stained Class.* Lawyers for the family claimed there were subliminal messages in several songs that were "causative factors" in the suicide.

At the trial, it was revealed that Belknap had been an abused child, had a history of heavy drug and alcohol use, and had been intoxicated when he shot himself. The lawsuit was dismissed.

Amidst all the attacks on rock and rap music, Jeff Ayeroff and Jordan Harris of Virgin Records formed an organization called Rock the Vote to encourage young people to make their voices heard in politics. I was happy to support them.

Ayeroff was filled with zeal. He pounded the phones to get support from hundreds of music executives. He commissioned a spectacular poster called "Censorship Is Un-American" that showed a young black man with a restraining hand over his mouth.

Former California governor Jerry Brown, who had recently become the chairman of the state Democratic Party, agreed to be the main speaker at Rock the Vote's inaugural event.

Although I had met him only a few times, I was apparently the only person in the holding area before the event who Brown knew at all. He motioned me over to him and asked in a whisper what was going on and what I suggested he say to the crowd. I explained to Jerry that the people in the audience made a good living and could be not only Democratic voters but also significant contributors.

Most of them had families, I told him, and had been in the music business for all of their adult life. Most of them were liberals who had been busy with their careers for the last decade and hadn't been politically active since the end of the Vietnam War. They were proud of what they did for a living and deeply resented being called pornographers by politicians.

"All you need to do," I said, "is include a couple of sentences saying that you respect the music business and are against censorship in general terms, and you've got them for life."

Brown peered at me with his intense, intelligent brown eyes. "I got it," he said. He then proceeded to give a brilliant but rambling and impressionistic speech about the failures of the Reagan and Bush administrations in dealing with poverty, international suffering, and the drug war. Brown spoke for about forty-five minutes and never mentioned free speech, censorship, popular music, or entertainment of any kind.

Ronald Reagan, undoubtedly influenced by his background as an actor, had an honest fascination with popular culture that would have helped humanize many policy-wonk Democrats. His wife Nancy shared some of his qualities. I met the former president and First Lady at an event to mark the release of an album to benefit the Pediatric AIDS Foundation, of which the Reagans were honorary cochairs. I accompanied one of my clients, Pat Benatar, who had donated a song, as had Bruce Springsteen, Michael Jackson, and others.

I was introduced to the Reagans shortly before they were to appear at a press conference. Nancy Reagan, diminutive and intense, immediately grabbed my hands and said, "I know you." It turned out that she'd seen me as a guest on her son Ron's syndicated late-night TV talk show.

"We're changing the show," she told me, never losing eye contact. "The producers have him doing too much serious stuff. People want more humor and entertainment." I nodded silently and agreed wholeheartedly when she said how wonderful her son was. In truth, Ron Reagan was a gracious, self-effacing, and very funny guy.

Only a year or two out of office, President Reagan, though eighty years old, looked extraordinary. With his cheeks as pink as apples, a full head of hair, and a muscular build, he could have easily passed for a man twenty-five years younger.

He raved to his wife about the buffet table, which served Mrs. Fields chocolate chip cookies. "They're my favorite cookies in the world," Reagan said to me, evidently having decided that if I warranted his wife's attention, I should get some of his, too.

"When we were in the White House, I was very excited when they told me Mrs. Fields herself was going to visit. I imagined a matronly older woman, but Mrs. Fields is only in her forties and has young children. Can you believe it? Can you believe that Mrs. Fields is a young woman?" Mrs. Reagan interrupted his reveries and grabbed him by the elbow and snapped, "Come on, Ronnie, let's do the press conference." Once behind a microphone, Reagan spoke eloquently about AIDS, a subject he'd largely ignored as president.

In January of 1992, I was hired by Atlantic Records CEO Doug Morris to be the label's senior vice president on the West Coast. My first job at Atlantic was to help bring in some rock bands that would appeal to the now huge alternative rock audience. During my time at Atlantic, I was instrumental in signing Stone Temple Pilots, Hootie and the Blowfish, and Jewel. I also brought in the Matador label, which released the critical faves Pavement and Liz Phair.

As the 1992 election loomed, actor Ron Silver formed a New York–based group called the Creative Coalition. Silver visited Los Angeles to recruit support and was widely critical of the left-wing slant of some of the existing Hollywood organizations. Patrick Lippert, executive director of Rock the Vote, showed Silver a TV spot featuring a scantily clad Madonna urging people to vote. It remains one of the best-known public service announcements ever created. But Silver lectured us on how inappropriate it was. "It's like fighting fire with fire," he said, indicating that his New York actors would do something much classier.

Patrick had spent hundreds of hours launching Rock the Vote, first convincing MTV to get on board, then convincing celebrated artists to make the commercials, and finally getting the TV spots actually produced. The crowning jewel of a year's effort for Patrick, his staff, and Rock the Vote's board was the Madonna spot, which had gotten more media attention than any voter registration spot in memory. I exploded at Silver for his rudeness, which I felt was laden with exactly the sort of elitism that undermined numerous progressive causes.

The Southern California ACLU was extremely busy in that period as Los Angeles seethed with racial tension and anger, much of it directed at the Los Angeles Police Department. In April of 1991, the brutal beating of Rodney King by four LA policemen horrified millions of Americans when an amateur videotape was shown repeatedly on national TV news. For almost a decade, civil rights groups in Los Angeles and the ACLU had been complaining about the LAPD and in particular about Chief Daryl Gates. Long before the term "racial profiling" entered common usage, activists in Los Angeles charged that people of color were far more likely to be stopped or searched by the LAPD than whites. Several black athletes successfully sued the city of Los Angeles for inappropriate and unwarranted stops, apparently based solely on the color of their skin.

Still, Chief Gates retained the support of the vast majority of the Los Angeles elite. In part, he still benefited from the afterglow of the relatively crime-free 1984 LA Olympics.

The Rodney King tape changed the political reality, with the kind of effect on majority opinion that Bull Connor's police dogs attacking nonviolent civil rights demonstrators had generated a quarter of a century earlier. Years of pent-up resentment of Chief Gates came exploding forth.

Ramona Ripston and the ACLU legal staff had been documenting police abuses for more than a decade, and the ACLU played a pivotal role in the ensuing fight against Gates and abusive cops. Ramona put together a campaign and, within a few weeks, got more than 20,000 signatures on a petition calling for Gates's resignation "more than we got for Nixon's," she told me. A few weeks after the King beating, actor Wesley Snipes was stopped and detained by the police for no reason while driving through Beverly Hills, and he called Ramona fuming with indignation. We organized a press conference for Snipes, Blair Underwood, and several other black actors who had had the same experience.

Not long afterward we had a public forum at which actor Ed Asner played the role of Daryl Gates, reading actual quotes of the embattled chief, including his notorious statement, "In some blacks, when the choke hold is applied, the veins or arteries do not open up like in normal people."

Mayor Bradley, a former police chief, had refrained from criticizing Gates publicly despite many years of pressure from civil rights groups. Now Bradley too said it was time for the chief to go, and he appointed Stanley Sheinbaum president of the police commission, the five-member body to which the chief officially reported.

Bradley also asked Warren Christopher, the eminent Los Angeles attorney who would later be named Bill Clinton's secretary of state, to create a bipartisan commission to investigate police practices. The Christopher Commission concluded that the vast majority of the 7,000 Los Angeles police officers were excellent, law-abiding officials, but that there was a group of 200 to 300 who were regularly "racist and brutal," and that these officers were responsible for creating a breakdown of trust between the police department and the black community.

It was not until May of 1992, when the streets of Los Angeles exploded in a riot after the policemen charged with beating King were acquitted, that Gates was finally pushed out of office. More painful changes in the Los Angeles Police Department were to come over the next decade, as the full extent of the brutality and corruption of a small but powerful group in the department was revealed.

A year before the Rodney King beating set all the changes in motion, the LA group NWA released an album called *Straight Outta Compton*. It is considered the first "gangsta rap" album. *Straight Outta Compton* sold 2 million copies despite getting virtually no play on radio or MTV.

Public Enemy star Chuck D. had called rap music "the CNN of the ghetto." If the Los Angeles establishment had been tuning in, they might have wondered why an album with so little marketing clout behind it would have sold so extraordinarily well when its best-known song was called "Fuck tha Police."

CHAPTER 8

Mend It, Don't End It

When I first was involved with the music business, the record companies were run by real gangsters. Now the records are rapping about gangsters. From where I sit, this is progress.
—Reverend Al Sharpton, urging Time Warner record labels not to give in to pressure to remove gangsta rap from their rosters

I N THE EARLY PRIMARIES for the 1992 Democratic presidential nomination, I raised a little money for Senator Tom Harkin, who seemed to be the most progressive viable candidate. But Harkin never created excitement anywhere. By the beginning of May, Arkansas governor Bill Clinton had the nomination all but locked up. After three losses in a row, many Democrats saw a winner in the telegenic moderate Southerner, and Clinton had an intellectual depth on issues that attracted many progressives as well. I was very busy at Atlantic and with the ACLU, and I watched from the sidelines.

In May, Vice President Dan Quayle tried to energize the lethargic Bush reelection campaign by launching an attack against the morals of a woman who did not exist. In a campaign speech, Quayle criticized Murphy Brown because the sitcom character played by liberal Democrat Candice Bergen had a baby out of wedlock.

The Murphy Brown jab was not one of Quayle's famous gaffes, but had been carefully planned. It almost certainly came from Quayle's advisor, William Kristol, who was considered one of the bright lights of intellectual conservatism. ("Dan Quayle has one of the best minds in Washington," was the running joke in the nation's capital, "and it belongs to William Kristol.")

Quayle's point was that kids of unmarried mothers, especially poor mothers, are more likely than other kids to have unhappy or destructive lives. Few people of any political philosophy disagreed with the overall statistics he cited, despite the many successful and happy people who have been raised by single parents.

A TV portrayal of a happy, prosperous mom who chose to have an out-of-wedlock birth, Quayle argued, encouraged such behavior among poor teenage girls. His supporters noted that environmental lobbying groups seemed to think recycling could be "taught" by a fictional TV series. So why didn't single pregnancy fall into the same category? This echoed the argument of the Parents Music Resource Center: If corporations spend hundreds of millions of dollars on TV commercials, they must know that TV influences behavior.

From a common-sense point of view, I've always felt viewers may decide to wear a different brand of T-shirt or to recycle trash after watching TV. But that doesn't mean they make profound life decisions, such as whether or not to kill someone, or to have a baby and raise it as a single parent, because of feature films or TV sitcoms or song lyrics. These are forms of storytelling that are understood to be layered with comedy, romanticism, sentimentality, irony, hyperbole, and all the other devices of fiction. People understand that Murphy Brown is a made-up character in a made-up story, not a real woman living alone in a house that needs a lot of work.

"If Dan Quayle wants to assure that Murphy Brown doesn't have any more children out of wedlock," said the show's executive producer, Diane English, "he should work to assure her that she will be able to have safe, legal abortions." Dazzled by the political adroitness of Diane's riposte to the antichoice Quayle, Ramona Ripston and I suggested that she join the honorees for an upcoming ACLU dinner. Diane promptly agreed and supplied us with a montage of scenes from the show she felt were appropriate for the ACLU. We all felt particularly pleased that she would be part of our program, which also was honoring Mayor Tom Bradley.

At the last minute, we were derailed by the kind of self-destructive freak-out that is so common on the political left. English's production company was feuding with TV unions over procedures on another series. One of the unions threatened to picket the ACLU dinner unless we withdrew the award to English.

LA activist Paul Schrade, who saw himself as the staunchest labor advocate on the ACLU board, hounded Ramona and me to give in to the union. I pointed out to Schrade that the award to English had nothing to do with the TV show he was objecting to, and that to set up a picket line around a dinner for the ACLU, which had absolutely nothing to do with TV production of any kind, was a secondary boycott that was both illegal and a violation of ACLU policy. "Of course you feel that way," Schrade snapped. "You're management."

To my dismay, Ramona felt she had to compromise with the union to avoid the embarrassment of a picket line. She came up with the idea of asking English to allow us to show the montage without coming to the dinner herself.

We sent English the award privately the next day. It was immediately returned. English understandably felt betrayed by the ACLU for caving in and has never spoken to me since. It was the only time I considered resigning from the ACLU, but I didn't want to negate the many good things I felt about the organization because of this one disagreement.

Less than a month later, in mid-June, Bill Clinton launched his own attack against popular culture in one of the defining moments of his campaign. Speaking to Reverend Jesse Jackson's Rainbow Coalition, he harshly criticized Jackson for including on a panel at the group's annual conference an obscure rapper named Sister Souljah.

Sister Souljah had suggested it would have been more rational for blacks to attack white neighborhoods instead of their own in the LA riots. Her statement was clearly ironic—if anything, it could be interpreted as a black critique of the senselessness of the riot.

But Clinton saw it as an opportunity to differentiate himself from Jackson and from previous Democratic nominees. Focus groups of swing voters in Michigan had revealed that many white working-class Democratic voters had switched to Reagan and Bush because they felt that the Democratic Party was too deferential toward blacks, as evidenced by the visibility at the 1988 convention of the Reverend Jesse Jackson.

In July, Clinton named Al Gore as his running mate. On the slow news day before the Democratic Convention started, CNN asked me for a comment. I said that I'd rather have Gore a heart-beat away from the White House than Dan Quayle. The morning the sound bite aired, I ran into John Dukakis, Michael Dukakis's son, in a Hollywood dry cleaner's. John was the business manager for Boyz II Men and other musical acts. Usually diffident and soft-spoken, he gave me a hug and enthused, "I'm glad you played it that way, we need to stick together right now." Many of my friends in the music business felt differently. Music journalist Dave Marsh and others, including my wife, accused me of selling out.

Not long afterward, the 1992 campaign bumped up against the music business in a controversy about a song by Ice-T called "Cop Killer." It had been on an album released by Warner Brothers the year before, and had neither sold well nor garnered much critical acclaim. When several police associations found out about the song, in which an aggrieved black man fantasizes about killing a police officer, they made it a cause célèbre.

Time Warner chairman Jerry Levin initially defended the album as a valid artistic work in a *Wall Street Journal* op-ed piece. President George Bush, Bill Clinton, Al Gore, and especially Dan Quayle, the four major candidates in the upcoming national election, weighed in with opposition to the song, each trying to outdo the other in terms of pro-police rhetoric. Police groups and their allies, including National Rifle Association president Charlton Heston, decided to make an issue of "Cop Killer" at the 1992 Time Warner stockholders meeting.

I was then working for Atlantic Records, which was, like Warner Brothers, a division of the Warner Music Group. Although relations between Atlantic and Warner Brothers were usually chilly with corporate sibling rivalry, Warner Brothers chairman Mo Ostin asked me to brainstorm with his staff. Mo was a staunch defender of artistic freedom.

"I'd put out an anti-Semitic record if my A&R people told me the music was valid," said Ostin, who is Jewish. It seemed to us that the lyrics had to be considered in the context of the humiliation and frustration many Los Angeles–area African Americans had been feeling about the LAPD under Daryl Gates. Lyrics to songs were typically filled with symbolism and exaggeration. Most important, we did not believe that people decided to become violent because of song lyrics.

I sat quietly in the disruptive shareholders meeting as Charlton Heston urged Time Warner to get rid of the no-longer obscure "Cop Killer." Impassioned police officers spoke in outraged tones about being wounded in the line of duty. No one attempted to make any connection between those tragic assaults and a song, but the sheer existence of "Cop Killer" was considered an affront to many police.

The next week, Time Warner's board of directors called for a retreat. Opera diva Beverly Sills was said to have been particularly hard on Mo Ostin. Articles outlining the violent and perverse plot lines of numerous classic operas did nothing to assuage her.

Under intense corporate pressure, Ostin reluctantly negotiated the return of the album to Ice-T and dropped him as a Warner Brothers artist. Howie Klein, the Warner executive closest to Ice-T, recalls, "Before the controversy, the album had sold a disappointing two hundred thousand copies. Afterward, because of all the publicity, it sold one million. I made up a 'platinum' plaque to present to Dan Quayle to thank him for selling so many more records, but Mo didn't want me to actually give it to him."

Having established his credibility with swing white voters by going after Sister Souljah and Ice-T, Clinton showed the political skills that made him a legend. He tacked back toward black and popular culture by playing the saxophone on *The Arsenio Hall Show* and by cooperating with MTV correspondent Tabitha Soren in the network's "Choose or Lose" voter registration campaign, done in partnership with Rock the Vote.

President Bush avoided MTV until the end of the campaign. When he finally consented to be interviewed by Tabitha, he did so while drinking a cup of coffee, exuding body language of discomfort and even contempt. By comparison, Clinton looked like the hippest of hepcats.

The 1992 election was the first since 1972, when eighteen-year-olds became able to vote, in which the voting rate among young people increased, and Clinton won that demographic by twelve points.

Shortly after Clinton was elected, I met his younger brother, Roger, who was looking for a record deal. A week later, I went to a TV show produced by Clinton friend and media advisor Harry Thomason where Roger performed as a warm-up act with a pop/R&B band he called Politics.

Thomason, white-haired, gregarious, and friendly, speaking with a slight stutter, assured us that the president-elect cared deeply about his brother and wanted him to be able to emerge as a performer. Roger, it turned out, had a decent rock/R&B voice, which he used to sing a few oldies and several forgettable new songs. He clearly was talented enough to get gigs as a singer in a bar band, and clearly not unique or special enough to warrant major-label attention were it not for his last name. He was, however, an extremely likable, earnest guy whose brother was going to be president.

Caught up in the moment, we recorded a single song, a cover of Sam Cooke's "A Change Is Gonna Come," backed by the popular R&B group En Vogue. We later gave the rights to the recording to Roger, who included it on an album he released on Pyramid Records.

Late in the afternoon of Inauguration Day there was a reception at the offices of the *New Republic* magazine in Washington, D.C. Al and Tipper Gore attended. As I passed them on my way out, I made eye contact with Tipper and, over the din of the party, mouthed the word "Congratulations." To the astonishment of my friends, she reached over and gave me a big hug.

That evening, the celebrity-laden MTV Ball attracted an extremely high turnout from members of the new Clinton administration. The new president came and thanked Rock the Vote and MTV for their role in his election, but when Roger Clinton emerged to do his version of "A Change Is Gonna Come," the president was nowhere to be found. I later heard he was angry at Roger for some indiscretion.

MTV's Judy McGrath was still aglow from attending a long meeting with Bill Clinton. With her had been Rock the Vote's executive director, Patrick Lippert, a longtime activist for progressive causes, who was thin and drawn from AIDS. Judy recalled, "Clinton looked at Patrick and then at me, and in one instant I could see that he knew the condition Patrick was in, and he gave Patrick this giant long hug and thanked him for everything he had done. We were all crying."

The Clinton years brought many Democrats and some progressives to the halls of power. I was not a so-called Friend of Bill's, but many of my friends and colleagues found themselves in a relationship with the president of the United States for the first time. People who'd been shunned by the White House for more than a decade suddenly had the opportunity to sleep in the Lincoln bedroom. David Geffen and Barbra Streisand had each raised seven-figure sums for the Democrats, were at the apex of accomplishment, and were compelling, charismatic figures. Stories of their visits to the White House and their conversations with the president quickly made the rounds.

Stanley Sheinbaum, who was more doggedly left-wing than most Clinton friends, and less significant as a fundraiser, also had access to the president. When Clinton had first become governor of Arkansas, Stanley and his wife Betty had often let the Clintons stay at their Brentwood home. Stanley's primary concern, once he left the LA police commission, was the conflict in the Middle East, and he frequently peppered Clinton with a far more evenhanded perspective than that which came from the official emissaries of the Jewish community.

But no matter who was in the White House, political attacks on popular culture never went away. Booth Gardner, the newly elected Democratic governor of Washington, proudly identified his state as the home of Nirvana in a 1993 address to the legislature. By then, Nirvana had become the most successful and influential rock band in the world. A few months later, the state legislature passed a bill making it illegal for kids under eighteen to attend rock shows that included profanity, even when there was no liquor present.

I called the governor to ask him to veto the bill, which would effectively end rock concerts in the state of Washington and also signal a terrible disrespect to the music scene in Seattle that he seemingly took pride in.

Gardner replied, "I'm going to sign it, but it's unconstitutional, so it will never be enacted." I asked why he was going to sign it if he knew it was unconstitutional. "I think it sends a message," he responded. I asked just what the message was, the message that he wanted me to give Nirvana. "It sends a message that needs to be sent. I think the message speaks for itself," the governor concluded, before hastily hanging up.

Rap came under heavy fire as the music became bigger than ever. The most successful label was Death Row out of LA. Its artists included Dr. Dre, Snoop Dogg, and Tupac Shakur. Death Row was affiliated with Interscope Records, which in turn was affiliated with Atlantic Records. One of my responsibilities at Atlantic was to act as a liaison with Interscope, and I talked to Interscope president Jimmy Iovine every day as the attacks on his artists mounted.

At one point, I set up a meeting between Congresswoman Maxine Waters, Snoop Dogg, and Death Row's controversial owner, Suge Knight. Snoop Dogg was under investigation because his bodyguard had killed someone who supposedly intended to attack Snoop. (Snoop was later acquitted of all charges.) At the meeting, the tall, extremely thin, gangly rap star was soft-spoken and as polite as the choirboy he had been in his younger years.

After Snoop left the meeting, Suge told Maxine that he intended to build some playgrounds in the poor neighborhoods of her district. Maxine stared at him and said, "I'm not here to talk about playgrounds. You know I speak up for you and that I respect what you do. And as far as I'm concerned, anything you want to put onto your albums is fine. It's your art form. But you have to make sure that there isn't any more violence around you or the people in your business. There are enough people who want to stop you. Don't give them the chance to shut you down."

Maxine talked with emotion about the promising young people she had known who were now in prison. Suge was polite and appeared to listen thoughtfully to everything she said. But subsequent violent events, which led to Suge Knight spending five years in prison, indicated that her message didn't have much impact.

The profanity and aggressiveness of rap music strained generational lines as no music had since the political rock of the sixties. Some middle-aged rock artists who had once been attacked for their music found themselves in strange positions. When Luke Skyywalker was arrested in Florida in 1990, I'd asked Allman Brothers drummer Butch Trucks, a Floridian who supported progressive causes, to make a statement opposing the arrest. Butch demurred. "I hate it when my son listens to that rap shit," he said. "I'd feel like a hypocrite defending it."

Some black intellectuals, like Henry Louis Gates of Harvard, defended hip-hop as an authentic art form. And some older African American musicians saw rap as an exciting new vanguard of creative expression. At a Time Warner forum during which Maya Angelou questioned the morality of some rap artists, arranger/composer Quincy Jones, well into his sixties, got up and said, "I'm with the rappers."

But many African Americans who had lived through the civil rights struggle were embarrassed by the anti-intellectual and, at times, seemingly illiterate persona of rap music.

One night, I was at a dinner party at the home of journalist Jack Newfield with former governor Mario Cuomo, his wife Matilda and Stanley Crouch. Prompted by Cuomo, I was describing the tensions between the teen and political cultures when Crouch, who is a great authority on jazz, interrupted and began berating me for defending rap music. I told Crouch that I wasn't comparing rap tracks

to the virtuosity and brilliance of Duke Ellington, but was defending the need of each generation to express its rebellion and unique-
ness through its own culture.

Crouch snarled that the whole idea of teenage rebellion was a
creation of the media and added that he had recently explained to
his nineteen-year-old daughter that she was too young to have
valuable opinions about anything.

Newfield, who shared my feelings about pop culture and generational snobbery, and who stood on the front lines of political and
cultural battles for decades, stared into his soup, hoping this unexpected moment of tension between two of his friends would go
away. Cuomo turned to me and asked, "Do boys and girls still
dance?" I nodded that they did. Cuomo responded with a theatrical hand flourish and replied, "As long as they still dance, it's okay."

And the tension left the room.

Not long after being elected, President Clinton appeared on MTV
and fielded some questions from the studio audience. When a
teenage girl asked whether he wore "boxers or briefs," Clinton
laughed and answered, "briefs." The Washington political establishment condemned him, arguing that answering the question de-
meaned the presidency. Clinton advisor Paul Begala told me later
that he thought the answer had been a serious mistake.

I disagreed. American political culture desperately needs connective tissue with young people. However, Clinton was highly sensitive to elite criticism, and he backed away from "lowbrow" media
and popular culture early in his first term.

One afternoon in 1993, I was invited, along with a few hundred
others in the entertainment business, to hear President Clinton
speak at the offices of Creative Artists Agency (CAA). Mike Ovitz,
president of CAA at the time, was one of the most powerful men in
the entertainment business. As Ovitz and the president walked

down to the lobby, Tom Epstein, whom I'd met on the Hart campaign and who was now an assistant to the president, beamed with adulation. He whispered to me, "I think Clinton has something really interesting to say today."

After enthusing about American entertainment, Clinton advanced a theory about the effects of violent entertainment on poor children with disengaged parents. People from conventional backgrounds, such as those listening to him that afternoon, could easily distinguish between reality and fantasy, he said. But poor, neglected kids treat the media as a parent and emulate it the way normal kids emulate their parents.

Those of us responsible for the content of films, TV, and recordings, the president said, needed to imagine the effect of each work on kids who supposedly view the media as their "third parent."

I would hear this theory repeated many times over the years. I think it is complete nonsense.

According to Justice Department studies, the biggest predictor of violent behavior in individuals is whether or not they have been abused as kids. Compared to the trauma of abuse, the influence of a rap song or horror movie is virtually nil. It bordered on obscene to substitute clichés about entertainment for action on the problems that Congressman George Miller and his colleagues had described to us several years earlier: terrible nutrition, bad education, flawed foster care programs, lack of mentors, physical and mental abuse, and the other soul-destroying effects of poverty and neglect.

Many authorities do not agree that children tend to imitate evil deeds depicted in fiction. Renowned child psychiatrist Bruno Bettelheim discusses this point in his classic book *The Uses of Enchantment: The Meaning and Importance of Fairy Tales*. According to Bettelheim, the violence and villainy of classic fairy tales help kids work out their anxieties and forge their identity.

There is no era or culture with a modicum of freedom whose art and entertainment doesn't include the darkest human impulses as themes. Many artists I've worked with who've written lyrics about alienation and violence get emotional letters from fans thanking them for making them feel less alone.

At an ACLU dinner, music manager Jeff Kwatinetz noted that a high school in Michigan had suspended a student for wearing a T-shirt with the logo of the hard rock band Korn, his client.

"Sure," he said, "Korn's music has not always been free of profanity, but their use of language is always reflective of intense emotions and true, visceral feeling."

He said the band received thousands of letters saying essentially the same thing: "I thought I was all alone, but after hearing your music, now that I know I'm not, I can go on with my life and look forward to better times in the future."

In any event, it would be crippling for artists to limit their work based on the possible reaction of the most emotionally damaged members of their audience. Should the Beatles have tried to imagine the effect "Helter Skelter" would have on the psychopathic mind of Charles Manson and tailored the song accordingly?

Just prior to the 1994 midterm election, I got a call from MTV's Judy McGrath, who had been so excited at the inauguration less than two years earlier. "As far as our viewers go," Judy said to me in disgust, "this election is going to be a disaster for the Democrats. Again and again in focus groups we keep hearing young people say, 'I thought Clinton was one of us and it turns out he was one of them.'"

Republicans won the House of Representatives for the first time in forty years.

By then, Rosemary and I had moved back to New York with our three-year-old daughter, Katie, and our new baby son, Max. My boss, Doug Morris, had named me president of Atlantic Records. I stepped down as chair of the ACLU Foundation of Southern California and accepted the more ceremonial role of foundation president, a title I still hold.

After we got settled in New York, Henry Siegman, the executive director of the American Jewish Congress, suggested that I get involved with that organization.

In the 1960s, the New York–based American Jewish Congress had played a leading role in the civil rights movement. I felt that in recent years the organization had focused more on defending Jewish interests than on fighting for minorities and the poor, which I and many Jewish liberals historically viewed as core Jewish values. My father, Victor Goldberg, felt very strongly that to be a good Jew, one must actively care about the most disadvantaged people. He was retired from the textile business and was interested in becoming involved in promoting those beliefs.

After meeting with the board of the American Jewish Congress, I accepted the post of executive vice president, with the understanding that my father and I would create an institute for intergroup relations that would focus initially on repairing black-Jewish relations.

Unfortunately, Henry Siegman chose this time to leave the AJC, and the board named his deputy, Phil Baum, as an interim executive director.

I became nervous almost immediately when Baum began criticizing Siegman for having been too far "left" on Middle East issues, since Siegman had favored dialogue with the PLO. Shortly afterward, Baum issued a statement criticizing the Reverend Jesse Jackson for "trivializing the Holocaust" in a speech at a New York synagogue. Jackson's speech was primarily a plea for intergroup tolerance. In referring to the intolerance of Pat Robertson's right-wing Christian Coalition, Jackson said that Nazi Germany had had groups like that as well.

I thought Baum's attack on Jackson, who was clearly reaching out to the Jewish community, was incredibly inappropriate. I did not want to be accountable for Baum's behavior so I publicly resigned, citing the attack on Jackson.

Jackson called appreciatively, and he visited me at Atlantic several times. From time to time, Reverend Jackson has lectured on tertainment companies about content in a way that seems overreaching to me, such as in the eighties when he criticized the Rolling Stones for their lyrics, and more recently the film *Barbershop*. But because of his experiences in the civil rights movement, he sees music and other forms of entertainment as a valuable tool in political organizing. His daughter Santita is an R&B and gospel singer. The longtime civil rights leader also had an extensive history with Steve Ross, the recently deceased CEO of Time Warner, who had financially supported many of Jackson's projects.

In my experiences at major corporations, I found Jackson to be very different from the cartoon version that conservative critics have drawn. While he would seek donations from time to time, there was never any sense that his friendship was conditional on them. On the contrary, with Steve Ross's death, Time Warner decreased its support of Jackson, and I was in no position to do much about it. Over the years, he's done much more for me than I have for him. When Jesse includes me among those to whom he delivers his monologues about current events, I am always dazzled by his brilliance. His observations are more penetrating than those of 99 percent of elected officials, academics, and pundits.

Early in 1994, Marge Tabankin accepted a fellowship at the Kennedy School of Government at Harvard. We had long ago become close friends as we fought for common causes, and she invited me to come up to Boston and take part in a forum on entertainment and politics. At a dinner afterward, I sat next to Marvin Kalb, the venerable newscaster, author, and professor, a pillar of the intellectual media establishment.

Kalb asked me about what kinds of records sold well and I told him that sales were dominated by the tastes of teenagers, who bought more albums per person than anyone else, resulting in big sales for rock and roll, pop, and rap music. Kalb looked mournful and asked me, "What percentage of total sales are original cast recordings of classic Broadway shows?"

I told him far less than 1 percent. He shook his head sorrowfully. I asked him when the last time was that he had bought a cast recording, and he said he couldn't remember. Then he said that it reflected very badly on the culture that such "classics" didn't sell.

The implication of Kalb's disapproval was that popular culture and the culture of younger generations was illegitimate, even though he himself had limited passion for the culture of the past. It was a classic paternalistic posture of "do as I say, not as I do."

That same year, a corporate drama began unfolding that would dramatically bring together politics and culture, my professional life, and my activist persona.

Atlantic, where I worked, was one of three record companies in the Warner Music Group, a division of Time Warner. The other two were Elektra and Warner Brothers Records.

Since the mid-1960s, Warner Brothers Records had been run by Mo Ostin, one of the most talented and effective music executives of all time. From a tiny, virtually invisible label, Mo had created the number one record company in the world, with a roster that included Madonna, Rod Stewart, Prince, REM, Van Halen, the Red Hot Chili Peppers, Neil Young, and Green Day.

Following Steve Ross's death in 1994, an internal battle began. Mo Ostin was forced out by Warner Music chairman Robert Morgado. Following more corporate machinations, I was asked to leave Atlantic and become the new chairman of Warner Brothers Records.

A few months later, as I struggled to get acquainted with the vast artist roster and executive team at my new company, Morgado was replaced with HBO chairman Michael Fuchs. The chemistry between Fuchs and my boss, Doug Morris, at that point chairman of Warner Music for the United States, was dreadful from the beginning, so I knew my own situation was precarious.

In the spring of 1995, while we were going through these gut-wrenching corporate changes, Senate majority leader Robert Dole, the front-runner for the Republican presidential nomination in the 1996 election, made a scathing speech about an entertainment culture that he said was rife with "nightmares of depravity." According to *The Choice*, Bob Woodward's book about the election, Dole was urged by political advisor Bill Lacy to gain political ground by an "attack [on] Hollywood directly on the grounds of sex and violence in movies and popular music."

The speech, written by Mari Will (wife of conservative columnist George Will), excoriated "a culture business that makes money from 'music' extolling the pleasures of raping, killing, torturing and mutilating women—from 'songs' about killing policemen and rejecting law."

"The mainstreaming of deviancy must come to an end," Dole proclaimed. "We will name their names and shame them as they deserve to be shamed. One of the companies on the leading edge of coarseness and violence is Time Warner.

"I would ask executives at Time Warner a question," he continued. "Is this what you intended to accomplish with your careers? Must you debase our nation and threaten our children for the sake of corporate profits?"

Dole specifically attacked the films *Natural Born Killers* and *True Romance,* and named heavy metal act Cannibal Corpse and rappers Geto Boys and 2 Live Crew, but the most intense criticism was of Atlantic's joint venture with Interscope and its Death Row Records roster of gangsta rappers.

When reporters asked Dole for more detail about the films and records he'd attacked, he sheepishly admitted that he hadn't watched or heard any of them and had based his comments on what others had told him. He admitted he hadn't seen *True Lies* either, although he had bizarrely cited the gory R-rated action film starring Arnold Schwarzenegger as a family-friendly film. *True Lies* was as violent as the movies he condemned, but Schwarzenegger was one of the few big movie stars who regularly campaigned for Republicans.

Notwithstanding the incoherence and hearsay underlying Dole's position, his speech made front pages around the country and was widely praised by media pundits and politicians of both parties.

I asked Clint Eastwood, a Republican, what he thought of Dole's speech. Eastwood is one of America's great patrons of jazz, and I had set up Malpaso Records at Warner Brothers for jazz artists he wanted to support. "You know politicians," Eastwood grumbled in his gravelly voice. "They'll say anything to get their name in the paper."

The Dole speech triggered intense pressure on Doug Morris to "do something" about Interscope, either to sell Time Warner's half ownership of the label or get it to tone down the Death Row rappers. Jimmy Iovine and Ted Field, who owned the other half of Interscope, had no intention of asking rappers to change music that their fans obviously loved. Dr. Dre's recent album had sold 5 million copies and Snoop Dogg's had sold 6 million, putting them among the most popular recordings of the year.

A press conference to attack rap music and Interscope was called by C. Delores Tucker, a former civil rights activist who had become the most outspoken African American opponent of rap; William Bennett, the former drug czar in the Bush administration; and Democratic senator Joseph Lieberman of Connecticut. The triumvirate got a meeting with top Warner executives Jerry Levin and Doug Morris, where Bennett challenged Levin to read Dr.

Dre's lyrics out loud. Raps, like other lyrics, are obviously not written to be recited by businessmen without accompaniment, but this gimmick would become a staple of confrontations between cultural reactionaries and entertainment executives.

Carla Hills, who had been the U.S. trade representative in the George Bush administration, was a member of the Time Warner board and was said to have been mortified when Dole teased her about the company's rap records at a Republican fundraiser.

Shortly thereafter, the Reverend Al Sharpton asked to meet with us. I joined Doug Morris, Elektra Records chairman Sylvia Rhone, and Ken Sunshine, who had recently been hired by Warner Music as a corporate PR expert, in the Time Warner conference room, where Sharpton urged us not to get rid of rap music.

From his days as a child preacher, the New York civil rights leader had been friends with James Brown. He had later worked with the Jackson family. He had a vivid memory of the fifties and early sixties, when R&B music was banned from pop radio playlists and shunned by many major labels for supposedly moral reasons. Afterward he told a battery of news crews he had urged us not to give in to conservative pressure, which he viewed as racist.

Reverend Jesse Jackson, Representative Maxine Waters, Professor Michael Eric Dyson of the University of North Carolina, and Professor Henry Louis Gates, director of African American Studies at Harvard, were among the black leaders who subsequently echoed Sharpton's sentiments.

Clinton campaign advisors James Carville and Paul Begala called Sunshine and me and gave us a private pep talk, helping us brainstorm about how to spin the issue, but there was no interest elsewhere in the white political or pundit world in refuting the attacks. To the best of my knowledge, no white Democratic officeholder has ever publicly disagreed with the damning of pop culture by Dole and Lieberman.

On a short corporate leash, I did make one public comment criticizing the critics. Asked by the *Washington Post* if I would've signed Nine Inch Nails, one of the Interscope artists who had been attacked, I replied:

"Nine Inch Nails is a Grammy Award–winning, critically acclaimed artist who millions of people love. Why should a corporation listen to a bunch of middle-aged people who don't like the music and don't listen to it and ignore the people who do love it and who do buy it?"

Doug Morris had encouraged me to respond to the attacks on Interscope, but now his boss Fuchs insisted I stop, so I canceled a scheduled appearance on *Face the Nation*. Guest William Bennett gloated at my absence: "I'm not surprised that Warner wouldn't want Mr. Goldberg to represent them. He's with the extreme left of the ACLU."

And Robert Bork would soon slam me for the *Washington Post* quote in his best-seller *Slouching Toward Gomorrah*: "The reason the corporation should listen to those middle-aged people is that they are attempting to uphold some standard of decency, for the protection, among others, of those who love and buy the filth."

Having been too young to make Nixon's enemies list, I figured that being attacked by Bork and Bennett is the closest I can come. As all this was going on, Interscope's Jimmy Iovine called me, laughing, and said, "It's your curse to defend what makes me rich."

In July, Doug Morris was fired by Fuchs. I was out in August, and by the end of the year Fuchs himself had been fired by Time Warner chairman Levin. Early the next year, Time Warner sold its half of Interscope to Universal for $200 million.

In January 1996 I accepted a job as president of Mercury Records, a New York–based label that was a division of Polygram. My predecessor, Ed Eckstine, son of jazz legend Bill Eckstine, had discovered and signed several important R&B artists, including

Vanessa Williams, Brian McKnight, and Toni Tone Tony. Bon Jovi and John Cougar Mellencamp had been on the roster since the seventies.

A creative soul whose best work came in the recording studio, Ed was burned out on executive life, but he had left Mercury with two hits, a platinum album (1 million copies sold) by the so-called hippie band Rusted Root, and a brilliant Joan Osborne album titled *Relish* that would sell over 4 million. As I arrived, "One of Us," a single from *Relish*, was becoming a huge hit around the world.

"One of Us," written by Eric Bazilian, was one of those very rare songs that was both instantly catchy and genuinely meaningful. The lyrics imagined God physically walking the earth and even taking a bus.

Rather than rejoice that a piece of pop culture was dealing with spirituality on a very human level, William Donahue of the Catholic League attacked the song as "anti-Catholic" because of the supposedly irreverent reference to the Pope. Joan, who was raised as a Catholic, was disgusted.

The furor reminded me of my management days, when one of my clients, the Christian heavy metal band Stryper, was attacked by televangelist Jimmy Swaggart. Regardless of the lyrics, Swaggart maintained, rock and roll was inherently evil because of the sensual rhythm and music. The members of Stryper and their families had been great admirers of Swaggart and ended their concerts by throwing Bibles into the audience. They were devastated by his irrational attack on them.

This kind of wrongheaded, stubbornly narrow interpretation of religious orthodoxy, a kind of spiritual version of political correctness, was not restricted to Christian leaders in the late nineties. Both of my kids were fans of the Nickelodeon TV show *Rugrats*, and one of the things I particularly liked about the program was that it depicted the Pickles family as unambiguously Jewish. *Rugrats* even created Hanukkah and Passover specials. I cannot think of any other TV show, animated or otherwise, in which Jewish traditions were so clearly expressed in the context of a mass appeal entertainment.

Rather than celebrate this remarkable development, the Anti-Defamation League attacked *Rugrats*, followed by the *Washington Post* editorial page. Supposedly, the drawings of the Pickle grandparents resembled anti-Semitic drawings from the 1930s in a Nazi newspaper. Albie Hecht, the Jewish president of Nickelodeon, was flabbergasted by the absurdity of this accusation.

At the same time, Jenette Kahn, the Jewish president of DC Comics, directed that an issue of *Superman* be devoted to the superhero traveling back in time to the days of the Holocaust. Rather than congratulating DC Comics for dramatizing the murder of millions of Jews for a younger generation, the ADL's Abe Foxman criticized the comic because the victims were not explicitly identified as Jewish—despite the fact that they all had Jewish names and spoke Yiddish.

Meanwhile in Washington, a new technology called the V-chip was being eagerly endorsed by many pundits and politicos. The V-chip is designed to let parents program their television sets to block children from watching shows with adult themes.

Dr. Rosalyn Weinman, who was an NBC executive at the time, recalls, "The V-chip proposal came about because Senator Paul Simon, while staying in a hotel, saw some of *The Texas Chainsaw Massacre* on Spectravision and confused it with broadcast."

Spectravision was a pay cable service that could only be accessed through a credit card, usually as part of the billing in hotels. In other words, it was virtually impossible for a kid to stumble upon a Spectravision movie accidentally.

Painstaking and repeated explanations to Simon and his staff that his experience had absolutely nothing to do with network television, or even conventional cable TV, did not seem to get the point across. "He couldn't distinguish between the box and what came out of the box," recalls Dr. Weinman. "And his staff refused to acknowledge the distinction as well."

A series of meetings on the V-chip ensued, first with Simon and other members of Congress, later with top representatives of the Clinton administration. All embraced the gimmick.

Dr. Weinman, as executive vice president of standards and practices, was NBC's chief spokesperson and strategist on dealing with government pressure. She recalled, "The conversations were tautologies. They were truly going around in circles. It was 'whose definition?' Good violence versus bad violence."

Simon focused on graphic violence because it supposedly led to real violence. But Janet Reno, who has admitted that she did not own a TV set prior to becoming attorney general, was concerned about violence that wasn't graphic enough. Sanitized violence, she believed, could mislead kids into underestimating the consequences of violent behavior.

"The more we talked," Dr. Weinman recalled, "the more frightful it was in terms of who gets to decide on the definition of what is or is not deemed as violent entertainment."

Advocates of the V-chip, like others who have attacked entertainment media over the years, insisted that there were numerous scientific studies that "proved" a connection between television and antisocial behavior. In fact, there is a vast range of scholarly disagreement on the subject.

No respected scientist would argue that smoking has not been shown to cause cancer. But a number of academics and researchers question the validity of studies suggesting that television causes violence. Jib Fowles of the University of Houston dissects many supposedly scientific studies in great detail in *The Case for Television Violence*. Civil liberties authority Marjorie Heins does the same in *Not in Front of the Children*, which in 2002 won the American Library Association's award for the best book on intellectual freedom.

In November of 2000, Fenton Earls of Harvard and Jonathan Freeman of the University of Toronto, among others, debunked the TV/violence research in a thoroughly investigated *Rolling Stone* article by Pulitzer Prize–winner Richard Rhodes.

These and other scholars and journalists conclude that the much-publicized studies linking TV and violence lack credibility because they are based on completely artificial testing environments. Moreover, a phenomenon called "researcher expectation" makes subjects, particularly children, tend to want to give researchers the answers they are looking for.

In some studies, those exposed to supposedly violent TV clips actually exhibited less aggression than control groups. One study even showed that exposure to *Sesame Street* and *Mister Rogers' Neighborhood* tripled aggressiveness in preschool kids.

"It's lousy science," says Dr. Weinman dismissively. "Kids watching a cartoon and then loudly saying 'pow, pow' is neither a reliable nor valid finding that television violence causes real-world violence."

Ultimately, government officials admitted there is no proof that violent entertainment causes violent behavior, but they said there is a "correlation," a conclusion that is worthless in showing cause and effect. There is also a correlation between being admitted to the hospital and dying.

Violent people may be disproportionately attracted to violent entertainment. But that does not mean that the entertainment itself makes them violent. Millions of people watch violent movies and live nonviolent lives. In Japan, extremely graphic violence is a staple of television. Japan has a very low rate of violent crime.

Dr. Weinman was frustrated by congressional staffers who refused to consider research that contradicted their biases. "A good deal of shoddy academic work was heralded by people in government," she said. "One particularly egregious study stated that the most violent program in the year the study took place was *Laugh-In*'s twenty-fifth anniversary show."

The whole endeavor, she said, was undermined by the refusal to even look at the effects of television news. She said, "Every piece of legitimate research showed that if there was a truly problematic effect, it was a result of kids watching real news, especially young children watching during the five o'clock to six o'clock local-news time period, when producers often follow the maxim, 'If it bleeds it leads.'" But, Dr. Weinman said, politicians and their aides shied away from stirring up the ire of journalists.

During that period, at a dinner with television executives, Vice President Gore remarked, "TV violence is like salt. Salt doesn't hurt most people, but for a few it was bad for their health." President Clinton had been working from a similar arrogant assumption when he suggested that entertainment executives tailor their shows and recordings based on their possible impact on the most emotionally damaged and vulnerable members of the audience.

Television executives were repeatedly frustrated when they tried to talk specifics with congressional aides. Dr. Weinman recalls, "I would ask them to give me an example of five shows that they thought were violent, so I could get a flavor of what they wanted blocked. And they'd be silent, so I'd say, 'Tell me four, tell me three, tell me two.' And they literally would say, without any embarrassment, 'Well, I don't really watch much TV.' They were unable to give any examples of any specific shows that they deemed violent."

In February, the Telecommunications Act of 1996 was signed by President Clinton, mandating V-chips for half of all TV sets with thirteen-inch screens or larger sold after June of 1999, and all sold after June of 2000. The networks agreed on a ratings system that they hoped would conform to V-chip capability.

Within a few years, the failure of the plan was clear. In July of 2001, the Kaiser Family Foundation released a survey showing that only 17 percent of parents who had one of the new TV sets and 7 percent of all American parents used the V-chip, despite wide-spread publicity from the networks and parents' publications. And there were very few calls to an 800 number set up for anyone who wanted to complain about programming. Says one network executive, "This was strictly a creation of the Beltway."

Shortly after I interviewed her for this book, Dr. Weinman called me to add a thought. "There were hundreds and hundreds of hours spent by very intelligent people on the V-chip. Instead of all that effort being made for political expediency, that combination of government officials and TV producers could have done *something* that was actually helpful," she said mournfully.

The liberal snobs inside the Washington Beltway did not let up on their attacks on popular culture. Senator Joseph Lieberman and others complained when NBC moved the time slot of the popular TV sitcom *Friends* from 9 p.m. to 8 p.m., when more children presumably would be awake. *Friends* is filled with sexual innuendo among its young adult characters, but it is far from graphic in either its images or its language.

"We got virtually no complaints about *Friends* being at eight o'clock," said NBC's Dr. Weinman. "If there was a news interrupt or an Olympics interrupt in regular programming in that time frame, you could get as many 2,000 to 3,000 phone calls complaining that regularly scheduled shows were preempted. So it's not as though people who wanted to contact the networks to complain about programming couldn't figure out how to do it."

Political scientists can do a far better job than I can in evaluating President Clinton's first term, but it seems almost impossible to find a rational description of it. To his partisans he was a genius who saved America's economy. To the right he was an incarnation of the worst aspects of the sixties. To many on the left his presidency was, as Harry Belafonte says, "a betrayal" because of his failure to

get universal health care, his uncritical support of big business interests, his mostly moderate judicial appointments, and his luke-
warm support for civil liberties. Belafonte laments, "We invested in
Clinton and he helped put the knife into liberal character, and liberal minds."

To me, Clinton was what he always said he was: a political moderate, more progressive than recent Republicans and less so than
liberal Democrats. Although I share a lot of the progressive critique
of Clinton, there is no denying that on some crucial cultural issues
he made a huge positive difference. No previous president acknowledged the gay and lesbian community the way Clinton did,
and his actions, big and small, helped break down an ugly and immoral wall of prejudice. And most significant, when affirmative action for minorities and women was under assault by both
conservative forces and middle-of-the-road Democrats, Clinton
guaranteed it for another generation with his impassioned and effective speech in which he said, "Mend it, don't end it." It was no
accident that African Americans became one of Clinton's most loyal
group of supporters, and it reflects on Clinton's best side.

After losing the 1996 presidential election, the would-be moral
leader Bob Dole began appearing on TV and in print ads as a
spokesperson for the newly available impotence drug Viagra. With his
newfound image as a virile older guy, Dole then appeared in a Pepsi
commercial sitting next to a hound dog and watching sexily dressed
teenage pop singer Britney Spears dance and gyrate suggestively.

As the commercial ends, Dole glances up at the screen, then at
his dog, and says, "Down, boy."

CHAPTER 9

Clinton's Second Term

Said the Presidential skeleton, I won't sign the bill,
Said the Speaker skeleton, Yes you will.
—Allen Ginsberg, "Ballad of the Skeletons"

I
N MY PROFESSIONAL LIFE, I got lucky again when Russell
Simmons and Lyor Cohen, the co-owners of Def Jam, chose to
become affiliated with Mercury. That gave us an immediate
presence in rap through artists such as LL Cool J.

The success we had with Def Jam and Joan Osborne gave me
the chance to fulfill a long-held desire to produce some spoken-
word records. Poetry and other spoken-word albums sell a limited
amount but cost very little to produce, and I like to think of them
as a way of connecting the record business with literary tradition.

The first release was from Paul Krassner, the longtime editor of
the *Realist* and one of the founders of the Yippies. Krassner had
been a hero of mine since high school.

Then came Timothy Leary. Tim and I had been friends for more
than a decade, and when he learned that he was dying of cancer, he
said he wanted to record as much of his last days as possible. We
agreed. I visited him often in that period. We did audio recordings

of deathbed interviews, and Danny Schechter shot them for a home video.

It's always painful when a friend dies. Not being able to call Tim on the phone or drop by to listen to him chat with excitement about some new technology or some old feud is an irreplaceable loss. But the way Tim handled his death, with equanimity, humor, and feistiness, was inspiring and underlined for me the depth of his spiritual core. One day, about a month before he died, I was with him when he called William Burroughs at his home in Kansas. I sat as Leary listened to Burroughs talk for a few minutes, only getting in a few grunts.

After he had hung up, Tim said to me, "Jesus, if there was one person I thought I could count on to be unsentimental it was Burroughs, and here he is blubbering away like a child." Tim's face was emaciated by illness, but he grinned at me with a wry sparkle in his eye.

Tim was reviled by drug warriors and was arrested dozens of times. But he saw psychedelics as a consciousness-expanding sacrament and thought they should be taken only under supervision. He never advocated hard drugs like heroin or cocaine or amphetamines. I didn't agree with everything Leary said or did, but I grew to love him personally. I think he was much more of a force for good, and for enlightenment, than for bad.

Of all the great people he had met in his life, Leary once told me, the greatest was Allen Ginsberg. I reconnected with Allen after seeing him perform his poem "Ballad of the Skeletons" with members of the Patti Smith Group for Tibet House at Carnegie Hall. The poem, an impressionistic commentary on the Clinton era, included the couplet:

> Said the Middle Kingdom skeleton, we swallowed Tibet
> Said the Dalai Lama skeleton, indigestion's what you get.

I thought the ballad was one of Allen's most successful mixes of poetry with rock, and Mercury recorded Allen chanting it with musical help from Paul McCartney, Lenny Kaye, and Philip Glass. Sophisticated about the limits of radio freedom, Allen made me a "clean" profanity-free version as well as the full-length "dirty" version. Allen asked many of his artist friends, such as David Hockney and Julian Schnabel, to do drawings for the packaging. We released it on Bill Adler's Mouth Almighty imprint.

Allen Ginsberg had helped create modern culture and remembered in detail his early battles. Neoconservative Norman Podhoretz had attended Columbia at the same time as Ginsberg and Jack Kerouac. Allen recalled, "I was the editor of the Columbia literary magazine and refused to publish Podhoretz's poetry. He was a terrible poet."

Later, when On the Road and "Howl" were published, Podhoretz viciously denounced the Beat movement.

"All through the years," said Allen, "he's attacked us, and over these many years, every time I need to debate an idea, I argue with him in my imagination. I'm going to call him and thank him for having been a kind of spiritual teacher over so much of my life, representing a force that sharpens my arguments and commitment."

Allen, a devout Buddhist, actually did try to get in touch with Podhoretz. In his memoir Losing Friends, Podhoretz boasts that he refused to return Allen's call because he could not forgive him for the "damage" he'd done to American culture. Soon afterward, Allen was dead.

Tom Freston and Judy McGrath of MTV were both huge Ginsberg fans. A low-budget video of "Skeletons" was directed by Gus Van Sant, and MTV played it for many weeks. At the time of Allen's death, we were planning an "Unplugged" concert that would feature Bob Dylan and many others who owed so much to Allen.

The recording, which was to be Allen's last, gave the great poet a connection with yet another new generation of rock fans. We also released spoken-word recordings by Burroughs, Jim Carroll, and Spalding Gray, among others.

On the more commercial side, Mercury ushered in a new generation of teen pop with Hanson, who sold more than 10 million copies worldwide of their debut album, propelled by the song "MMMBop." Hanson was the first group I worked with that my kids personally appreciated.

When Hanson played *Saturday Night Live*, both Lisa Marie Presley and Caroline Kennedy brought their kids to the rehearsal to get the group's autographs. I got a huge kick out of knowing that a group that I helped launch meant something to the grandchildren of John F. Kennedy and Elvis Presley.

Another notable success was the acquisition of half of Phil Walden's Capricorn label. Walden, who had managed Otis Redding and the Allman Brothers, had signed some great new rock bands. We quickly got two of them, 311 and Cake, to platinum.

In May of 1997, two controversies involving popular culture and free speech collided at an ACLU dinner in Los Angeles.

Gloria Steinem and several other feminists objected to our honoring director Milos Forman for his film *The People vs. Larry Flynt*. Steinem felt that the film glamorized a vile pornographer whose *Hustler* magazine debased women, pointing out that he had once run an illustration of a woman's body going into a meat grinder.

Forman grew up in Communist-controlled Czechoslovakia and had a deep personal and emotional commitment to free speech. To him, the movie was about the First Amendment. He also found the attack aesthetically baffling. "Why," he wondered, "would portraying a character be described as glamorizing him?"

Flynt's character, played by Woody Harrelson, did many unsympathetic things and comes across as a morally flawed and deeply unhappy person. But his victory in the Supreme Court over Jerry Falwell's libel suit was a landmark decision for freedom of the press.

In fairness to Steinem, Forman did choose to give Larry Flynt a cameo role and included him in a lot of the film's publicity, somewhat undercutting his argument that it was not the man but free speech that the film was celebrating. Nonetheless, Ramona Ripston and I considered Forman to be a major and serious artist and saw the film as a rare dramatic depiction of an important First Amendment fight. Free-speech advocacy often involves defending the rights of people whose views are repellent. From a practical standpoint, we also knew that honoring Forman would attract financial support from the film industry.

The second dispute, a related one, was the most bizarre. Courtney Love had starred in the film as Larry Flynt's wife, and I asked her to present the award to Forman. Courtney delivered a thoughtful and moving talk about free speech and about what Milos Forman meant to her. After Forman accepted his award, a young man with a British accent walked confidently onto the stage and started railing about how hypocritical it was for Courtney to talk about free speech when she herself was so uncooperative with the press.

It became apparent to me that the speaker was about to bring up the crazy Internet rumors that Kurt Cobain had not committed suicide but had been murdered. Knowing how depressed Kurt had been in the days prior to his death, I have zero respect for this theory. But most important, I didn't want Courtney subjected to this painful diatribe about her late husband after she had been gracious enough to appear at the dinner. I ran onto the stage and shouted at the intruder, "You're not part of the program, get off of the fucking stage." He immediately walked away.

I later found out that the man was filmmaker Nick Broomfield, who was working on a documentary called *Kurt and Courtney*. The scene at the dinner is included in the movie, accompanied by his self-righteous narration about the paradox of a free-speech organization stifling speech. Broomfield's simplistic attack ignores the fact that the First Amendment does not give anyone the right to rudely crash a private event and seize the microphone.

In late 1997, Polygram increased my responsibilities, promoting me to chairman of the newly created Mercury Records Group. The group included Motown Records and the Polygram classical labels, as well as Def Jam and Mercury Nashville. Early the following year, Phillips, the Dutch electronics company that owned 75 percent of Polygram, announced it would sell it to Universal. It took most of the year for the deal to go through, and I carried out my job in the midst of uncertainty.

Two of my personal signings to Mercury were Lucinda Williams and Shelby Lynne, both strong, fearless, sexually frank singer-songwriters whose records had not done very well commercially. Lucinda, a critical favorite who had never sold more than 75,000 albums, had been a longtime legal client of Rosemary's. For months, I had heard Lucinda's completed but unreleased album *Car Wheels on a Gravel Road* on Rosemary's car stereo. The album had been recorded for Rick Rubin's American Records but rejected by his two distributors, Warner Brothers and Columbia Records.

To my ears, the songs on *Car Wheels* were powerful, and some of them had strong potential commercial appeal. I also thought the production, by Steve Earle, made it more musically accessible than her previous work. We bought the album from Rubin and released it on Mercury, and it became a hit. *Car Wheels* eventually sold over 500,000 copies, making it Lucinda's first gold (500,000 units sold in the United States) album. It won a Grammy Award for best contemporary folk album.

Shelby Lynne's *I Am Shelby Lynne* also went gold and won a

Grammy. She was named best new artist, despite the fact that she had been making records for over a decade.

The most successful project during this period was Shania Twain's superb country album *The Woman in Me*. Shania's previous album had sold 7 million copies, making her the biggest female star in country music. We promoted *The Woman in Me* to a pop audience as well, and it sold over 20 million copies worldwide.

On the classics side, we focused on Andrea Bocelli, who became the first operatic tenor since Pavarotti to sell over a million albums. But perhaps the most interesting, enlightening, and fulfilling work I did involved Motown.

Polygram had been unhappy with Motown's profits ever since it acquired the label in the early nineties. Motown's chairman, Clarence Avant, and I were asked to find a new president. Clarence suggested movie producer George Jackson, and I immediately agreed. George and I had become friends in Los Angeles where he had coproduced such films as *New Jack City* and *Krush Groove*.

Until I worked with George Jackson and Motown I had not fully realized how meaningful the company was to the African American community. To me, Motown was the source of classic pop and R&B music, and its recordings by Diana Ross, Marvin Gaye, Smokey Robinson, the Temptations, and others were America's answer to the Beatles and Rolling Stones in the 1960s.

In the African American community, however, Motown was also a symbol of black entrepreneurship. Founder Berry Gordy was one of the preeminent African American business success stories of the era, and certainly the most prominent one in the entertainment business.

Diana Ross held a dinner at her home welcoming George Jackson to Motown, and sitting next to Berry Gordy I felt that I was with a historical figure as significant as Jackie Robinson.

George and I made many appearances in front of young mostly

African American audiences who wanted information about entering the entertainment business. Intellectually, I had long understood the terrible legacy of racial discrimination. But I had not
realized until then how close to the surface the feelings of vulnerability of young African American men and women are, many of
whose parents were blocked from avenues to business success that
many whites take for granted.

In the middle of trying to help George and Clarence revive Motown, I was asked to get involved with a racial contretemps at
Polygram.

In a deposition, Polygram executive Eric Kronfeld was asked
about the criminal record of a black employee. Kronfeld went off
on a bit of a tangent, decrying the American criminal justice system
for its treatment of blacks, and stated that ex-convicts were so common among black men of a certain age that it was hard to hire a
black staff without including some with criminal convictions.

In the cold light of a written transcript, taken out of context,
Kronfeld's remarks could be interpreted as saying that most black
men were criminals. An excerpt was quickly emailed and faxed
around the country, and public pressure began building on Polygram to disavow Kronfeld's statement and fire him.

Kronfeld made a public apology. He was strongly defended by
Clarence Avant, known as the "godfather of black music" because
he was a key advisor to most senior black music executives, including Quincy Jones. But fallout from the deposition was so great, and
the underlying emotions so bitter, that the issue kept getting bigger.
One afternoon, I was asked to join top Polygram executives and
Clarence Avant in a meeting on the problem with Jesse Jackson.

An outside litigator hired by Polygram warned that Jesse Jackson
was a "hustler" who was there to try to shake the company down,
but I told my colleagues that my experiences suggested otherwise,
and asked them to keep open minds.

After listening to our side of the story, Jackson suggested that Polygram as a company should apologize, and that Clarence Avant be given a seat on a largely ceremonial company policy board. We agreed. Jackson issued a statement that he was satisfied with the solution, and the furor died down. Jesse Jackson never asked Polygram for a dime.

In 1998, the Mercury Records Group led all its competitors in over-the-counter sales. Despite our success, in early 1999 the new owner, Universal, dismantled the group and spread its companies over various new divisions. George Jackson and I were among the Polygram executives who were asked to leave.

On April 20, 1999, two students at Columbine High School in Littleton, Colorado, opened fire with assault rifles on students and faculty. They killed twelve students and one teacher before turning the weapons on themselves.

Initial media reports suggested that the Columbine killers were fans of rocker Marilyn Manson, leading a Denver concert promoter to cancel a scheduled Marilyn Manson show. It soon was revealed that Eric Harris and Dylan Klebold didn't even like Marilyn Manson. They thought the band's music was "wimpy." There was, as it turned out, not the slightest evidence of a connection between the entertainment tastes of Harris and Klebold and their murderous behavior.

Similarly, Jim Carroll, author of the semi-autobiographical novel *The Basketball Diaries*, was attacked because of a scene in the movie version of the book—Leonardo DiCaprio, portraying Carroll, is shown having a dream in which he imagines killing kids and a teacher at school. Carroll is my wife's first husband and a close family friend. Nonviolent and socially conscious, Carroll was devastated by the attacks and asked for my advice on dealing with the media.

"When CNN shows the clip, they edit out the context that

shows it's a dream," Carroll told me. His pain and frustration evident on his face, he said intensely, "Artists have nothing to do with the deranged actions of a few celebrated nutcases. The guy who shot John Lennon, Mark David Chapman, loved *The Catcher in the Rye*. But how many millions of people have been helped by that book or by mine to feel less isolated, less alone, relieved to know there is someone else out there who understood how they feel?"

Although there was no evidence that the Columbine killers liked or even ever saw *The Basketball Diaries*, the film had been mentioned by a killer at a similar incident in West Paducah, Kentucky. In the wake of Columbine, MGM withdrew the home video.

President Clinton, under siege because of the unfolding Monica Lewinsky scandal, ordered the Federal Trade Commission to investigate entertainment marketing practices. And Senator Lieberman renewed his attacks on teen-oriented films, saying, "None of us wants to resort to regulation, but if the entertainment industry continues to move in this direction and continues to market death and degradation to our children and continues to pay no heed to the real bloodshed staining our communities, then the government will act."

Meanwhile, the annual National Rifle Association convention went on as scheduled in Denver, a few miles from Columbine. NRA president Charlton Heston proclaimed, "We cannot, we must not, let tragedy lay waste to the most rare, hard-won right in history . . . the right to bear arms."

In the spring of 1999, I started an independent company called Artemis Records in partnership with Michael Chambers, who had produced several movies, including *Kids*, and started a small heavy metal label. Our first album release, in the fall of 1999, was *Somewhere Between Heaven and Earth* by singer-songwriter Cindy Bullens. The album was a tribute to her daughter, who had died of

Hodgkin's disease at the age of eleven. A most remarkable expression of love and grief, the album has become a cult treasure for people who have lost loved ones. Some of the Columbine families emailed their thanks to Cindy when the album was released and wrote about it on their websites.

Other early Artemis releases included gold albums from rapper Kurupt and the female heavy metal band Kittie, and new recordings from Steve Earle, Rickie Lee Jones, and Warren Zevon.

During the late 1990s, the music business was rocked by the Internet. Start-up companies such as MP3.com and Napster tested the limits of copyright law by providing free access to thousands of recordings. The RIAA, representing major record companies, sued to stop this practice. I kept Artemis out of these disputes. On one hand, we certainly needed strong copyright laws to protect our releases, as did all intellectual property businesses. On the other hand, we were an independent label and I didn't want us associated with the rigid approach of the majors. We often experimented with the Internet in ways the majors wouldn't; for example, by releasing songs to publicize albums and producing Internet radio shows.

I had gotten to know Rabbi Michael Lerner, founder and editor of *Tikkun* magazine, when I lived on the West Coast. Started during the Lebanon war, *Tikkun* importantly gave voice to American Jews who disagreed with Israel's policy and who identified with the Israeli peace camp. My attraction to *Tikkun* was also based on Lerner's analysis of American politics. I admired some of his insights about the American left, particularly the belief that spirituality could and should be a part of the way progressive ideas are expressed. Much as some of us had implored the left to learn from Ronald Reagan's media savvy, Michael urged progressives to respect the spiritual yearnings addressed by organizations like the Moral Majority.

Michael and his colleague Peter Gabel, both of whom had been

Berkeley radicals in the sixties, tried to make connections between modern politics and what they saw as the best qualities of the sixties.

I disagree with Lerner and Gabel about some civil liberties issues. Michael and Peter are die-hard supporters of free speech, but they feel that excessive focus on such civil liberties as gay rights and the rights of the accused (as in the O.J. Simpson case) can tear apart a sense of community. In this respect, Lerner and Gabel are similar to the communitarian intellectuals who had influence on President Clinton.

I feel that these communitarians have it exactly wrong. The fight for civil liberties, as I have experienced it, is about championing the rights of other people, about supporting those with whom we may have little in common. It creates community. Principles like freedom of religion, freedom of speech, freedom from racial and sexual discrimination, and the right to a fair trial are connections that everyone in a free society can plug into.

However, Michael Lerner always relished debate, and I greatly respect his voice. In 1997, Michael asked me to become publisher of *Tikkun*. With the magazine based in San Francisco, he was looking for funding and editorial input from New York. By coincidence, my father, Victor Goldberg, was getting a little restless in his job as associate publisher of the *Nation* but was still eager to stay involved in progressive causes.

From 1997 to 2000, my dad and I were copublishers of *Tikkun*, and ran a small editorial office out of New York. We got pieces from Mary Gordon, Nick Von Hoffman, and Michael Tomasky. Jack Newfield did a series of interviews with Mario Cuomo, Frank Rich, Budd Schulberg, Jesse Ventura, and his old nemesis Ed Koch.

I usually tried to inject a civil liberties spirit into the magazine that was otherwise lacking. For example, when gay activists around the country urged a boycott of sponsors of Dr. Laura Schlessinger's TV program because of antigay remarks she had made, I opposed the boycott. I can't stand Dr. Laura Schlessinger's self-righteous, narrow-minded, and bigoted concept of morality. But the ACLU, for good reason, has always opposed boycotts intending to block ideas in the media, whether the target is books, movies, or TV shows. Seductive as such campaigns are when one is wounded by something in the media, the result is a narrowing of "safe" subjects for discussion, and such a narrowing ultimately always serves the status quo and dampens the possibility of progressive change.

Progressives were disappointed with much of Clinton's second term, as they had been with his first and for the same reasons: too much concern with the interests of the superrich, and too little concern with civil liberties. On the other hand, he adroitly stymied the scary reactionary agenda of Newt Gingrich and Tom DeLay in a way that other, less media-savvy Democrats would have had difficulty doing.

The Washington response to the Monica Lewinsky scandal mirrored a lot of the disconnect between politics and culture that I had previously observed. Large majorities of Americans were more appalled by Kenneth Starr's persecution of Clinton than by Clinton's sins. Yet most Washington politicos and pundits, including many nominal Democrats, sided with Starr. The public be damned.

Although we were never part of Bill Clinton's campaigns, Rosemary and I did get invited to White House Christmas parties during the last two years of his presidency. The president and I never discussed anything of substance, although he chatted in a friendly way with our son, Max, then six and rather shy.

I attribute the White House invites to our friend Sidney Blumenthal, the Clinton advisor who was required to testify in the impeachment trial. Sid has always rolled his eyes at my complaints about liberal snobbery, but he is no snob himself. His son, also named Max, interned at Mercury one summer and later became an accomplished rap producer.

Meanwhile, Clinton himself continued to mix liberal snobbery with a more positive attitude toward the entertainment business. Not long after he'd demanded a Federal Trade Commission investigation into marketing practices in the film, video game, and music businesses, he and the First Lady appeared at Walden Woods in Massachusetts to celebrate a remarkable accomplishment by Don Henley, one of the strongest voices against liberal snobbery and culture bashing.

Early in the nineties, Henley had been outraged to learn that real estate developers planned to build an industrial complex in the woods that Thoreau had immortalized in *Walden*. Many environmentalists considered Walden Woods to be the birthplace of their movement. Having been inspired by Thoreau in his college years, Henley impulsively called me and Betsy Kenny of Norman Lear's office to accompany him on a visit there. We were all transported by the beauty of the woods, as Thoreau had been a 150 years earlier. Henley began a quest to buy the land as a public trust and to build an environmental museum there.

Over the next few years, Henley raised $18 million, the bulk of it by staging benefit concerts with a number of musicians, including his former group, the Eagles. In 1998, I was at the dedication ceremony for the Thoreau Institute and the surrounding ninety-six acres of protected Walden Woods, with Betsy Kenny, now Betsy Lack, and her husband, then NBC president Andy Lack. At the time, Washington pundits and politicians, including many so-called liberals, were pounding Clinton on Monicagate, misreading the attitude of the public, much as they did on popular culture. President and Mrs. Clinton, who attended the ceremony, were radiant in describing the importance of Thoreau's legacy. President Clinton was at his best, joking about the irony of walking in pristine woods while trailed by a TV camera. As the president drew connections between the world of art, philosophy, and the environment, Lack looked at me with a shrug of his shoulders and a rueful smile as if to acknowledge that the president, who his own correspondents were relentlessly belittling, could still rise to an occasion such as this with an effectiveness and eloquence rare in public life.

In the spring of the presidential election year of 2000, I was asked by the Creative Coalition to attend a meeting with Joseph Lieberman, Republican senator Sam Brownback of Kansas, and conservative moralist William Bennett, who had been drug czar in the George Bush administration. Besides my disagreement with Bennett about pop culture, I have a deep moral aversion to the war on drugs. If today's drug laws had been in force when I was arrested in the late sixties, my life would have been ruined by imprisonment. Millions of poor people who do not have access to good lawyers languish in prisons for nonviolent drug crimes despite ample evidence from other countries that treatment of drug abuse as a medical issue instead of a criminal problem creates far less social chaos.

About twenty of us from the entertainment business packed into a conference room at HBO's New York offices, including NBC's Roz Weinman, legendary film industry spokesman Jack Valenti, TV and film producer Steven Haft (*The Dead Poets Society*), and Creative Coalition president William Baldwin, the actor.

I first met Joe Lieberman in 1988, when he was asking for money for a run for the Senate. To my lasting regret, I responded to the argument that the Democrats would have a better chance of controlling the Senate if Lieberman defeated Republican Lowell Weicker. I had given Lieberman $250. Thus, in a tiny way, I was complicit in the defeat of Weicker, who was notably sensitive to civil liberties, and the victory of cultural conservative Lieberman. Beneath his affable demeanor, Lieberman has a self-righteous, intolerant, Puritanical streak. "Hollywood is a place that doesn't understand piety," Lieberman once said.

Lieberman led off the meeting at HBO by invoking Columbine

and asked, in his scratchy, folksy voice, how we would feel about overall standards for all entertainment, similar to the very strict ones in the movie business from the 1930s to the early 1960s. Lieberman expressed his vision, shared by Bennett and Brownback, for the creation of universal ratings for films, television shows, video games, and recordings with a set of standards that all parents could use.

Billy Baldwin asked me to respond first, and I pointed out that music, films, and video games were totally different forms of communication and did not lend themselves to similar types of categorization. As to "standards," people of goodwill often disagreed about subjects like sex and violence in entertainment. I gave, as an example, Oliver Stone's *Natural Born Killers*, which many social critics had accused of glorifying violence. To me and many others, it was a black comedy satirizing the news media's infatuation with violence.

I cited *Natural Born Killers* in part because I was sitting next to one of its stars, Juliette Lewis. She reiterated that the film was a satire and then pulled out research indicating that all of the murderers in the previous eight schoolroom shootings, including Columbine, had only one thing in common. It was not their taste in entertainment. All of the young killers had been given prescription drugs for psychological and behavioral problems. Lewis pointed out that millions of young children are on these drugs, and cited studies showing that 1 percent of kids taking them could have psychotic reactions. The explosion of violence in schools had come at the same time as the indiscriminate increase in the use of such drugs.

Lieberman had received large campaign contributions from pharmaceutical companies. His wife, Hadassah, had formerly worked for Pfizer, which made some of the mood-affecting drugs used to treat kids. He refused to acknowledge Lewis's comment and acted as if she didn't exist.

None of us agreed with Lieberman, Brownback, and Bennett on universal ratings. "That's off the table," said Haft firmly. But many of the entertainment people said they shared the concern about the state of the culture and welcomed a dialogue.

As the meeting was breaking up, Bennett, who surrealistically has claimed to have dated Janis Joplin, tried to play the part of the genial Washington hipster. He started riffing about the music of Buddy Holly. I quickly left. I couldn't stomach schmoozing with the architect of the war on drugs. I do have some standards.

CHAPTER 10

The 2000 Election
Ralph Nader, Joe Lieberman, and Eminem

There is a swelling sense that much of our culture has become toxic. That
our standards of decency and civility are being significantly eroded by the
entertainment industry's shameless and pervasive promotion of violence,
sex, and vulgarity, and that traditional sources of values in our society
such as faith, family, and school are in a life and death struggle with the
darker forces of immorality.

—Senator Joseph Lieberman, *In Praise of Public Life*, published in
September 2000

I N THE SPRING of 2000, Ralph Nader asked for my support
in his run for the presidency. I had long admired him for his
public interest work, and there was no question that he was
willing to speak about the environment, economic justice, and other
issues that would otherwise be slighted or absent in the national
campaign. However, Nader's self-righteousness in recent years had
begun to grate on me. He seemed to feel that his approach to any
problem was the only possible choice for a moral person.

Famously out of touch with culture, he had said in a recent interview in the *Nation*, "Television watching teaches children that

violence is the preferred solution to life's problems. They are taught
to value cheap sensuality in everything from sex to self-image to
food and they become addicted to entertainment that shortens
their attention span." When I complained about this outburst,
Nader, who has no children of his own, told me he thought kids
would grow up better "if they performed their own versions of Eu-
gene O'Neill plays or *Romeo and Juliet* instead of watching movies
or TV."

"Ralph," I responded in frustration, "I've seen two O'Neill plays
in the last year and they were filled with alcoholics and depressing
monologues. *Romeo and Juliet* ends with a murder and suicide.
Frankly, I'm much happier that my kids have memorized large sections of *Austin Powers*." It was clear from the dead silence on the
other end of the line that Nader had no idea what *Austin Powers* was.

When Nader again parroted the conventional wisdom about violence and popular culture, I got angry and yelled, "You don't know
what you are talking about, and you're needlessly alienating millions of young people who might support you!"

"I do know what I'm talking about!" Nader yelled back, and
hung up.

In April, before the presidential campaign had really heated up,
ABC News announced that movie star Leonardo DiCaprio, who
was chairman of Earth Day 2000, had interviewed President Clinton for a network special on the environment. Columnists ridiculed
the idea, and ABC News stars Sam Donaldson, Peter Jennings, and
Diane Sawyer were widely reported to be furious that a mere movie
star had been assigned to interview the president.

ABC News president David Westin, apparently intimidated by
the snobbish Washington media, backed away. He characterized the
interview as merely a brief and unplanned chat, just part of a walk-
through in which Clinton showed DiCaprio how the White House
had been made environmentally friendly.

Ken Sunshine, who handles DiCaprio's PR, told me at the time, "This is such bullshit. I have emails from ABC specifically asking about the interview and scheduling it." It quickly became known that ABC had spent hours setting up cameras for a lengthy interview and had submitted questions to the White House ahead of time. At a Washington correspondents' dinner, Clinton got a big laugh by twitting Westin with: "It's not the mistake that causes problems, it's the cover-up."

In May, Rosemary and I hosted a fundraiser at our house for Hillary Clinton in her race for the Senate. One of our cohosts was Ken Sunshine. In the midst of a successful evening of schmoozing with people who were delighted to meet her, including our children, Katie and Max, Mrs. Clinton made a point of saying, "I'm glad that President Clinton spoke to Leonardo DiCaprio."

However, ABC had used only a brief fragment of DiCaprio's interview with the president, depriving them (and the Democrats) of the chance to reach a younger audience on environmental issues. Inside-the-Beltway snobbery had prevailed once again.

In early August, about a week before the Democratic National Convention, Al Gore named culture basher Joseph Lieberman as his running mate. Lieberman had publicly castigated Clinton about the Monica Lewinsky scandal, and naming the Connecticut senator to the ticket was widely judged as part of Gore's campaign to distance himself from the president. Voters were suffering from "Clinton fatigue," according to influential pundits and campaign consultants.

Elite Washington's misreading of the public's feelings about the Clinton scandal fatally infected the Gore campaign from the beginning. The public consistently showed that they detested the self-righteousness of Clinton adversaries like special prosecutor Kenneth Starr and Henry Hyde, the Republican chairman of the House Judiciary Committee. The heavy-handed moralism of the

Gore-Lieberman campaign may have calmed the anxieties of some anti-Clinton swing voters, but it probably hurt more than it helped with millions of Americans who were much more appalled by the excesses of the president's enemies than by anything Clinton had done.

Lieberman turned off other voters with his incessant references to his orthodox Jewish faith, which became so extreme that even the Anti-Defamation League, which was formed to fight anti-Semitism, criticized him for making religion a litmus test of political virtue. Many civil libertarians felt like feminist Ellen Willis, who wrote in Salon.com that she was supporting Ralph Nader specifically because she was so turned off by Lieberman's excessive religiosity. "He's a Christian rightist in Jewish drag," she wrote, and slammed both Lieberman and Gore for "pandering to religious and moral conservatives."

Gore made his antipathy for popular culture a major part of his 2000 campaign. In his acceptance speech at the Democratic National Convention, Gore said, "To all the families who are struggling with things that money can't measure, like trying to find a little more time with your children or protecting them from entertainment that you think glorifies violence and indecency, I want you to know: I believe we must challenge a culture with too much meanness and not enough meaning."

Of course, he left open the question of just who was to decide the difference between meanness and meaning.

During the convention in Los Angeles, Congresswoman Loretta Sanchez had scheduled a fundraiser at the Playboy Mansion. Christie Hefner, CEO of *Playboy*, has raised millions of dollars for the Democratic Party and its candidates over the years. Because of the moralistic tone that Gore wanted for his convention, enormous pressure was put on Sanchez to cancel the event. A still-outraged Hefner told me later, "They told her that Al Gore would not campaign for her, and that if he were elected he might campaign for a primary opponent in future elections, and that she could be stripped of her committee positions and party leadership roles."

Representative Patrick Kennedy, Ted Kennedy's son, announced that the fundraiser "totally contradicts what our party stands for in terms of equal rights and civil rights for all people, respect for human dignity of every individual."

Playboy has long been a part of mainstream American popular culture and has consistently taken strong stands over the years for civil rights and civil liberties.

"Months earlier," Hefner told me, "Patrick Kennedy had raised thousands of dollars at my house for an Illinois House candidate. How come that was okay, but suddenly it was immoral for a Latino congresswoman to do the event at the mansion?"

Further to the left, there still seemed to be little connection between generations. Antiglobalization protesters, mostly young, demonstrated in front of the convention. They were largely ignored. At the same time, older dissidents had convened a "Shadow Convention" to focus on issues ignored by the major parties. I participated, and I was inspired by the concern with poverty and the war on drugs. But after several elders went on about the need to create a "movement," a young *Tikkun* staffer suggested that they drive a few blocks to where the antiglobalization protesters were being harassed by police. The leftist elite nodded politely and stayed where they were.

Once Al Gore announced that Joe Lieberman was going to be his running mate, Nader called again. He gleefully asked, "How do you feel now that Gore has picked the arch critic of entertainment as his running mate?" I told Nader I agreed with him about many issues but I was worried about his effect on the outcome of the election.

Nader told me, as he would many others, that his goal was to get

5 percent of the national vote, enough to funnel millions of dollars in federal financing into the Green Party for the next election. He said his plan was to pick up most of his votes in large states where he would not affect the outcome: the Republicans were a shoo-in in Texas, and the Democrats were sure to win in New York and California. So progressives and young people in those three states, the largest in population, could vote for Nader without affecting the outcome. It was a well-thought-out argument that he had obviously repeated many times. He faxed me a Molly Ivins column calling for progressives in locked-up states like Texas and New York to vote "with their hearts" for Nader, and voters in key swing states to vote "with their heads" for Gore.

Ralph Nader assured me he would not be campaigning in swing states.

Right after Labor Day, the Federal Trade Commission issued a report criticizing the marketing of violent entertainment. The key point of the study, which had been commissioned by Clinton after the tragic shootings at Columbine, was that entertainment rated unsuitable for children was marketed through media whose audience included many children.

Gore, Lieberman, and Clinton immediately condemned the entertainment companies. The day the report came out, Gore said on *The Oprah Winfrey Show* that if he were elected he would give the companies six months to "clean up their act," and if they did not, he would consider action by the federal government. His wife, he said, had been "successful in convincing the recording industry to use warning stickers when material is inappropriate. We're going to try to persuade the companies to abide by what they said they would do."

Intriguingly, Republican presidential nominee George W. Bush was silent—as supporters in Hollywood like producer Jerry Weintraub did not hesitate to point out.

At that point, much of the furor about popular culture focused on the white rapper Eminem. His album *The Marshall Mathers LP* was full of profanity and flaunted sexist attitudes toward women and lyrics that offended many gays: "My words are like a dagger with a jagged edge/That'll stab you in the head whether you're a fag or lez," he rapped.

There was a vigorous debate among music critics about the album. Some, such as R.J. Smith in the *New York Times*, argued that Eminem had crossed a moral boundary with his lyrics. Many critics, however, praised the album as a brilliant evolution of rap and saw Eminem as a wisecracking ironist who used exaggeration in a humorous way to make a point.

In *SPIN* magazine, rock and roll/country legend Johnny Cash praised Eminem and pointed out, "The biggest-selling song of the nineteenth century was a song about a bandit and an outlaw and a killer. It was called 'The Ballad of Jesse James.'

"Those themes," he said, "have carried through up until now. I watched Elvis go through it—people saying, 'You're leading our children to hell.' I've been hearing it all my life. But I have yet to hear anyone take it seriously and actually shoot a man in Reno just because my song said so."

I empathize with those who feel that when gays are still physically attacked in America, lyrics such as Eminem's can be inflammatory. But Eminem is a legitimate artist, one who populates his songs with many characters, some clearly unsympathetic, to express conflicting ideas. His songs do not have the ugly, leaden quality of Guns N' Roses' late-eighties lyrics cursing "niggers and faggots." Elton John, the most successful openly gay recording artist, praised Eminem's album and performed the song "Stan" with him on the internationally televised Grammy Awards.

Teen culture has always included male adolescent misogyny, but it has also empowered women to express themselves in important ways. It is hard to think of any feminist culture that reached as many young women as the Lilith Fair tours of 1997–98, with the passionate songs of dozens of artists like Sarah McLachlan, Jewel, and Alanis Morissette, and it's impossible to imagine a code of content that would eliminate Eminem's sexist lyrics but give Alanis and Ani DiFranco the freedom, honesty, and frankness that created their intense connection with their audience.

Following the release of the FTC report, congressional hearings were hastily convened for September 13 by the Senate Commerce Committee, chaired by Republican senator John McCain. I was asked to testify, along with the RIAA's Hilary Rosen and Strauss Zelnick, the CEO of BMG's Music Division, a major recording distributor.

We met ahead of time at the law office of David Kendall, a senior partner in the venerable D.C. law firm of Williams and Connolly, which the RIAA had on retainer. Kendall is an expert on First Amendment law but is best known as President Clinton's impeachment lawyer. I was excited to meet the guy who had cross-examined Kenneth Starr.

Kendall was neat in appearance, with perfectly coifed brown hair and slightly graying sideburns. He radiated the physical energy common to many successful people. He turned out to be a master schmoozer, far more vibrant than his stoic, dour, Monicagate TV persona.

Kendall's office displayed fascinating impeachment memorabilia: photos with the president, a framed *Washington Post* front page with the headline "Clinton Acquitted," a framed copy of the actual roll call of the impeachment vote, the "uncomfortable chair" he sat in as counsel for the president at the trial.

When Kendall listened to us talk, he shut one eye, appearing to concentrate intently, as if whoever was speaking were the most fascinating person he had ever met. There must be something in the water supply of Washington that enables its powerful people to do that so convincingly.

Other framed memorabilia identified Kendall as having served as a federal marshal in Oxford, Mississippi, to help enforce the Voting Rights Act. There was also, to my puzzlement, a *National Enquirer* front page revealing that Liberace had AIDS. Kendall explained that he had long represented the *Enquirer* and although it had been a "tough decision," he had advised them to run the story.

The Washington gossip about the hearing at which we were testifying, according to Kendall, was that Senator McCain had scheduled it to give committee member Joe Lieberman another positive media hit. The Arizona Republican had lost a bitter battle for his party's presidential nomination to George W. Bush and was said to be willing to do almost anything to undermine Bush, even while professing to support him.

"The Bush people are furious," Kendall said. They had pressured McCain into including as a witness longtime culture basher Lynne Cheney, the wife of the Republican vice presidential nominee. At that point in the election, national polls conducted by the *Wall Street Journal*/NBC and the *New York Times*/CBS both showed Gore and Lieberman overtaking Bush and Cheney.

Kendall drew my attention to an editorial in that morning's *Washington Post*. It remarked, "When it comes to children, movies, and violence it has always been hard to tell whether the H stands for Hollywood or hypocrisy. You have studios and recording companies piously invoking their cultural integrity and First Amendment rights as they peddle stuff with no discernible redeeming virtues. You have the movie theatre chains pretending they can't control the teens who buy tickets to PG-rated films at the multiplex and then stroll in to watch R-rated movies. And you have politicians like Al Gore whose sensibilities on the matter seem to depend on whether today is devoted primarily to soliciting money from the moguls or votes from everyone else."

The *Post* seemed to be suggesting that everyone in America except entertainment moguls—"everyone else"—hated the records and movies and TV shows that had mysteriously become so popular, or at least hated the way the records were sold. Perhaps the editorialists should have checked with the paper's music, TV, and film critics, who often gave their highest praise to the edgy works that had inspired the furor in the first place, including recordings clearly directed at a youthful audience.

Or perhaps they should have polled their readers.

"Seventy-four percent of people surveyed by the FTC are happy with the current record company parental-advisory labeling system," Kendall stressed. "That's in the FTC's own report."

But, he said, "The *Post* is very important here." I rolled my eyes and suggested that the intellectually inbred community in Washington that was so sure the public agreed with it on entertainment had also been certain that the American people wanted Clinton impeached. Kendall smiled and said, "I always used to laugh when people discussing Whitewater would talk about what a small community Arkansas was, as if this town isn't just as incestuous."

As the time to leave for the hearing approached, Hilary Rosen, who as RIAA president thoroughly understands the nuances of power, warned us to "expect AK-47 attacks from the dozen congresspeople who are speaking before you testify.

"Republicans want to outbid Democrats in attacking Hollywood," she said. "You guys are concerned with what you're gonna say. The senators only care about what *they're* gonna say."

As we walked to the Hart Senate Building, we ran into Massachusetts Democratic representative Ed Markey, one of several congressmen who were slated to testify. Hilary, who is well connected on Capitol Hill and exudes far more humanity, passion, and humor than the typical lobbyist, asked jokingly, "Where are you going—don't you want to speak and beat us up?"

Markey smiled and said, "I'll be back—there's so many people speaking I don't want to sit through all of it. It's gonna be like Mo Udall used to say: 'Everything's been said but not everyone has said it.'"

The main hearing room was filled with media and witnesses, approximately 150 people in addition to most of the twenty-three members of the committee. Joe Lieberman was nowhere to be seen.

McCain, in a blue shirt and red tie, had recently recovered from surgery for skin cancer and wore a bandage on the slightly swollen left side of his face. He read an opening statement, quoting the FTC report: "Individual companies in each industry routinely market to children the very products that have the industry's own parental warnings or ratings with age restrictions due to their violent content."

McCain cited ads for R-rated movies that ran on TV shows such as *Dawson's Creek* or *The Simpsons,* whose audience is mostly kids under seventeen. He then made it clear that he was miffed that only Jack Valenti, president of the Motion Picture Association, would be there to represent the movie industry.

"There'll be much said today, but thundering silence will be heard from motion picture executives," he proclaimed. "By some uncanny coincidence, every single studio executive was either out of the country or unavailable . . . Their hubris is stunning."

Praising those of us from the music and video game businesses who had agreed to testify, McCain announced, "I want to make clear that neither this report nor this committee intend to make the case for censorship. We make no threat against the First Amendment. It is not my place to pass judgment on the products of your industry." According to McCain, it was all about the marketing, a point that was quickly lost.

White-haired Ernest ("Fritz") Hollings from South Carolina was the ranking Democrat on the Commerce Committee and the first of a long roll of speakers. His pink face was mottled with age and he walked slowly and stiffly. Hollings was one of the few who had been on the committee in 1986 for the hearings on rock lyrics. He informed us in his deep Southern drawl that hearings about violence and TV had first been held in the early fifties, and that between 1960 and 1999, "this committee itself has had twenty hearings" on similar topics.

Hollings pitched what he saw as a solution to the half-century of wrangling: the Safe Harbor bill, initially proposed in 1995, which would forbid "excessive gratuitous violence" from nine in the morning until nine at night. Hollings said the practice was "proven and tried and true in Europe and Australia and down in New Zealand. They don't go into school down in Australia or in countries in Europe and shoot up the student body."

Hollings's remarks were completely unrelated to the FTC report and the purpose of the hearing, as just stated by McCain. He mentioned nothing about marketing practices. Nor did he mention that people in the countries he cited watch the same movies and TV shows and listen to the same music as Americans. They are, however, subject to much stricter gun control laws than Americans.

Oversized easels displaying lyrics from Dr. Dre's *Chronic 2000* and Eminem's "Kill You" were brought out for an attack on the record business by Republican Sam Brownback of Kansas, Lieberman's frequent sidekick. Excerpting the most offensive lyrics from rap or rock songs has been a favorite tool since I first started in the business. I, too, cringe at reading some of Eminem's words out of context: "I invented violence, you vile, venomous, volatile bitches . . ." but context is everything in analyzing the actual meaning of art and entertainment.

John Kerry from Massachusetts was the only senator who seemed to be living in the same country that I did. Kerry, at this point, was not the household name he would become four years later. Nonetheless, with his chiseled cheekbones and lush Kennedy-esque salt-and-pepper hair, he looked like a movie star. "Let's not assume the sort of pontificating role," he said. "Elvis Presley was unacceptable at periods of time. James Dean and *East of Eden* reflected alienated young people. Alienation among young people is something that's historical, part of adolescence. I think we ought to ask ourselves up here why so many kids reflect the kind of life they reflect. Why are so many kids out of school in so many communities in the afternoon with no parents at home? Why are there no after-school programs? Why is it that so many children are growing up at risk in this country at a time when we're the richest nation on the planet? If you want to empower parents to be able to make some of these choices, parents need to also be able to be home and be with their kids."

Tennessee Republican Bill Frist announced that he had three teenage children, ranging in age from thirteen to seventeen. Collectively, he said, they would "go to at least fifty movies this year, watch probably over five hundred hours of television, and probably listen to over a thousand hours of music.

"Much of what the boys are exposed to in music and in the movies is simply vulgar and violent . . . The impressions that it leaves I am absolutely convinced will affect them as individuals, in their emotional life, in their spiritual life, their happiness, their degree of fulfillment in the future." A Senate hearing, it seemed to me, was a rather impersonal way to communicate with his kids. (In 2002, Frist became the Senate majority leader.)

Senator John Ashcroft of Missouri is a dour and chinless fellow. (Ashcroft was soon to be defeated for reelection, losing to a deceased man, former governor Mel Carnahan, who had died in a plane crash weeks before the election. Carnahan's wife Jean was appointed to fill his seat and Ashcroft was then appointed attorney general by President Bush.) Ashcroft quickly rehashed the FTC report one more time for a sound bite on TV back home. "If the industry does not police itself and young children continue to be targets of violent promotional material," he threatened, "then government should target the industry with false and deceptive enforcement actions."

The most flamboyant looking committee member was John Breaux, a centrist Democrat from Louisiana. He wore square glasses, a silver-gray suit, a yellow tie, and a daringly dark blue shirt. He looked a little like Jon Voight. I had first met Breaux in the late eighties at a fundraiser at Don Johnson's house in Aspen. One of six Democratic senators on hand to raise money, Breaux told me he wanted to avoid getting his picture taken with Johnson because the folks back at home might not like seeing their representative hobnobbing with the star of *Miami Vice*.

Breaux said, "We have helped parents have tools to ensure their own children are protected, V-chips and rating systems. Are parents using those tools? Information I have is that ninety percent of the children tell us their parents have never discussed the ratings with them. How does Congress address that problem?" He did not dwell on the possibility that parents were not discussing the ratings because they did not perceive that there was a problem.

Although Utah's Orrin Hatch gave the ritual condemnation of violence in the media, he clearly understood more about the creative process than did most of his colleagues. The conservative Republican writes songs and had struck up an unlikely friendship with Marilyn Bergman, the famously liberal president of ASCAP, an organization that collects and disburses money to songwriters.

"It is clear you cannot regulate decency or legislate taste," Hatch said. "Some want to target Hollywood, but what in Hollywood are we targeting? Are we angry with those who gave us *Saving Private Ryan*, *The Patriot*, and *Schindler's List*? All of those movies are rated R for violence, and could not have been made in their present form under the movie code that prevailed until the sixties, and that some legislators wanted us to return to."

Like Donny Osmond, whose testimony in the eighties against a ratings system was partly inspired by experience with religious prejudice, Hatch is a Mormon. "Do we only object to the work of those with whom we have no cultural or personal connection?" Hatch asked. "As one who has written gospel music only to be told it was unacceptable because of my religious faith, I have seen both sides of this debate on a personal level."

At this point, Senator Lieberman walked in. Popping flashbulbs confirmed that he was the star of the hearing. Lieberman waved at several of his colleagues and walked across the room to give a friendly arm-grab to Republican congressman Henry Hyde, who had fought so hard to remove President Clinton from office.

Hyde, appearing as a witness, began his testimony by reading the "toxic culture" passage (it's quoted at the beginning of this chapter) from Lieberman's brand-new book, *In Praise of Public Life*. Lieberman broke in with a chuckle and said, "Thanks for the promotion, Henry." I wanted to throw up.

As he often did, Lieberman launched his culture-bashing diatribe with a reference to Columbine, "a psychic breaking point for our country." The tragedy in Colorado, said Lieberman, "was a warning that the culture of carnage surrounding our children may have gone too far and that the romanticized and sanitized visions of violence that our children are being bombarded with by the media have become part of the toxic mix that has now turned some of them into killers." "Culture of carnage" became the featured catchphrase for Lieberman's sound bite on the evening news.

Barbara Boxer, a liberal Democrat from California with a lot of support in Hollywood, changed the tone dramatically by focusing on what she considered to be the real causes of violence among young people. Quoting statistics from the National Institute for Justice, she compared Windsor, Ontario, in which there were four firearm murders in 1997, with Detroit, which had 354. Windsor and Detroit are only a few miles apart and essentially share the same electronic media. The same movies and television shows are shown and the same recordings are sold in both places. But Detroit has much more poverty, and many more guns, some of which would not be legal in Canada.

Senator Boxer pointed out that by far the biggest predictor of violence in young people, according to the NIJ, is an abusive father. She cited an FBI report that was critical of entertainment marketing but noted that it also looked askance at gun advertising aimed at the young and at Eddie Eagle, the NRA mascot.

A rumpled picture of the earnest bureaucrat, FTC chairman Robert Pitofsky was asked by McCain for an analogy between the marketing of entertainment and the marketing of tobacco. Pitofsky replied, "The harm from smoking is more documented, I suppose. Also, selling tobacco to kids is illegal. Selling violent movies and rap lyrics to kids is not illegal. And there's the First Amendment. There's no First Amendment protection to market cigarettes," the FTC chairman concluded mournfully.

After Lynne Cheney lambasted Eminem, it was my turn. I was part of a panel with Strauss Zelnick and three video game spokesmen. I went first. The lights were a bit brighter than I'd expected, but I could see that McCain, Hollings, and Brownback, at least, were listening.

I outlined my background in the record business and said, "I am speaking not only as a longtime record executive, but also as a father of a ten-year-old girl and a six-and-a-half-year-old boy. I do not believe either government or any entertainment industry committee has any business in telling me and my wife what entertainment our children should be exposed to."

McCain nodded in approval as I continued:

"The United States is a diverse country with hundreds of divergent religious beliefs, ethnic backgrounds, regional traditions, and opinions about art and entertainment. Unlike the visual media, the record business is being asked to categorize and label groups of words. For the same reason there is no ratings system for books, or for that matter congressional testimony. With one narrow exception, it is virtually impossible to rate words."

At the beginning, I found myself gasping for breath in nervousness. My anxiety at testifying before the Senate was abated, in part, by McCain's body language. He never lost eye contact and continued to nod at some of my remarks, as if he agreed with me.

"What kind of system," I asked, could "distinguish between the words 'I want to kill you' said in an affectionate, sarcastic, or ironic way and those same words being used literally? Song lyrics are by their nature impressionistic and are often used symbolically. No one really thought that the words 'killing me softly with his song' referred to murder.

"The one exception are the so-called seven dirty words, and for fifteen years, record companies, including my independent company Artemis Records, have been placing 'parental advisory' stickers on albums that have a lot of curse words."

The stickers, I pointed out, were strictly advisory, and contrary to recent statements by both President Clinton and Vice President Gore, record companies had never suggested there be an age limit on who could buy the records—that was up to parents.

"We placed such a sticker on our current album *Spit*, by the heavy metal band Kittie, because the teenage girls in the band use several curse words over the course of the album. There is nothing illegal about this, and I and critics across the country and the half a million people in the U.S. who have bought the album are morally comfortable with it as well. I know that there are many Americans who are offended by curse words and don't want children exposed to them. However, those people have no moral or legal right to impose such a standard on my family or the millions of other Americans who, like George Bush, are comfortable with cursing."

There were a few laughs, and a few groans. A recent news story had revealed that the Republican presidential candidate had called a *New York Times* reporter an "asshole."

"I respect the fact that many parents don't want their kids to watch R-rated movies," I said, "but I prefer a deeper analysis of each movie. I recently recommended the R-rated *Erin Brockovich* to our ten-year-old daughter Katie, who is a passionate feminist and environmentalist, because I had seen the film and knew the rating was because of cursing. Others may disagree, but this country will cease to be free the day that one group of parents can tell all other parents how to raise their children.

"Song lyrics are not literal. Listening to the blues often makes people happy. Angry weird songs often make adolescents feel less lonely and more connected to other kids. Millions of these teens and young adults feel ostracized when politicians and academics who obviously have no real understanding of their culture make sweeping generalizations about their entertainment, conveniently overlooking the fact that literally every generation has embraced entertainment with sexual and violent themes. Gangsta rap is the direct descendant of the gangster movies of the thirties and forties, the TV Westerns of the fifties, and critically acclaimed films like *The Godfather*."

I looked at McCain, who still seemed to be following every word intently. He nodded encouragingly.

"Mr. Chairman, I don't like every record. Spike Lee criticizes much of the rap culture in his new movie *Bamboozled*. Criticism and moral argument is appropriate and an integral part of the entertainment culture. In an Internet world, there will be ever-increasing ways for parents to find like-minded groups who can advise them on entertainment through the prism of their own particular values. However, so-called self-regulation achieved by political intimidation is the equivalent of censorship."

At the word "censorship," McCain's expression changed from friendly to grim. I took a sip of water and plowed ahead,

"It has become commonplace to assert that popular culture is popular against the wishes and values of its fans. But popular culture gets that way precisely because the balance of consumers—not record makers, not rule makers, but everyday people—enjoy it.

"Mr. Chairman, make no mistake, their tastes, their values, and their morality are under assault every bit as much as the entertainment executives who occupy the hot seat today.

"Washington is a culture of legislation and policy. Asking the FTC or the Washington media or the Congress to analyze popular entertainment makes about as much sense as going to Hollywood to restructure Medicare . . . Washington political leaders are out of touch with the real dynamic of the ways young people process entertainment and condemn youth culture. The only result of demonizing pop culture is to drive millions of young people away from politics. In the last Congressional election in 1998, less than 17 percent of eighteen- to twenty-five-year-olds voted . . . I believe that fifteen years of youth culture entertainment bashing in Washington has greatly contributed to alienation and apathy on the part of young people from politics."

I paused for a moment and peered through the bright lights at McCain before I concluded with, "Mr. Chairman and members of the committee, please help to stop this trend of pushing young people away from politics."

Strauss Zelnick followed, also identifying himself as a parent and acknowledging, "Certain of the messages that pervade our society make it difficult to teach our children the difference between right and wrong." But he stressed that "many of our artists legitimately comment on the problems of our society."

At the end of our testimony, McCain said, "Obviously Mr. Goldberg, in his statement, and Mr. Zelnick to a lesser degree, view this as some sort of coercion or censorship. I do not."

He asked the two of us to "engage in a little colloquy."

"Since I would feel free to interrupt you," he said, "please feel free to interrupt me." I shook my head vehemently, indicating I had no intention of interrupting John McCain. But he said earnestly, "Seriously, I think that's the only way we can have an honest exchange of views here, because I am concerned about some of the things you stated in your testimony."

McCain's personal charm is so strong that even from a distance, up on a rostrum, he is a highly seductive figure. Somehow, he made me feel that he had been hanging on my every word. He now said, "First of all, Mr. Goldberg, I think that young people are not involved in the political process simply because they don't believe they're represented here."

McCain, who had fought a long battle for campaign finance reform, blamed "special interests and big money" for making young people think they were not represented in the political process.

But I had a different point to make: "There are no young people testifying today. There are no groups of fans or consumers that have been invited."

McCain responded, "Well, I would be glad to do that, but we were reviewing a study of marketing practices as opposed to purchasing principles." Perhaps sensing that this was a dubious distinction, McCain added, "But I do agree with you. Perhaps we should have more young people come and testify before Congress. But I'll tell you what a lot of them would say: 'It doesn't make any difference because I couldn't afford the $500,000-ticket fundraiser.'"

Moving to labeling, McCain said he believed people have a right to know the contents of a product before buying it. Why, then, did I seem to view labeling as censorship?

"We label albums with curse words," I said. "That's exactly what we've been doing for fifteen years . . ."

McCain jumped in, saying he was talking about more specific recommendations. Couldn't we say something was not suitable for audiences of a certain age?

I replied that there were no universal criteria.

"A fourteen-year-old in one family, the parents may not want exposed to material that in my family, maybe we do. We have no idea how to further categorize words. I do agree with making all of the words available for parents who want to read them, subject to the copyright owner's permission to do so. But I don't understand what criteria could be used to create additional categories. Book publishers don't do it, magazines, newspapers don't. Words don't lend themselves to those kinds of categories except for profanity, which we already label."

McCain said, "I frankly recoiled at the lyrics Senator Brownback put up there. Isn't it pretty clear that something like that should be labeled? I want to emphasize, Mr. Goldberg . . . I can't speak for other members of this committee, I don't want to resort to censorship. We want to try to remove and eradicate a problem that's been identified by a respected agency of the government. Did you want to respond?"

"The Eminem album is stickered," I replied. "A lot of people like it anyway. And I realize that everybody here didn't like reading those lyrics isolated, disconnected from the music, disconnected from context, and you might hate hearing the whole album, even after meeting the artist. But millions of people like it, and in a free society, what do you do about that except tell your opinion? I think you also have to recognize that young people have a different language that they use, different symbols, and have a different feeling about this. Most young people I know feel that this is a humorous record not a violent record. You may disagree with them, but it

might be good for you to hear their point of view, the actual fans of
the music, instead of assuming how they interpret it."

Although McCain and I failed to reach a meeting of the minds,
I found his attempt at actual dialogue, even in the context of a public hearing room, more substantive than any conversation I'd had
over the years with Democrats.

Jack Valenti called to congratulate me on my testimony. In his
sonorous Texas drawl, Valenti said with typical hyperbole, "You
spoke truth to power. They're not used to hearing it." He reassured
me with the voice of experience, "Don't worry, after Election Day
things will be different."

Valenti's sanguine view was echoed by Jann Wenner, the publisher of *Rolling Stone*.

"There's not going to be any censorship," Jann told me. "I've
spoken to Tipper about it."

Wenner and VH-1's John Sykes put together an impressive
fundraiser for Gore that included performances by Sheryl Crow and
Jon Bon Jovi. An issue of *Rolling Stone* came out close to the election
with a passionate endorsement of Gore by Wenner and an interview
in which Gore quoted the Dylan line, "He not busy being born is
busy dying," that Jimmy Carter had used twenty-four years earlier.

Following the Senate hearing, I debated Jerry Falwell on a talk
show cohosted by Democratic power figure and former Clinton
counsel Paul Begala. After the show, I asked Begala if he thought
that the Democrats' obsession with culture bashing hurt them with
young voters.

"I don't think so," said Begala. "I think the reason young people
don't vote is because the issues of government don't affect people
until they're married and have children." I pointed out that this has
always been the case, but that younger voting had been precipi-
tously declining in the last decade. "Well," said Begala, "there were
bigger issues, like the Vietnam War."

Of course, the Vietnam War ended in 1975. More to the point, when Jesse Ventura ran a campaign for governor of Minnesota that was fueled by pop culture and straightforward language, youth turnout skyrocketed.

It was during the same time period that Artemis had its biggest and most unexpected hit with a song that was featured in a G-rated movie for kids. Steve Greenberg, who had worked for me at Atlantic and Mercury, had always been a big supporter of a relatively obscure Bahamian world-music group called the Baha Men, and when he played me their raucously joyful "Who Let the Dogs Out," I jumped at it. The recording would become almost ubiquitous in the fall and winter on the radio and as a sports anthem, played at countless baseball, basketball, and football games. It really exploded after it was used in the popular children's movie *Rugrats in Paris*. We sold over 3 million copies of "Who Let the Dogs Out," which helped Artemis achieve the ranking of the number one independently distributed label in the United States for 2000.

As the presidential campaign droned on, Rosemary and I became more and more disenchanted with Gore. We resented it that Democrats made sure that Ralph Nader (and for that matter, Pat Buchanan) could not participate in and broaden the scope of the televised debates. We decided to go with our hearts, as Molly Ivins had suggested, and support Nader in New York, where Gore was leading in the polls by twenty points.

We introduced Nader to Patti Smith, and she appeared with Eddie Vedder of Pearl Jam, Ani DiFranco, Michael Moore, and others at a sold-out Nader rally in mid-September at Madison Square Garden. In his speech, Nader connected his campaign with the spirit of our No Nukes concerts twenty-one years earlier. The next night, we held a fundraiser for Nader at our house, which was co-hosted by Tim Robbins and Susan Sarandon, among others.

By the middle of October, however, I and many other Nader supporters were having second thoughts. He had broken his promise not to campaign in swing states. Reportedly, he was persuaded by Green Party leaders that he needed to swell his vote total to get the 5 percent needed to nail down matching funds.

Democrats, finally waking up to the fact that Nader was a factor, dispatched venerable leaders of the party's left wing to urge their followers not to vote for him. The Reverend Jackson called and lectured me that Strom Thurmond and Jesse Helms were "licking their chops at the idea of Bush in the White House and all of the appointments they'll control."

I told Jesse that I felt that older Democrats were coming home to the party in swing states, even if they didn't particularly care for Gore, but that Nader was drawing huge crowds on college campuses. Young people were not moved by the middle-aged surrogates like Gloria Steinem and Jackson himself that the Gore campaign was sending out. Nader was articulating strong positions on the environment, on labor, on poverty, and on trade that were not even being discussed by Bush or Gore.

Over the course of the presidential debates, Gore managed to make it literally impossible for most voters outside of Washington to understand the differences between him and Bush. The most memorable thing that came out of the debates were the *Saturday Night Live* parodies. Darrell Hammond's devastating caricature of Gore, simultaneously stiff and sneaky, reminded people of everything they didn't like about him, whereas Will Ferrell's George W. Bush seemed like silly fun.

"How can you change anything if you don't understand TV?" Michael Moore regularly admonished the left. His TV show *The Awful Truth* and his films *Roger and Me* and *The Big One* had given more mass exposure to progressive ideas than the rest of the alternative media combined. His very active website had helped galvanize public opposition to the impeachment, earning the thanks of both Gore and Clinton. Like me, Michael had decided to support Nader's campaign as a way of broadening the national debate.

"I figured Gore would win by ten points," Michael said to me in wonder as Election Day grew near, and the pollsters declared the race too close to call. "The economy is terrific," said Moore. "The public opposed impeachment. Gore was supposed to be this great debater, facing an idiot. I never thought Gore would lose all of the debates and that it would be this close."

Moore is a charismatic speaker who often appeared with Nader at rallies, but he refused to campaign with him in swing states. He tried unsuccessfully to get Nader to stop it, and called everyone he knew in the Gore campaign, trying to find a way to bridge the gap.

Moore told readers of his website that he could understand why Nader supporters would vote for Gore in swing states. Nader supporter Ani DiFranco urged young people in swing states to vote for Gore.

"Maybe Gore could say that he'd be in favor of Ralph being included in debates for the next election," Michael suggested shortly before Election Day. Instead, Gore chose to completely ignore Nader and never referred to him, nor to the millions of people who followed him and voted for him.

Steve Earle, who records for Artemis, tried to encourage his fans at least not to vote for Bush. A longtime and active opponent of the death penalty, Steve and director Amos Poe made a music video of "Jonathan's Song," a farewell to a condemned man Steve had gotten to know in Texas. While Steve's lament played in the background, the video showed the faces of over 300 people executed in Texas while George W. Bush was governor.

The Sunday before the election, Barbra Streisand called me, explaining in her earnest New York accent, the real policy differences between Gore and Bush. I agreed with her. So did many people who'd been attracted by Nader at the beginning. The problem wasn't the middle-aged left, or the old left. The problem was young voters who didn't watch C-SPAN or read the editorial pages, people for whom the *Saturday Night Live* caricatures of Bush and Gore rang true.

I asked her to support Moore's efforts to get Gore to acknowledge Nader, but she said she no longer had any input to Gore's campaign. I told Barbra that Lieberman and Gore's attacks on popular culture hadn't exactly helped with young people. Barbra asked me plaintively, "Aren't they doing things on college campuses?"

The answer was, too little too late.

A major reason Gore lost in 2000 was a very severe case of liberal snobbery. With his unwillingness or inability to communicate in ordinary language ("Dingell-Norwood"?), his shrill attacks on popular culture, his selection of a running mate even more sanctimonious and elitist than he, and his obsessive need to distance himself from President Clinton, Gore turned off millions of voters he could have attracted.

Conservative Democrats and some pundits implausibly blamed what they called Gore's "populist" message for driving away swing voters. This theory totally ignores the voters who swung between Nader and Gore. Even if Gore occasionally said something that could be taken as populism, his style and affect remained hopelessly elitist. Gore had none of the common touch of true populists such as Ross Perot or Jesse Ventura. On the contrary, he always seemed like a lecturing professor, while Bush was able to portray himself as the solid voice of common sense next door.

Gore's dramatic drop in the support of younger voters alone cost him the election. The statistics are clear. Among voters aged eighteen to twenty-four, Clinton defeated Bob Dole, the archenemy of popular culture, by 19 percent in 1996. In 2000, Bush, who was not identified with attacks on youth culture, received half the 9 million votes in the eighteen to twenty-four category. If Gore had retained the Democratic margin among young voters from the previous election, he would have added almost 2 million votes to his national margin. That would have tipped the balance his way in several swing states (including, of course, Florida), and he would have won the electoral college and thus the election decisively.

Although I think Ralph Nader was too cavalier about his effect on the outcome, blaming Nader misses the point. Most people who voted for Nader had made up their minds that they didn't want to vote for Gore or Bush.

Rock the Vote registered over 500,000 eighteen- to twenty-one-year-olds at rallies around the country in 2000. Mario Velasquez, Rock the Vote's executive director, told me shortly after the election, "Young people were obviously not part of the Gore-Lieberman campaign strategy. For months we had events on college campuses where representatives of Bush and Nader would come, but not from the Democrats. Finally, the last few weeks of the campaign, when their polls showed the appeal of Nader to young people, Gore sent people, but by then it was too late." Not only was Gore hostile to youth culture, he made scant reference to issues that would move young people. There was almost no mention of the great moral purpose of politics, the ability of government to help the most disadvantaged, to create ladders that can lift people out of poverty or despair. There were no misgivings about a drug war that landed hundreds of thousands of people in jail for the same crime Gore himself admitted to having committed in his younger years. Gore, who had genuine passion about the environment and who had written a book about it, almost never touched upon the issue in his campaign, and on those rare occasions when he did, he failed to draw clear distinctions between his positions and those of Bush.

Judy McGrath, president of MTV, spoke of a similar failure: "We had a great relationship with Clinton, but it was almost impossible to get Gore to do anything on MTV. When he finally came on, the most telling moment for me was when a black kid with dreadlocks held up a copy of the Mos Def album and explained how there was a side to rap that was socially conscious, and that many young people such as himself combined their belief in music with their politics."

Mos Def is a politically oriented rapper who has never been criticized for misogyny, violent lyrics, or any of the usual catalogue of sins. "Instead of hearing what the kid was saying," Judy told me, "Gore totally ignored his comment and used it to lecture him on how women would feel about the word 'bitch' in songs, an answer that had nothing to do with what the kid was saying. He just squashed him. And our audience."

CHAPTER 11

The Media Marketing Accountability Act

Hip-hop culture is imprinted with the very economic and social misery that it intends to confront, to which it responds very valiantly and sometimes self-destructively. The real obscenity is not the vulgarity that emerges out of the mouths of these young people, the real vulgarity is the economic and social and racial misery and gender misery that they continue to confront.
—Michael Eric Dyson, professor of religious studies at DePaul University

I N THE BATTLE FOR FLORIDA that followed the 2000 election, the Democrats made some of the same mistakes that had plagued their campaign. Stiff, sour-visaged Warren Christopher was not a compelling spokesperson, and David Boies, the brilliant litigator, took courtroom arguments and put them on TV, lecturing the public in colorless legalisms. He came across as what he is, a shrewd lawyer, reinforcing the Republican message, "They're trying to steal the election." Democrats certainly could have said the same thing.

The Republican spokesman, former secretary of state James Baker, spoke in coherent, media-friendly sound bites that rallied the troops.

The Democrats virtually ignored a potentially powerful story line, the disenfranchisement of black voters. The Gore forces seemed anxious to keep the Reverend Jesse Jackson and other black advocates at a distance, and to rely on the lawyers and the courts. In the months that followed, Democrats studiously avoided the circumstances that led to Bush's "victory" in Florida. Two years later, when a group of first-time filmmakers released the documentary *Unprecedented* outlining the systematic exclusion of African American voters in Florida in 2000, many Democrats wondered why the case had not been made at the time.

Gore won several hundred thousand more popular votes than Bush. As Rick Hertzberg pointed out in the *New Yorker*, Gore could have used this fact as the basis to give monthly speeches on behalf of the plurality of Americans who had voted for him to criticize Bush's policies when he disagreed with them and advocate his own. Instead, Gore disappeared from public life for almost two years.

On the morning of April 18, 2001, Senator Joseph Lieberman came to another Creative Coalition meeting. This one was on the third floor of the imperial office building of talent agency CAA on Wilshire Boulevard in Los Angeles.

Around thirty-five actors, producers, and directors filled the conference room. The many actors included Richard Schiff and Bradley Whitford, whose show *The West Wing* was already providing millions of Americans with a fictional Democratic alternative to the new Bush administration. Also present were columnist Arianna Huffington and Tom Hayden, who was in the midst of an unsuccessful runoff for election to the LA City Council. I was the only person from the music business.

Lieberman made an unpretentious entrance accompanied by a

single aide. In the wake of the election, and the widespread feeling among Democrats that it had illegitimately been decided by the Supreme Court, even I felt some goodwill toward the defeated Democratic candidate for vice president. Lieberman quickly, however, reverted to type.

"Since I was out here to speak on foreign policy at USC," he said in a casual tone, "I thought I'd meet some people from the entertainment business to continue a dialogue. Entertainment became a source of concern to me when I walked by the TV set and my then-five-year-old daughter was watching *Married with Children* with my then-seventeen-year-old son. I had no problem with my seventeen-year-old watching it, but I did remove my five-year-old.

"A society expresses itself through stories," he said. "Culture affects us. Social scientists seem to say it affects behavior. I never say it causes violence, teen pregnancy, sexually transmitted diseases, but that it contributes. Kids are affected, especially vulnerable children are affected.

"Can we do better?" he asked plaintively.

Lieberman said that a new Federal Trade Commission report on entertainment marketing would be issued imminently.

"I've said I'd introduce legislation to empower the FTC to have authority to enforce ratings issued by companies," he said. He did not again refer to legislation at the meeting. Instead, he asked us to focus on a paper he distributed on "media literacy," which was basically about learning how to understand, analyze, and use modern mass media. It was filled with feel-good generalities.

Actor Daniel Stern, who teaches a media literacy course to ninth graders and has enormous passion for it, spoke up excitedly, "I was in the *Home Alone* movies, and kids came up to me to ask if heavy objects really hit me in the head." But, Stern admonished, "Regulation is a slippery slope. Education is the key. But it takes money, Senator."

Lieberman appeared flummoxed. He said he wanted foundations and charitable groups to sponsor and teach media literacy, not the federal government. Seeing the disappointed looks in the room, he added, "The typical way we do this is to give incentives to states— maybe that's a good idea."

Pulp Fiction producer Lawrence Bender, a host of the meeting, adroitly changed the subject by reading an article detailing how TV news had exaggerated violence in society and had been unfair to minorities in covering crime. He was obviously not calling for censorship of TV news but trying to create some perspective on violence and the media.

Lieberman sighed and said, "I've noodged TV. It's harder to do because news is local." Quickly returning to movies, he said, "We need to limit or educate or inform the public regarding violent intake." I cringed at the implications of the innocent-seeming word "limit."

Boaz Yakin, in his mid-thirties but appearing younger, with his look-of-the-moment stubble and short hair, said, "I am the director of *Remember the Titans* for Disney, as gentle a movie as you could want. I'm sure you would want children to see it." The film, which stars Denzel Washington, is the achingly sincere, true story of a black football coach taking over a previously all-white team in the South in the early 1970s.

"We got letters from Saudi Arabia saying they really wanted to release the movie there," Boaz recalled. "But they asked us to make some changes, including removing scenes showing crosses, showing short skirts on girls, and scenes of males and females holding hands. When we got the letters we all laughed and said to ourselves what a fucked-up society they have. We think that because we have freedom here. I see freedom of ideas as a way to protect me.

"I was educated at a Yeshiva. I was brought up in an insular, narrow way. A rabbi there told me black people were inferior because they were descendants of one of the sons of Noah—he called them *schvartzes*. When I finally met a black person he was Catholic and he told me that he had been taught that there was a special place in hell for Jews."

Lieberman interrupted to quip, "A very special place."

He got a laugh, but Boaz wasn't done. Lieberman was well-known as a strong advocate of funding religious groups to provide a variety of social services, including schooling. Boaz said, "You want to give money to religious institutions like these to teach. What are they going to teach? I was able to expand my mind by reading William Burroughs and Henry Miller, whose works were once banned, because of the way they dealt with complex issues that I had to work through as a human being. Who will be teaching this media literacy? What if they're bigots? I believe in letting all the ideas be expressed, and the best ideas will win. Sometimes someone crazy will shoot someone and have liked a movie—that's the price you pay for a genuinely stronger society. This is about fear of ideas, fear of real communication."

There was dead silence. The room belonged to Boaz, and Lieberman didn't want to take him on. "Given the choice of freedom or limitation, I'd always choose freedom," Lieberman claimed.

Lieberman complimented the MPAA ratings system as a good basis on which to build more "consumer information." Producer Tom Baer interjected, "Don't be so enthusiastic about ratings. *Billy Elliot* is an R, and I'd like every nine-year-old to see it."

Arianna Huffington agreed. In her thick Greek accent, she told Lieberman that she and her husband had two kids, aged eleven and thirteen. "I don't want less choice, I want more choice," she said. "I insisted they see *Traffic* and *Erin Brockovich*. *Traffic* has changed the debate on the drug war." There was much nodding in approval.

I took a turn. "Senator, first, thanks for a more collegial approach compared to confrontational."

"I'm sooo glad you appreciate it," interjected Lieberman, his voice dripping with sarcasm.

I kept going. "As a Democrat, I am concerned that young people are turned off to voting. They feel politicians of both parties attack what they think is their culture. We didn't think Woodstock was Warner Brothers culture, it was our culture. Democrats have lost the edge they had with younger voters, from a nineteen-point margin in 1992 to zero in 2000."

Lieberman implausibly replied, "I didn't know those numbers," and had no comment on how to motivate young people to participate.

Toward the end of the meeting, Richard Kind, an actor in the TV series *Spin City*, began railing at Britney Spears, declaring that her revealing outfits were a bad influence on young teenagers. I suggested that Britney Spears's image might be empowering to pubescent girls, and that her lyrics were substantially less risqué than those of the previous decade's female icon, Madonna.

"Well, I wasn't too crazy about her, either," the actor countered.

"What about Janis Joplin?" I asked.

Kind, who was born in 1956, looked at me with misty eyes. "I loved Janis Joplin," he said.

I said that I loved Janis Joplin too, but reminded him that Joplin posed for nude photos, cursed like a sailor from the stage, and was an unapologetic drunk and druggie.

In the elevator to the lobby, Lieberman said to me sarcastically, "My thirteen-year-old daughter will be so thrilled that you defended Britney Spears."

The next day, under the headline "Senator Joe Lowers Boom on H'wood," the *New York Post* reported, "Lieberman claimed Hollywood has failed to police itself so he'll introduce a bill allowing the FTC to fine companies that direct explicit films, music, and video games toward young audiences." That was certainly a lot more information than Lieberman had given us directly the day before.

Lieberman, the story continued, "feels the movie industry hasn't done enough and the music business has done nothing."

On April 24, the Federal Trade Commission released a new report on entertainment-business marketing. The report charged, "The Commission found advertising for explicit content–labeled music recordings routinely appeared on popular teen advertising programming. All five major recording companies placed advertising for explicit content music on television programs and magazines with substantial under-17 audiences, in some cases more than 50 percent under 17."

One particularly surreal part of the report was a criticism of record companies for advertising stickered albums on the World Wrestling Federation's *Smackdown*, which features scantily clad, insanely aggressive men and women screaming vitriol and pretending to knock the living daylights out of each other. Thirty-six percent of the program's audience is under eighteen, it turns out. Well, at least they could be protected from rap music.

Two days later, three Democrats—Joe Lieberman, Senator Herb Kohl of Wisconsin, and, shockingly, Senator Hillary Clinton of New York—formally introduced the Media Marketing Accountability Act of 2001. It would expand FTC authority to crack down on businesses that engaged in "false and deceptive advertising practices." Senator Clinton explained, "If you label something as inappropriate for children and then go out and target it to children, you are engaging in false and deceptive advertising."

The proposed new law would require record companies and film studios to have "an age-based rating or labeling system" with more teeth than the traditional movie ratings. And the FTC would be given authority to decide if "advertising or marketing is . . . directed or targeted to minors." In practice, the FTC could decide which music and movies could be mass-marketed and thus, by and large, which ones would be released. The bill would, in essence, criminalize the marketing and sale of most rock and rap albums to kids under seventeen.

Jack Valenti, head of the Motion Picture Association of America, attacked the bill with unusual intensity: "The bill defiles the Constitution. There's a difference from putting labels on cereal boxes and Hershey bars. You're dealing with Supreme Court–ordered protection. The bill will be dead on arrival at the first federal court to hear it. What's next, books, newspapers?"

I called Valenti to congratulate him on his comments and I told him that Lieberman had dissed him at the Creative Coalition meeting, complaining about his resistance to supplying more detailed information in film ratings. Valenti sighed.

"I know," he said. "I refuse to attack him by name publicly, though. I say Joe Lieberman is my friend, he and I just clash on this issue. I'm a staunch believer in the First Amendment, and I thought he was, too."

I asked Valenti if he'd pointed out the First Amendment implications of the bill to Lieberman, and he sighed again. "When people get very religious and they believe their course of action is sanctioned by a higher authority, there's not much you can do to communicate with them—left, right, whatever," Valenti pointedly concluded.

Uncharacteristically irate, Valenti kept fuming. "And Hillary Clinton," he said. "She's a lawyer. How could she say that labels are appropriate for foods and forget that there's a First Amendment?"

I called Chuck Schumer, the other Democratic senator from New York. "I'm against it," said Schumer. "If I say anything publicly now, it would look like I'm picking a fight with Hillary. The media is constantly harping on our supposed rivalry. If it ever comes to a vote, I'd be against it and speak against it—it's ridiculous. But don't worry, the bill is not going anywhere."

Jerry Nadler, a staunch First Amendment supporter and the con-

gressman whose district includes our Greenwich Village neighborhood, agreed. "The bill isn't going anywhere, so what difference
does it make?" The implication is that the whole process was grand-
standing to make some Democrats more politically palatable to culturally conservative swing voters. But the effect of that symbolism
cuts more than one way. To me, the "difference" that congressional
rhetoric makes in cases like this is to further alienate young people
and fans of pop culture from politics in general. I believe that the
cost of such alienation in terms of creating nonvoters and third-
party voters is far greater than any gain for Democrats.

Washington gossip had it that Lieberman had spent a lot of energy trying to get a Republican senator to cosponsor the bill, but
that Orrin Hatch and John McCain, among others, had declined.
Valenti told me that Senate majority leader Trent Lott saw the legislation as a PR vehicle for Lieberman's national aspirations, and
that he would make sure that no Republican signed on as a cosponsor. None did. Thus, for those paying attention, Republicans came
across as less snobbish and less elitist than Democrats.

A conservative columnist for the New York Post was one of the
few media pundits to attack the legislation. Andrea Peyser wrote,
"It's much easier to target Hollywood and Nintendo than to suggest
that guns should be removed from the reach of already damaged
and emotionally disturbed kids. It is much easier to blame rap music for violence than it is for some parents . . . to sit down with kids
and discuss the lyrics they've heard. Censorship is easy, which
makes it popular. Trouble is, it's doomed to failure."

While the controversy was building, I had a business meeting
with Ray Daniels, a big Canadian rock manager. He told me an an-
ecdote about one of his clients:

"With the Matthew Good Band, at the request of Wal-Mart in
the United States, we had to change the title on the package of *A
Boy and a Machine Gun* to *A Boy and* followed by three dots. In

Canada we can say what we want on the album cover, but you can't buy guns in the same store. At Wal-Mart, you can't have the word 'gun' on an album cover—but they sell actual guns!"

In June, the Creative Coalition issued a statement condemning the proposed legislation as a violation of the First Amendment and urged Senators Lieberman, Clinton, and Kohl to withdraw their support. Among those signing were actors Robin Williams, Ben Stiller, Lauren Bacall, Chevy Chase, Bo Derek (who publicly campaigned for George W. Bush), Olympia Dukakis (cousin of the former Democratic presidential nominee), Hector Elizondo, Richard Belzer, Harvey Fierstein, and Kathleen Turner. Ron Reagan signed it, as well as Jane Alexander, head of the National Endowment for the Arts under Clinton. Creative Coalition president William Baldwin went on television news shows to oppose the bill.

Responding to a Creative Coalition letter, President George W. Bush straddled the issue with a note from his ranch in Crawford, Texas: "I believe that government must be engaged but restrained. I will take your views into consideration in the coming months."

In the spring of 2001, powerful black record executive Russell Simmons organized a rap summit, both to defend rap and to move it in more socially responsible directions. Dozens of rappers and record executives attended, along with several members of the Black Congressional Caucus, Minister Louis Farrakhan, Martin Luther King III, and Harvard professor Cornel West.

Simmons, one of the founders of the seminal rap label Def Jam, with his shaved head and his stand-up comedian's sense of timing, had become the best-known rap impresario. He set a balanced tone for the meeting.

On one hand, he said, "I want to defend forever the right of rappers to say, 'Fuck the police.' We have to be able to comment on and express our lives just like every other group and every other generation."

On the other hand, Simmons called for rappers and executives to take a closer look at lyrics, particularly those involving women. "I know the relationships a lot of you have with your wives," he said, "so why talk like a pimp? If this culture is about truth, then tell that truth as well."

Russell Simmons was also a key player in a meeting between Hillary Clinton and several of us who had enthusiastically supported her run for the Senate, and who were particularly annoyed at her cosponsorship of the Lieberman bill. Simmons's wealth and his house in East Hampton had given him access to New York's elite, yet he always kept in close touch with "the street" through the rappers who congregated around him. He was and is an indispensable link to young African Americans for black political leaders, and for white ones, like Hillary Clinton, who courted the black vote. Hillary Clinton was one of the few white politicians with any currency among African Americans, and Simmons was concerned that she would lose some of that.

We met at Senator Clinton's Manhattan office. She was ebullient, and looked striking in an orange pants suit. She quickly addressed our reason for being there. "I didn't realize how culturally divisive this bill would be. It was just after that terrible election and I wanted to be supportive of Joe. But this is a different time now. I thought we would build on the progress we made in the White House. We got a lot accomplished—such as the V-chip—and you all supported that."

I stared at her blankly. The only people who "supported" the V-chip were TV networks, and they were coerced into it.

"The bill is not going anywhere," she assured us. "There are no Republican cosponsors. Joe sees the world in a different way than I do, but I can't offend another senator—it's a very small body."

Echoing her husband's remarks years before, she talked about kids at risk and turned to me, recalling her encounter with Katie and Max at the fundraiser at our house the previous year. "I saw you with your kids and could feel the relationship you have with them," she said. "What's scary is a lot of parents aren't there or aren't doing their job. To these kids entertainment becomes a co-parent."

Russell Simmons demurred. "If you were a kid with nothing in your head, the DMX album would be a positive influence. When he listens to the devil he goes to hell. When he talks to God he goes to heaven. DMX is a profound American poet—his lyrics will be taught someday like Shakespeare." Senator Clinton's staff took notes. I hoped that at least one of them eventually listened to a DMX album.

I explained that 80 percent of the music targeted by the FTC came from black artists. During the election, Senator Clinton had been interviewed by Angie Martinez of Hot 97, the number one hip-hop station in New York, and the station aired the interview repeatedly with obvious pride. Now Senator Clinton was aligning herself with attacks on the culture that the station celebrated. The racial undertone of attacks on hip-hop was so obvious that Hot 97 had created sarcastic "bumper" spots with a voice in an echo chamber that intoned, "Warning! Explicit Negroes."

Simmons, who had arranged the Hot 97 interview, told the Senator, "I'm not worried about this bill personally. I'm not going to jail. My artists are going to make the music they want. When there are political attacks it actually helps us. I make more money."

Simmons laughed, and then his face grew serious and he spoke with emotion directly to Hillary Clinton: "I don't want you associated with this. I don't care what Lieberman says—but you shouldn't be against youth."

Clinton responded, "I don't relish the role I'm in now. Chelsea was horrified that I supported this. She was saying to me, 'What about country and western songs with lyrics about killing,' and so on . . . She has told me about media literacy in Canada and I asked her to get more info on it from the Internet. Maybe that's a positive area." Clinton sighed wearily. "I'm going to talk to Joe."

On our way out, Russell said to me, "She sure was nice, but basically we got nothing, right?" Russell indeed was correct.

On July 24, all of us from the meeting got a fax from Senator Clinton that had all the hallmarks of a form letter sent to thousands of constituents. Citing Columbine and the FTC report, she wrote, "Since we met, I spoke with Senator Lieberman again about these issues. As I have explained to you and many others, I view the Media Marketing Accountability Act as a measure of last resort."

I sent a reply, saying, "The carefully balanced approach that you and President Clinton employed in the past is very different from the radical step embodied in the legislation proposed by Senator Lieberman . . . There is no question that the Media Marketing Accountability Act would involve the heavy hand of government in regulating the marketing of entertainment in a way unprecedented in the United States or any western democracy."

I cannot imagine how to explain to a young rap artist that his or her words couldn't be marketed to teenagers, but that the exact same language and concepts in more traditional literary packages were free from restrictions. I was gratified when an umbrella publishing group called the Media Coalition came together to fight the bill. Its members included all of the major book and literary organizations, and large associations of book and magazine publishers, distributors, and sellers.

In late July, hearings began on the Media Marketing Accountability Act in the Senate Committee on Governmental Affairs, chaired by Joe Lieberman. Republican senator Fred Thompson of Tennessee expressed the sharpest criticism of the bill. "We can't keep our vital national security secret," said the Tennessee senator, a sometime film and TV actor. "You think we'll keep entertainment out of the hands of kids?"

Russell Simmons was initially refused a slot to testify, but Lieberman eventually gave him some time, after several witnesses complained about the bizarre exclusion of African American voices. The essence of his testimony was laid out succinctly by Simmons in a *New York Times* op-ed piece on August 3.

"Hip-hop," Simmons argued, "is an important art form, really the first new genre of music to emerge since rock and roll. To condemn it without understanding it is irresponsible. To disregard its huge audience is arrogant. To deny its power and artistic merit in an attempt to silence it is downright dangerous . . . If the government can target young African American artists for censorship, no one's freedom of expression is safe.

"Studies created by government bureaucrats and papers prepared by academics can only go so far," he wrote. "At some point, to truly understand the anger, profanity, joy, humor, and celebration of hip-hop you have to go to the artist."

I and many people in the entertainment community have supported Al Gore and Bill and Hillary Clinton and others whose perspectives on art, entertainment, and free speech diverge from our view of the world, and if electoral logic called for it, I would do so again. However, I would never under any circumstances support or vote for a ticket with Joe Lieberman on it. Not only is he one of the most conservative Democrats with a national profile, but his self-righteousness about religion and venom toward popular culture would make him a serious threat to a free and intellectually diverse American society if he were to gain more power.

CHAPTER 12

September 11

In the dark times, will there still be singing? Yes, there will be singing about the dark times.
—Bertolt Brecht

I WAS IN THE MIDDLE of writing this book when planes crashed into the World Trade Center and the Pentagon. For weeks after September 11, 2001, the wind would occasionally blow smoke north from the devastated ruins of the Trade Center into the Greenwich Village neighborhood where my family lives. Like almost everyone in New York, I knew several people who died on September 11. I shared the sense of stunned horror, anger, and fear that so many Americans felt in the weeks following the attack. Even if we could have forgotten, our children regularly reminded us with their fearful questions about the newfound sense of peril that accompanied their lives.

On TV, David Letterman and Jon Stewart wept, and Larry King asked Jerry Seinfeld without irony, "When will it be okay to be funny again?"

A month later, the tragedy was still haunting New Yorkers, as became clear at a panel on Music in the Time of War at the annual conference of college radio programmers and music professionals sponsored by the CMJ music network. The panel, which I participated in, was chaired by *Village Voice* music editor Bob Christgau, who has probably listened to and written about more rock and rap records than anyone else in history.

Christgau sobbed during his opening remarks, and said that because of his grief for the deaths of September 11 he was having a hard time listening to new music. *Newsweek* music writer Lorraine Ali, an Arab American who had been in Cairo during the attack and had been temporarily assigned to write about the reaction in Arab countries, also spoke of how difficult it was for her to imagine going back to writing about music.

I said I felt that the voices of people in the arts needed to be part of national conversations in times of emergency or tragedy. But I also felt that we in the music business needed to be sensitive to the physical and emotional horror and pain wrought by the killing of thousands.

Radio programmers told Artemis Records that they didn't want to broadcast a song by our group Sugarcult because of the phrase "everybody is blowing up the neighborhood." The band didn't hesitate to rerecord a new phrase. The reference had clearly been to teenage partying, but they could certainly understand how it now could be construed as insensitive.

Similarly, the Strokes, who my wife Rosemary represents, eliminated a song on their debut album on RCA that referred derisively to New York policemen. These changes didn't seem like censorship to me, but were made by artists themselves in recognition of a radically changed context.

But cultural reactionaries couldn't wait to take advantage of the tragedy. On Pat Robertson's *700 Club*, Jerry Falwell said that the destruction of the World Trade Center was God's punishment to America for "feminism, gay rights, and groups like People for the American Way and the ACLU." The attack had an effect, but not the one Falwell intended. The ACLU experienced the greatest membership increase in its history in the months following September 11, growing from about 250,000 members to around 350,000. In October, we organized the first LA-style fundraising dinner for the New York Civil Liberties Union, honoring Nickelodeon president Albie Hecht and film director Ang Lee. It was the most successful fundraiser the NYCLU ever had.

Susan Sontag wrote a thoughtful and thought-provoking piece in the *New Yorker* in which she mentioned that President Bush's reference to the terrorists as "cowards" seemed an odd way to describe people willing to die in flames for their beliefs. Conservatives, who had long hated Sontag, attacked her as if she were urging support for Osama bin Laden.

Bush's use of the word "coward" was also mocked by Bill Maher, host of the TV show *Politically Incorrect*. Maher was sternly rebuked by White House press secretary Ari Fleischer, who said, chillingly, "Now is a time when people have to watch what they say." With happy visions of blacklisting dancing in their heads, conservatives convinced a few sponsors to pull out of *Politically Incorrect*, but they were soon replaced. ABC did fold the show the following summer, but its ratings had been low for some time.

Liberal snobs also jumped at the chance to use the national crisis to advance their pet cultural theories. Singer-songwriter Paul Simon wrote in the *New York Times* that the tragic deaths at the World Trade Center were "ameliorated" by what he anticipated as a forthcoming decline in "violent entertainment." I found it quite extraordinary that Simon would be on a hobbyhorse about entertainment violence. The last time I had seen him was during my brief tenure as chairman of Warner Brothers Records. Simon spent much of our lunch together expounding on his passion at the time, the forthcoming Broadway musical *Capeman*. It was the story of an infamous murderer of the 1950s.

But the great majority of the American public had no appetite for conservative cultural obsessions. Clear Channel, the Texas-based company that owns more music radio stations than any other—at this writing, about 1,300—dispatched a memo listing 200 songs that might be offensive in the wake of the tragedy. The list ranged from all work by the political rock band Rage Against the Machine to many long-popular songs with lyrics that could now be interpreted differently, such as Peter, Paul and Mary's "Leavin' on a Jet Plane" and John Lennon's "Imagine."

The outcry at the reported banning of "Imagine" was enormous. What was the "inappropriate" line—the one that says "Imagine all the people, living life in peace"? or the one that asks us to "Imagine there's no countries"? In the wake of widespread criticism, not a single executive at Clear Channel would admit to having had anything to do with the memo. "Imagine" quickly became one of the most frequently played songs on the radio, including stations owned by Clear Channel. When celebrities raised hundreds of millions of dollars for families of the victims of September 11 in a national telethon, Neil Young's performance of "Imagine" was generally considered to be the emotional and artistic high point of the event.

To me, the most striking symbol of the adverse relationship between critics of popular culture, liberal or conservative, and most of America came at Madison Square Garden in late October 2001. The occasion was the nationally televised "Concert for America." Six thousand policemen and firemen and their relatives were invited to sit in the best seats. Many rock stars from the sixties and seventies performed. Much of the audience that night consisted of white ethnics, union members, and working families, exactly the kind of swing voters political consultants say are swayed by cultural conservatism.

Artists such as the Rolling Stones and Billy Joel, performing songs that had been filled with alienation and anger when first recorded, touched some kind of emotional chord in the audience, transcending many cultural differences. The passionately applaud-ing audience seemed to represent a much bigger slice of America than the one that resided in the imaginations of either Jerry Falwell or Joe Lieberman.

Then Hillary Clinton was introduced. She was loudly booed.

Yet the same people applauded rapper Jay-Z, who had recently pled guilty to assault, and cheered the publicly gay musicians Elton John, Peter Townshend, and Melissa Etheridge.

Why I Love !?!?! New York, a short film by director Kevin Smith that consisted of profanity and bleep-filled interviews, was met with enthusiastic cheers, as was the appearance of Howard Stern, whose suggestive radio broadcasts have led to countless fines over the years from the FCC.

So what motivated those who booed? My guess is that it was a combination of factors. Some of the men in the audience just didn't like strong women. Some were economic conservatives, and many, I suspect, perceived Senator Clinton as a politically correct liberal snob.

Meanwhile, George W. Bush's brilliant political advisor, Karl Rove, met amid much fanfare with film industry leaders to discuss ways that Hollywood could support government policy in the war on terrorism.

CHAPTER 13

2002

The Beat Goes On

I'm just kiddin', America, you know I love you.
—Eminem, "White America"

I N THE MONTHS AFTER SEPTEMBER 11, terrorism remained a real threat. Escalating violence between Israel and the Palestinians was not only a tragedy to people who lived in the region but a reminder of the vulnerability of any society. The Bush administration's approach to the threat of domestic terrorism was debated by both the left and right. American corporations experienced a series of scandals that helped plunge the stock market into a dramatic decline. The environment, health care, and the drug war continued to have a real effect on the day-to-day lives of Americans.

These were important issues, some of them profound. For people like me, it was a moment when a progressive critique of conservative assumptions was vital. Yet the cultural overlay in which political discourse was formed continued to weaken both Democrats and the political left. The progressive agenda still suffered because huge chunks of America's population were turned off to politics.

My business again bumped up against these forces in the reaction to Cornel West's CD *Sketches of My Culture*. I first met Cornel through *Tikkun* editor Michael Lerner, with whom he'd written the wonderful book *Jews & Blacks: A Dialogue on Race, Religion, and Culture in America*. After my father and I became publishers of *Tikkun*, Cornel had cohosted an event for the magazine at our house. With his three-piece suit, retro Afro haircut, and eloquent theatrical speaking style, Cornel is the epitome of the "public intellectual," balancing serious academics with mass media communication skills.

To my dismay, Cornel had indulged in some left-wing culture bashing in his book *The War Against Parents* written with Sylvia Ann Hewlett, in which they stated, "The entertainment media has moved from celebrating to denigrating parental role and function . . . Hollywood feeds off psychobabble, narcissistic individualism, and market-driven hedonism." I respectfully but strongly criticized those passages in *Tikkun*. I feared that Cornel might be less than friendly when I encountered him again, but when we talked about it many months later, he shrugged it off. He had developed some friendships with rappers such as Chuck D and KRS-ONE, and when he spoke at the rap summit he balanced criticism of sexism and homophobia with deep respect for hip-hop's place in the history of American and African American culture.

In the spring of 2001, while on leave from Harvard, Cornel played me an album he and his brother Cliff had just finished recording called *Sketches of My Culture*. Artemis released the CD later that year.

Sketches is a concept album that includes R&B instrumental tracks, a little bit of singing, and rap, as well as West's poetic and charismatic monologues on subjects ranging from the heroes of the civil rights movement to the sweet soul music of the 1970s. While the album recognizes the artistry and relevance of hip-hop culture, one of its songs, "N Word," urges young rappers to stop using the word "nigger."

The connection of spoken word and contemporary music on the album reminded me of Allen Ginsberg's best recordings. Although Cornel hoped that some rap fans would learn about African American traditions from his album, it seemed more likely to me that older black audiences would learn from Cornel the connective tissue between the civil rights generation and the hip-hop scene.

In October 2001, Henry Louis Gates, chairman of the department of Afro-American Studies at Harvard, hosted a "welcome back" lecture and dinner for Cornel in conjunction with the release of the album at the Kennedy School of Government at Harvard. Cornel combines a keen intellect with a preacher's emotional range and is a compelling public speaker. The lecture hall was packed with close to a thousand students. Ironically, Cornel used the very colloquialism he criticized on his album, referring to September 11 as "the niggerization of America," explaining that "all Americans now know what it feels like to be hated, and to feel unsafe." Blacks, he suggested, could teach other Americans how to persevere in such circumstances.

At a time when there was an American consensus about rebuilding infrastructure in Afghanistan, Cornel mused, it seemed appropriate to marshal political will to rebuild infrastructure in America's poorest neighborhoods as well. Firemen, postal workers, police officers, schoolteachers, and emergency workers were correctly being acknowledged as heroes, and there was a political opportunity to push for higher pay for such workers, a long-held progressive goal.

I found myself wishing that Cornel's ability to see a progressive opportunity in the tragedy could be translated to the general media environment.

At a dinner for Cornel after the lecture hosted by the Afro-American Studies department, there was an emotional and bittersweet feeling in the room because Cornel's doctors had detected a resurgence of prostate cancer. Cornel would take another leave shortly to have an operation. Although the prognosis was good, I found it impossible not to worry about the forty-seven-year-old professor's future, and to appreciate his contributions in a more vivid light.

This combination of personal vulnerability and extraordinary value to his colleagues and students made Cornel's encounter the following week with the new Harvard president, Larry Summers, all the more odious. West and Gates and most of the Afro-American Studies department at Harvard had joined the university under Summers's predecessor, Neil Rudenstine, and Cornel was summoned to a meeting with the new president.

Summers, like West, was an academic prodigy and was in his late forties. He had been one of the youngest tenured professors in the history of Harvard and had most recently been secretary of the treasury in the final months of the Clinton administration.

Cornel later told me of a very confrontational meeting. Cornel said that the new Harvard president admitted he had never read any of West's sixteen books, but he nevertheless attacked them as lacking academic gravitas. He had never listened to *Sketches* but attacked Cornel for "embarrassing" the university by having recorded a CD. "To ignore the medium of musical recording," Cornel related to me afterward in disgust, "is like living in the nineteenth century and ignoring the cultural significance of the novel."

Summers also criticized Cornel's activism on behalf of Bill Bradley and Ralph Nader and his recent public appearance with Reverend Al Sharpton when the latter was released from jail following a protest over military bombing on the Puerto Rican island of Vieques. The Harvard president suggested that Cornel had missed classes to engage in activism. The charge was patently false. Cornel had not missed a class in eight years and had done all outside activities at times that didn't conflict with his classroom schedule. Summers could easily have discovered this information. It appeared to Cornel that Summers was trying to smear him for contrived academic reasons rather than directly confront him ideologically or culturally.

News of the dispute broke on the front page of both the *New York Times* and *Washington Post* in early January. The articles singled out *Sketches* as a primary reason for Summers's unusual attack on an eminent professor.

Many political conservatives were cheered at the attack on Cornel for ideological reasons. However, many liberal snobs joined in because of their implacable bias against his populist style. Journalists who supported Summers repeated the false charge that West had missed classes and claimed that Summers was really worried about "grade inflation"—a concern that too many professors gave out too many A's. But why single out West for a conversation on that topic when scores of Harvard professors had the same tendency? In *Harper's* magazine, Shelby Steele nastily suggested that West's role at Harvard was to relieve "white guilt," but West's following on campuses around the nation as well as at Harvard consists primarily of young black academic stars. Cornel's real sin to liberal snobs is that he himself is not a snob. He insists on making connections between classical philosophy and theology and modern colloquialisms and issues. He is a challenge to the snobs' need to feel that they are better than average people, and his embrace of a populist medium like music epitomizes it, which is why the CD became such a flashpoint.

Cornel waited until April, a couple of months after his successful prostate operation, to formally announce his departure from Harvard and his renewed affiliation with Princeton. As Cornel traveled around the country promoting his CD he spoke brilliantly on many R&B radio shows, effortlessly connecting, for example, current events, the ideas of Aristotle and Christ, and the art of

John Coltrane or Lauryn Hill. There are few other academics in the United States with the gift for reaching such large numbers of people. It said something about Harvard that Cornel West taught there, and it says something about Harvard that he no longer does. And it is another sad footnote to the recent history of the Democratic Party that it is a liberal snob from the Clinton administration who is responsible.

Reactionaries tried to grab political and cultural space in the wake of September 11. The American Council of Trustees and Alumni, formed in the mid-nineties by Senator Lieberman and Lynne Cheney, issued a report that listed the names of academics along with statements they made questioning the Bush administration in the wake of the World Trade Center attacks. "College and university faculty have been the weak link in America's response to the attack," the report hysterically concluded.

William Bennett, in his post–September 11 book *Why We Fight: Moral Clarity and the War on Terrorism*, a fierce defense of George W. Bush's military policies, attacked various college professors by name and incongruously bemoaned that "some Americans have ended up tolerating, protecting, or apologizing for evil—like those rap songs or those movies" that Bennett disapproved of. The very title *Why We Fight* was culturally savvy on Bennett's part since it had been the name of the group of films that director Frank Capra made at President Roosevelt's request to explain to American soldiers the purpose of World War II. Unlike Bennett, Capra never portrayed his fellow Americans as the enemy.

In July, cultural conservatives in the American media turned their rhetorical guns on Artemis artist Steve Earle because of his song "John Walker's Blues," which was part of his album *Jerusalem*.

Steve Earle was the first artist I had signed when I started Artemis. His combination of artistic brilliance and political consciousness reminded me of Bonnie Raitt and Jackson Browne. Steve has been a passionate anti–death penalty activist. Although Steve lives outside of Nashville and uses country, bluegrass, and blues in his music, he is not a "country" artist as defined by current country music radio. A leader of a subgenre called "alt-country," or Americana, Steve has drawn an audience composed primarily of rock fans of artists like Bruce Springsteen, Tom Petty, and Lucinda Williams.

After September 11, Steve wrote several songs for his album *Jerusalem* that had a political tinge, including the prayer-like title song and "John Walker's Blues," a poetic first-person musing on the thought process of the young American who joined the Taliban. In the know-nothing tradition of other distorted attacks on entertainment, some right-wingers claimed that the song was "glorifying" Walker. Steve Gill, a talk-radio host in Nashville, said that Earle was "in the same category as Jane Fonda and John Walker and all those people who hate America." Both Fox News and CNN had Gill debating music critics about Steve's patriotism and artistry.

Steve was on vacation in Europe when the controversy broke but had done an interview about the album for our press kit in which he said clearly: "I do not condone what Walker did. Fundamentalism, as practiced by the Taliban, is the enemy of real thought and religion, too." The song, a minor-key lament sung in Walker's voice, begins, "I'm just an American boy, raised on MTV/And I've seen all those kids in the soda pop ads/But none of them looked like me/So I started lookin' around for a light out of the dim/And the first thing I heard that made sense was the word of Mohammed/ Peace be unto him." The lyric is subtly sarcastic when it refers to Walker's delusion that he was doing God's work: "Allah had some other plan/Some secret not revealed/Now they're draggin' me back with my head in a sack/To the land of the infidel."

To my ears and those of the music critics around the country who scoffed at the attacks on the song, "John Walker's Blues" is obviously in the folk tradition of songwriters getting inside the head of criminals such as Bruce Springsteen's songs in the voice of criminals on *Nebraska*, Johnny Cash's "Folsom Prison Blues," and Steve's own "Jonathan's Song." Earlier in American history there were popular songs about such criminals as Pretty Boy Floyd, Jesse James, and Stagolee. Jackson Browne leapt to Steve's defense, telling *Entertainment Weekly*, "It's a beautiful song, a very soulful thing to do."

The authoritative voice of American conservatism, the editorial page of the *Wall Street Journal*, devoted a long editorial to an attack on Earle headlined "Terror Tune—A Country Song Celebrates a Man Who Betrayed His Country." The smug author, Collin Levey, wrote of Earle, "His apologists seem to have taken a rather watery line of defense: If you look at the body of Mr. Earle's work, you'll see he regularly sings from the perspective of society's rejected without necessarily endorsing their actions. That's an interesting tack, and one frequently employed by gangsta rap aficionados. Their violent use of misogynistic lyrics are said to simply hold a mirror to life in the streets. Uh-huh." The *New York Times* soon thereafter published an editorial comparing Steve's song favorably to other post–September 11 songs, and critical response to the album was overwhelmingly favorable. Its first-week chart position of number fifty-nine was the highest Steve had ever attained.

Meanwhile, Eminem's new album, *The Eminem Show*, released in the summer of 2002, was easily the best-selling album of the year. Its opening song, "White America," included the lines, "Fuck you, Ms. Cheney; fuck you, Tipper Gore. Fuck you with the freest of speech this divided states of embarrassment will allow me to have." Eminem's sold-out "Anger Management" tour began with a montage of video excerpts of Cheney, Lieberman, and C. Delores Tucker from the Senate hearing where I had testified.

Was the vast segment of American society who enjoyed these entertainers really less moral than William Bennett and the staff of the *Wall Street Journal*?

In the summer of 2002 Robert Shogan, a *Newsweek* and *LA Times* political writer, published a book called *War Without End: Cultural Conflict and the Struggle for America's Political Future.* Shogan's well-written and researched book reflected the Washington media's conventional wisdom about the cultural tensions with which I've been involved. According to this narrative, the protests of the 1960s galvanized the religious and cultural right, who in turn have driven American politics in recent decades. Referencing Gertrude Himmelfarb's book *One Nation, Two Cultures: A Searching Examination of American Society in the Aftermath of Our Cultural Revolution*, Shogan refers to "one culture shaped by the 1960s . . . permissive, secular, and bent on individual gratification," and "the other, drawing its beliefs from the 1950s and earlier decades . . . God-fearing, moralistic, and devoted to traditional values, particularly the importance of the family."

Of course, this formulation is a cartoon of two nonexistent cultures. Many on the cultural left are religious. The civil rights and peace movements emerged from churches. Believers in Eastern religions are not "secular." Nor is there any evidence that cultural conservatives love their families more than other Americans.

Shogan, echoing establishment Washington's obsession with the Monica Lewinsky scandal, hypothesized that Al Gore lost the 2000 election because of his association with Clinton. Amazingly, in a sixty-page analysis of that election, Shogan never mentioned Ralph Nader or the 2.5 million people who voted for him! The ludicrous inference is that the Nader voters as well as the Bush voters were motivated by a reaction to Monica Lewinsky and not by the issues championed by Nader, such as the environment, corporate corruption, and campaign finance.

Counterintuitively, Republicans seemed more comfortable with popular culture than their Democratic counterparts. Bush's secretary of the treasury Paul O'Neill completed a trip to the poorest nations in Africa with U2 lead singer Bono. Secretary of State Colin Powell did an interview on MTV in which he talked about subjects as diverse as foreign policy and AIDS. Without embarrassment or overt reproach from the administration, Powell endorsed the use of condoms as a health measure. CNN covered Attorney General Ashcroft's rendition of his own patriotic song "Let the Eagles Soar," and Ashcroft appeared on the *Late Show with David Letterman* punctuating his theories about how to fight terrorism with a performance on the piano of the Beatles' "Can't Buy Me Love."

In the spring of 2002 there was a piece in the *Daily Sun* by former Reagan and Bush speechwriter Peggy Noonan about the MTV series *The Osbournes*. Describing Ozzy Osbourne's visit to the 2002 White House Correspondents Dinner, Noonan wrote of Ozzy: "His presence was so electric that wherever he and his entourage walked, they eclipsed all in their wake. President Bush in his remarks mentioned Osbourne's hit 'Sabbath Bloody Sabbath' and quipped, 'Ozzy, Mom loves your work.' Afterwards when Ozzy suggested that the President wear his hair in magenta-tinged locks, the President yelled with affection, 'Second-term Ozzy.'" The easy embrace of Osbourne by a Republican president and pundit was a marked contrast to the distance that most progressives and Democrats create between themselves and far less controversial entertainment figures.

I encountered a classic bit of leftist cultural tone deafness in response to a book I edited with my dad, Victor Goldberg, and TV and film producer/director Robert Greenwald. In addition to various Emmy-winning TV movies, Robert had directed the Abbie Hoffman bio-pic *Steal This Movie*, and Artemis produced the soundtrack, with sixties songs covered by Bonnie Raitt, Sheryl Crow, Steve Earle, and others.

Our book was called *It's a Free Country: Personal Freedom in America After September 11*. It was an anthology with a foreword by Cornel West and pieces by several ACLU officials, as well as Michael Moore, Michael Ratner, and others. A well-meaning leftist activist emailed me that many of her friends loved the galleys of the book but suggested we change the subtitle because the words "personal freedom" were associated with conservatives. That, of course, was exactly the point! Why should wonderful words like "responsibility" or "personal freedom" be hijacked by the right wing?

Although I don't pretend to know why the left has drifted away from populism, especially as it relates to mass communication, I keep coming back to my own generation, the baby boomers and their weird political and cultural alienation from younger generations.

In the spring of 2002 an old friend, Jim Steyer, published a book called *The Other Parent: The Inside Story of the Media's Effect on Our Children*, about the effect of entertainment media on children. I met Steyer in 1988 when he started the California-based children's advocacy group Children Now and asked me to join the board of directors. Jim taught law at Stanford and had started a TV production company, JP Kids, whose biggest success was *The Famous Jett Jackson* for the Disney Channel.

The Other Parent, which includes an afterword by Chelsea Clinton, has many important insights about how America could treat its children better, rooted in the policies he advocated at Children Now. However, the book also contains the now familiar litany of attacks on pop culture, such as convoluted attempts to connect violent-themed entertainment to the Columbine murders. With misguided baby-boom nostalgia, Steyer wrote, "Before our mass media culture became so explicit and so pervasive, before large media companies began to realize huge profits by pushing sex and sensationalism, things were different."

The fact is that there has never been a time when violence was not part of the media. I grew up in the 1950s when network television's primary genre aimed at kids was the TV Western. These were televised dramas in which guns were always used to solve problems, with titles such as *The Rifleman, Wanted Dead or Alive,* and *Have Gun Will Travel.* Also popular were crime shows such as *The Untouchables* and *Dragnet,* or the legal drama *Perry Mason* in which a murder was depicted every week. I did not know any boys in the Republican Westchester suburb where I grew up who did not have toy guns.

As I got older and became fascinated with the culture that my parents had grown up in, I found that the male icons of the 1930s and 1940s, Humphrey Bogart and James Cagney, had become famous playing gangsters. Subsequent generations have given the highest awards to gangster-themed dramas such as *The Godfather* and *The Sopranos.*

Admittedly, the fact that "things have always been this way" is not a serious moral argument. There were decades in which racial segregation and sexism were the status quo as well. If there is a serious moral argument that entertainment is bad for kids or adults, it should be given weight, but the same people who attack teen culture seem completely comfortable with the violence of their own generation's entertainment.

The same generational double standard exists about sex. In May of 2002, *U.S. News and World Report* had a cover story, "'Teens and Sex," with the breathless bullet points "They're Starting Earlier" and "The Growing Health Risks." In an article in *Extra* magazine, which critiques mass media, Mike Males debunked the middle-aged newsweekly's alarmism. He pointed out that the birth rate among ten- to fourteen-year-olds is lower than in 1950, and that sexually transmitted diseases (STD) are at the lowest level among boys ages ten to fourteen since 1958 and at the lowest among girls of that age since 1972, according to the Centers for Disease Control report on STD 2000.

I don't deny that sexual behavior has a moral component. Pregnancy is one of the most important events a human can experience and should never be considered lightly. And nobody denies that there are profound health consequences to sex that kids should be aware of. What I don't get is the bizarre notion that baby boomers handled these issues better than today's young people. As Males wrote, "The junior high sexual revolution happened thirty to forty years ago and kids have gotten much safer since." He pointedly concluded, "The main danger to young girls remains older men."

As to comparisons between baby-boom teen entertainment and today's, let's not forget that the Woodstock movie, the biggest youth culture phenomenon of its time, showed rock fans parading around nude and smoking pot, and featured Country Joe and the Fish chanting the letters F-U-C-K. What contemporary artists are more overtly sexual than Jimi Hendrix or Janis Joplin? John and Yoko posed nude on an album cover. The Rolling Stones appeared in drag on the single sleeve of "Have You Seen Your Mother, Baby, Standing in the Shadow?"

What is it with liberal baby boomers? Is it guilt about drugs and sex? Is it, for some, a sense of failure because of the lowered economic performance of so many compared to their parents? Is the baby boomer's angst somehow connected with Vietnam? Is all the adulation for "the greatest generation" causing generational self-esteem problems?

Instead of more studies on teenage behavior, maybe we need studies of why middle-aged people turn on teenagers. For parents who treasure the cuddly and relatively safe years of young childhood, the inevitable independence and risks of adolescence are understandably frightening. And it's not just the kids who keep getting older. We miss our formerly unlined faces and smaller pants size. We don't like being older than most celebrities, older than most cops, older than all athletes, and now older than many presidential candidates. We don't like seeing an increasing proportion of obituaries of people younger than us. We don't like colonoscopies or mailings from the AARP. Sometimes we're jealous of those fellow baby boomers who are at their peak of power, and other times we're fearful we'll be pushed into early, unwanted retirement. But these pressures and others do not give us the right to attack or dismiss younger generations.

As media critic and author Jon Katz wrote in *Wired* magazine, describing the avid young users of the Internet that he calls the "digital nation": "They share a passion for popular culture—perhaps their most common shared value, and the one most misperceived and mishandled by politicians and journalists. As much as anything else, the reflexive contempt for popular culture shared by so many elders has alienated this group. For much of their life, these young people have been branded ignorant, their culture malevolent. The political leaders and pundits who malign them haven't begun to grasp how destructive these perpetual assaults have been, how huge a cultural gap they've created."

We baby boomers seem to have a hard time knowing our place in the world. Sometimes it seems we have an inability to acknowledge that we, the "youth generation," are middle-aged. I'm all for staying vigorous as long as possible, but that's no reason for us to confuse ourselves with actual young people.

To turn our aspirations and anxieties into hostility toward the younger generation is morally wrong and, for progressives, politically wrongheaded.

CHAPTER 14

War Clouds, the Midterm Election, and the Democrats' Downward Spiral

*Where have we betrayed ourselves? We're sitting here like deer numbed
in the brightness of oncoming headlights of catastrophe.*
—Harry Belafonte, explaining his frustration with the Democrats
and the political left in the wake of the Bush administration's plans
for war in Iraq

A FEW MONTHS BEFORE the 2002 election I opened an
envelope from the Democratic Senatorial Election Committee (DSEC) to find an invitation to a fundraiser featuring Senate majority leader Tom Daschle. The entire front page
of the mailing consisted of the following quote: "Never before in
modern history have the essential differences between the two major political American parties stood out in such striking contrast, as
they do today." The quote was from former president Franklin Delano Roosevelt and dated 1945. It seemed to me a terrible commentary on today's Democrats that they had to go back to the
1940s to evoke a contrast with Republicans.

The differences between the parties were indeed vivid fifty-seven years ago in the wake of the New Deal and during the end of World War II. The Democrats' problem is that the differences between the parties today are not clear to many of their own supporters, not to mention nonvoters, Nader voters, and swing voters.

One Democrat who seemed to get this was Senator Jon Corzine of New Jersey, who wrote in a note to me convening a meeting to support the Century Foundation, a progressive think tank: "In my view, progressives must do a much better job of competing with conservatives in the areas of education, research, and publicity." Corzine lamented the lack of progressive counterparts to Charles Murray, William Bennett, Irving Kristol, Abigail Thernstrom, Dinesh D'Souza, Lynne Cheney, and others.

I listened over lunch at the Harmonie Club with Century Foundation president Dick Leone and several dozen progressive funders, academics, and activists, as Corzine explained, "When I speak against privatization of Social Security on the floor of the Senate, the response comes first from the Cato Institute and Heritage Foundation, followed by editorials in the *Wall Street Journal*. Then they have organs like the *Washington Times* and Fox News and Rush Limbaugh, and we have nothing to compete with that and we don't have enough coherence."

Arthur Schlesinger Jr., former aide to President Kennedy and one of America's leading historians, spoke next and pointed out that September 11 discredited those who demean government. "Ronald Reagan in one of his inaugural addresses said that government was not the solution to problems, government was the problem. That idea wouldn't be so popular today."

Schlesinger also commented on one of my pet obsessions, the presence of so many good-looking young conservatives on cable news outlets. "Does this mean that young people are becoming reactionary? Do these young fogies speak for their generation?" he rhetorically asked.

Senator Corzine said that the big liability of the left is a failure to "stay on message." I reminded him that Al Gore was incredibly disciplined in 2000 as he repeated his description of the Bush tax proposal as a "risky scheme" and the need to protect Social Security in a "lockbox" so many times that it became fodder for TV comedians. Richard Gephardt in the House and Tom Daschle in the Senate had "message teams" on a few maven-approved issues. The problem, as I see it, isn't a lack of superficial PR technique, but the failure to make a deeper level of connection with a wide constituency who could feel and express what "progressive" means in their bones with the same level of intensity that conservatives have had in recent decades.

As the meeting was breaking up I asked Senator Corzine if his vision included the mobilization of young people. He winced empathetically, "I've asked about that. But no consultant in Washington can do anything to reach young people. Bob Schrum and his team are the best—the best! But they say that it can't be done!" I assured him that organizations like Rock the Vote and candidates like Jesse Ventura and Clinton in 1992 and Nader in 2000 have proven that it indeed can be done to some extent, but not with national spokesmen like Joseph Lieberman.

Culture bashing receded from political discourse following September 11, but tone deafness was in full bloom. By the early summer of 2002 it was clear that the Washington consultants for the Democrats had determined that "swing voters" could be swayed by focusing on prescription drug benefits, protecting Social Security, and warning of the impact of Bush economics on the stock market. These were all perfectly valid issues, but again most Democratic candidates had deliberately avoided issues of interest to younger voters and to many other segments of the Democratic base. There was no overarching moral vision of the appropriate role of government, a role that could have been articulated vividly after September 11. There were little or no references to poverty, to public financing of political campaigns, or to national service. There was no questioning of the drug war nor any passion about the environment.

This all took place against the backdrop of a Democratic strategy in the years leading up to the election in which consultants treated all messages as if they were in the last stages of a hotly contested election. Instead of looking at long-term opinion growth, they were focusing year-round on the sliver of "swing voters" who represent approximately 10 percent of the voting public. No attention was given to the half of the eligible people who choose not to vote. Far too little attention was given to issues that inspire emotional intensity on the part of activists who can influence media and turnout. Even among "swing voters" the assumption was that they are undecided because they are centrist on every issue. In fact, many such voters have strong convictions but can't figure out which party's candidate represents their views. If one were to dig down and read every detailed position paper of the Democrats, in many cases one would find that there were indeed significant differences from Republicans. For someone like me, who places importance on judicial appointments, and who closely follows the Senate debates, it was not difficult to root for a Democratic Senate. But it was not at all surprising to me that most voters who follow the popular media had no idea what Democrats stood for.

Democratic strategists seem to have assumed that any reference to September 11 would automatically benefit Republicans. Rather than offering a much-needed debate about security and foreign policy, they naïvely tried to avoid the subjects that were uppermost in the minds of most Americans. As Arthur Schlesinger pointed out, the Democrats had traditionally been the party that stressed the need for collective action via government. Why hadn't there been a more aggressive government action to protect harbors, train stations, and nuclear power facilities? Why was it so important to the Bush administration to prevent new union members from being minted in a department of homeland security that the Republicans were willing to put off the creation of such a department? These were not esoteric challenges but ones that could have put Democrats at the emotional heart of the concerns of most Americans. Instead, most Democrats robotically repeated concerns about "prescription drugs" as their advisors had directed, as if all other issues were irrelevant.

I couldn't understand why the Democrats weren't calling for energy independence. It seemed obvious to me that oil profoundly affects our relationships in the Middle East, where so much terrorism originates. Moreover, Bush and Cheney both have oil industry backgrounds. Progressive publicist David Fenton suggested that a progressive goal of energy independence could be similar to President Kennedy's commitment to get a man on the moon. Neither Democrats nor environmental groups in Washington sparked to the idea, although around the same time EMA, the environmental group started by Norman and Lyn Lear, produced a public service spot calling for energy independence featuring movie stars Gwyneth Paltrow and Cameron Diaz. But a few airings of the spot were not sufficient to create political traction. Hollywood can be a wonderful echo chamber for political leadership, but it cannot be a substitute for it.

Why assume that Republicans had the unique ability to prepare the nation for future attacks? September 11 had occurred on the Republicans' watch. No one was held accountable for security lapses. Senate Democratic leader Tom Daschle had enormous moral authority on the subject of fighting terrorism because his office had been the target of an anthrax attack. Yet Daschle mysteriously avoided debating the Bush security policy and rarely mentioned that the search for the anthrax criminals had turned up no suspects, nor even any theories of the attack's source.

Another issue that Washington mavens avoided was the performance of Attorney General Ashcroft. Early in the year Bob Borosage, who ran a progressive think tank called the American Future, floated the idea to civil liberties groups and progressive Democrats that there should be a national campaign demanding the resignation of Ashcroft. Many progressives felt that Ashcroft had crossed the line on a number of important civil liberties issues and seemed oddly focused on unpopular cultural conservative issues. Weeks after September 11, when the nation was looking toward Washington for ideas about improving security, Ashcroft's Justice Department instead filed a lawsuit in Oregon to prevent implementation of a "right to die" law that Oregon voters had supported in a ballot initiative. For months Ashcroft had kept FBI agents focused on the drug war instead of the war on terrorism. Most absurdly, Ashcroft ordered covering for nude statues in front of the Justice Department building. However, neither public interest groups nor progressive Democrats chose to make Ashcroft an issue.

As summer turned to fall, the Bush administration's push for a preemptive war against Iraq intensified. Bush chief of staff Andy Card implicitly acknowledged the administration's PR strategy when he told a reporter that "August is not a good time to introduce a new product," in reference to the planned initiative to convert the American public to support of a war. Bush was said to have insisted to his staff that the resolution authorizing a war against Iraq be "so simple that the boys in Lubbock can understand it." Given the awkward and jumbled response of those Democrats who opposed Bush's policy, it was obvious that the antiwar forces were not thinking anywhere near as effectively.

I recognize that there are many progressives, people who are passionately pro-environment, pro–civil liberties, and deeply concerned about poverty, who nonetheless agree with the Bush foreign policy with Saddam Hussein and Iraq. However, much of the Democratic support of Bush's foreign policy was said to be based on the dubious theory that by avoiding debate on the war, Democrats could get the focus of the nation back on the economy, which pollsters indicated was a better issue for the Democrats.

The conventional wisdom of centrist Democrats on Iraq was laid out by Senator Zell Miller of Georgia in a *Wall Street Journal* op-ed piece in October. Cleverly entitled "That Seventies Show," the piece managed to get in the now fetishistic Democratic insult to entertainment stars who supported the party. Miller's thesis was that the failed McGovern campaign of 1972 was still, thirty years later, the key cautionary tale for twenty-first-century Democrats. Miller, who had been a delegate for Vietnam hawk Henry Jackson at the Democratic Convention in 1972, recalled smelling "tear gas mingling with marijuana smoke."

Miller opined that "the 'peace at almost any price' position is a loser for the Democrats," adding that "the extreme left will . . . put their money, their emotion, their Ms. Streisand's vocal cords" into an antiwar movement. Of course, no one on the antiwar side advocated "peace at any price." The debate was over whether or not to initiate an unprecedented preemptive war, and the most coherent arguments from the political world against war with Iraq had come from Republicans such as Brent Scowcroft, the national security advisor for the first President Bush, and conservative Democratic senator Robert Byrd of West Virginia. Miller advised Democrats to "respond with strength and boldness, not with the same failed script that doomed us thirty years ago."

No national Democrat saw fit to remind Miller that the biggest "failed script" of the early seventies was the continuation of the Vietnam War itself, nor that a "message" tailored for conservative Georgia might not be appropriate for national Democrats.

Instead, national Democrats, as expressed through the views of House leader Richard Gephardt and Senate leader Tom Daschle,

bought into Miller's argument and supported the president's request for authorization for a war against Iraq. Those Democrats
who disagreed with their congressional leadership made speeches
on the floor of Congress and dutifully voted against the bill, but
none of them spoke at antiwar rallies or staged teach-ins or expressed themselves in a way that was comprehensible to most
Americans. At a moment when the Bush administration was making a radical change in American foreign policy, Democrats allowed
the Bush administration to decide that a preemptive war was
morally and politically valid without so much as a spirited and detailed debate. Why would anyone other than lifelong Democrats be
attracted to candidates of a party who so stubbornly refused to engage this crucial issue?

Al Gore, who had been eerily absent from the public stage since
winning a plurality of votes for president, made one speech articulating reservations about Bush's plan for a preemptive war, but
rather than expanding on his position, he hastily retreated from
public debate on the issue. Hillary Clinton, like the Democratic
congressional leadership, voted in favor of Bush's war authorization
bill. Of those Democratic senators up for reelection, only the late
Paul Wellstone, who was tragically killed in an airplane accident
shortly before the election, voted against Bush. Wellstone was leading in Minnesota polls just prior to his death. When Minnesota Democrats picked as Wellstone's replacement former vice president
Walter Mondale, he followed the lead of national Democratic
leaders and avoided the issue of Iraq, emphasizing instead his detailed knowledge of Senate rules. He lost.

After both houses of Congress passed the resolution giving President Bush the authority to go to war with Iraq, *New York Times*
columnist Frank Rich pointedly wrote, "Perhaps more than he intended, Tom Daschle summed up the feeble thrust of his party's opposition on *Meet the Press* last weekend when he observed, 'The

bottom line is . . . we want to move on.' Now his wish has come true—but move on to what? The dirty secret of the Democrats is that they have no more of an economic plan than they had an Iraq plan."

As I mentioned in the introduction to this book, the Democrats in 2002 did such a poor job of defining their agenda that a *New York Times* poll published on the Sunday before the election showed that only 31 percent of the electorate thought that the party had "a clear plan for the country." What makes this heartbreaking for progressives is that there are plenty of excellent plans gathering dust in the offices of policy wonks in Washington. What was lacking was the political judgment to advocate progressive government, and what was present was a cultural myopia among political consultants that actively prevented Democrats from expressing a clear agenda.

On Election Day, the low Democratic turnout permitted Republicans to gain control of all three major branches of government for the first time in several decades. As Clinton media advisor and CNN commentator James Carville lamented on election night, "A party that won't defend itself is not going to be trusted to defend the country." Not long after the election I spoke to Congressman Jerry Nadler, who represents the lower Manhattan district where my family lives and which also contains the site of the former World Trade Center. Although Nadler easily won reelection, he was deeply upset at the poor performance of Democrats nationally. Nadler is one of the most progressive members of the Congress, and unlike the Democratic leadership, he had voted against both the Patriot Act, because of its civil liberties excesses, and the Iraq war resolution. "The party did much worse than the election results showed," he said. Nadler pointed out that although the Democrats lost only a few seats, the overall vote for Congress was 47 percent for Democrats, several points less than in previous elections. Nadler, who had grown close to many relatives of September 11 victims, wanted the party to focus more on fighting terrorism, which he saw as a long-term struggle similar to the Cold War. He pointed out the failure of the administration to allocate money to protect harbors or follow other recommendations of commissions that had studied homeland security. "If someone is worried about their safety," said Nadler, "it's hard to get them to focus on their job opportunities or health care costs."

I completely agree that Democrats need to focus on safety and that Republicans obsessed with tax cuts are vulnerable on these issues. Democrats and progressives are often as elitist and tone-deaf in their language concerning terrorism as they are on other issues. However, Nadler misses the fact that most Americans have no idea what the Democratic positions on the economy are. To the extent that concerns about economics, health care, corporate excess, or the environment motivated people, Democratic positions on those issues, even those of progressives like Nadler, were indistinct to most Americans because of the culturally parochial way in which the issues were being discussed publicly.

With regard to young people, more focus on issues such as education, the drug war, and a moral vision of the future was required to motivate participation. An issue of the *Nation* ran some instructive letters from alienated younger people. "The apathy of Generation X comes not from the fact that we watched too much MTV but from a frustration over a lack of liberal leaders. No one is out there capturing the leftist imagination which has historically been infectious," wrote one reader.

Another reader suggested some tangible steps to take for 2004: "(1) Advertise on MTV to reach sixteen- to eighteen-year-old future voters . . . speak about gun control, a woman's right to choose and the environment. (2) Get celebrity spokespeople young people have heard of—Shaq, Jennifer Aniston, Vin Diesel. (3) Advertise in magazines like *Vibe* and *Seventeen*. Stress pure air and water and explain to a sixteen-year-old who will vote in 2004 what the air will be like when she is fifty. (4) Have voter registration inserts in cosmetic products, X-box games, and at mall food courts. Think outside of C-SPAN and MSNBC."

Not all of these ideas are practical, and there are many other good ideas as well. I would say a good start would be to pay attention to the full range of culture that connects with young people and address it in terms of both content and style. Not only will there be an increase in the turnout of younger voters, but the mysterious "teen spirit" energy that affects the entire culture will be reconnected with progressive goals. Fashion, music, and all other aspects of culture are affected by teens. So are politics, but in recent years that ripple effect has been the ripple effect of apathy.

As the likelihood of a war with Iraq increased, most Democrats stayed silent. Even those against the war kept their comments limited to the *Congressional Record*. "Didn't you hear Senator Boxer's speech against the war resolution?" asked a staffer who requested that I organize a fundraiser weeks after the election. Since I wasn't tuning in to C-SPAN at the instant she made her speech, of course I didn't hear it. I admire Senator Boxer, but if she or Nadler or other progressive Democrats are going to be effective, they need a mass media strategy that reaches millions of people, not a micromedia one that reaches only die-hard political junkies.

Given the limited outreach of such antiwar politicians and the journalists who agree with them, and given the appropriately limited appeal of obscure radical left-wing groups who expressed their opposition in weird nihilisitic diatribes, several artists tried to fill the vacuum. Woody Harrelson, who was appearing in the play *On an Average Day* in London, wrote a column for the *Guardian* with the headline "I'm Tired of American Lies," saying, "The warmongers who stole the White House have hijacked a nation's grief and turned it into a perpetual war on any non-white country they choose to describe as 'terrorist.'" Sean Penn spent $56,000 of his own money to run an ad in the *Washington Post* urging the president to stop a cycle where "bombing is answered by bombing, mutilation by mutilation, killing by killing. I beg you," Penn continued, addressing President Bush, "help save America before yours is a legacy of shame and horror. Sacrificing American soldiers or innocent civilians in an unprecedented preemptive attack on a separate sovereign nation may well prove itself a most temporary medicine."

Singer Harry Belafonte, who four decades earlier had been a key advisor to Martin Luther King, burst onto the media stage when he told a radio interviewer: "There were those slaves who lived on the plantation and there were those slaves who lived in the house. You got the privilege of living in the house if you served the master exactly the way the master intended to have you serve him. Colin Powell has committed to come into the house of the master." He later told Larry King that this applied "even more" to Condoleezza Rice. Powell called the remark "a throwback to another time and another place that I wish Harry had thought twice about before using."

Some progressives were upset with Belafonte because they felt that Powell was the only senior official in the Bush administration urging military restraint and that he deserved to be supported, not undermined. However, the very fact that Belafonte's comment was racially charged is what gave it news value and what gave him a platform to go on numerous news and talk shows to discuss his reasons for opposing the war. When I called Belafonte to ask him about his statement, he said that he had not anticipated the attention his remark had received, but that he felt the controversy was a blessing because it created a "tiny opening to jump into this fray, to exacerbate the dialogue and get it into the arena of honorable debate."

David Fenton launched a campaign with "I want YOU to invade Iraq" posters and ads depicting Osama bin Laden in an Uncle Sam pose pointing his finger. The copy read, "Go ahead. Send me a new generation of recruits."

Several antiwar newspaper ads appeared sponsored by the group Refuse and Resist featuring the headline "Not in Our Name," with a heavy emphasis on the voices of artists. The group staged a rally in New York whose speakers included Tony Kushner, Andre Gregory, Ed Asner, Danny Glover, Howard Zinn, Marisa Tomei, and Pete Seeger.

I do not suggest that these eclectic voices were in any sense a substitute for a conventional opposition. By definition, such renegade voices had rough, impolitic edges. There was a need for progressive Democratic leaders to play a role on the left, similar to that played on the right by mavericks like Jesse Helms and Newt Gingrich during the Clinton administration, or that played by senators like Wayne Morse and William Fulbright during the Vietnam War. There was a need for more conventional progressive public interest opposition to doctrines like "preemptive war." But in the absence of such political leadership, the spontaneous mélange of unorthodox voices gave some clues as to how an opposition could be expressed.

Barbra Streisand remained the highest-profile progressive in Hollywood, raising $6 million for the Democratic Congressional Committees at a benefit concert at the Kodak Theater in Los Angeles. Streisand had long advocated that Democrats be more aggressive in challenging President Bush and she opposed his Iraq policy. Marilyn O'Grady, the Republican opponent to Long Island congresswoman Carolyn McCarthy, aired a TV spot saying, "The *New York Post* calls her Baghdad Babs, but Carolyn McCarthy calls her a contributor." This referred to a $1,000 contribution that Streisand had made to McCarthy in 1998. Despite the smear ad, McCarthy handily won reelection.

Liberal snobs in the media focused on some minor errors Streisand made in her remarks at the fundraiser instead of the substance of her implicit critique of the Democrats' lack of clarity. Ul-

timately, however, it was the "professional" Democrats whose strategy for 2002 failed, and the "Hollywood" push for a clearer and
more principled Democratic message that proved right. It wasn't
just the Iraq issue; it was the whole political philosophy of obscuring
differences between candidates instead of emphasizing them that
diluted the credibility of Democratic candidates. Democrats lost
control of the Senate, lost seats in the House, and overall had one
of the worst performances ever for a party not occupying the White
House in an off-year election.

Meanwhile in California, Arnold Schwarzenegger was made the
official spokesperson for the popular and uncontroversial Proposition 49, which would provide $455 million for after-school pro-
grams for the state's schoolchildren. Proposition 49 easily won a
majority vote, setting the stage for Schwarzenegger's ascension the
following year to governor in the wake of the recall of Governor
Gray Davis.

CHAPTER 15

2004

The Progressive Campaign

People ask me if I'm preaching to the choir. Well, sometimes you have to give the choir something to sing.
—Michael Moore

T HE 2004 CAMPAIGN began shortly after the midterm election. Actually, there were two national progressive campaigns in 2004. One was in support of John Kerry and other Democrats running for office, a subject to which I will return in more depth in the next chapter. The second was to build a new progressive movement in the United States that, over time, could rival the conservative movement as a source of ideas and leadership. The two campaigns supported each other and fed off one another, but they were far from identical. Elections are measured in months, weeks, and days. Building intellectual and populist infrastructures to counterbalance the "great right-wing conspiracy," on the other hand, would take years.

The personal popularity of some older Democrats, and the move to the center of others (Bill and Hillary Clinton fell into both categories), had masked the decline of liberalism as a political force since the Reagan years. The Iraq War was the issue that made it clear how distant the Washington leaders of the Democratic Party were from their base. Polls showed that more than two-thirds of self-identified Democrats opposed the war, yet the combination of an "inside the Beltway" notion of foreign policy and a political calculus which assumed that opposition to the war would be harmful at election time, caused the Democratic congressional leaders, Bill and Hillary Clinton, John Kerry, Richard Gephardt, John Edwards, and Joseph Lieberman to support the president.

After the Nader experience of 2000, most progressives' priority was to defeat George Bush above all else. But there was also a determination to build networks and organizations so that would-be Democratic leaders might never again ignore their constituency so cavalierly.

In 2004, at long last, a new progressive force was born. Although Kerry had neither the political weakness nor the emotional fervor of Barry Goldwater, the progressive campaign of 2004 had much in common with the intensity and seriousness of the conservative activism that the 1964 Republican campaign had launched.

I noticed an incredible increase in political awareness and passion. For the first time in decades, conservatives no longer had the monopoly on political intensity. Long-apathetic liberals became activists seemingly overnight. Business meetings and encounters with old friends or parents at our children's schools invariably included discussions of the election.

The Internet undoubtedly heightened the ability for the previously inchoate progressive subculture to respond to political events, but the sense of collective consciousness reminded me a lot of the 1960s and transcended any particular technology.

No single person embodied the progressive ideology of 2004 more than Michael Moore, who combines the idealistic anarchistic spirit of the Yippies with the discipline of Clinton-era Democratic politics. Michael and his wife and producer, Kathleen Glynn, grew up in

Flint, Michigan, and are Detroit sports fans. In the spring of 2003, Rosemary and I and our kids went with them to one of the Nets-Pistons playoff games at the Continental Airlines Arena in New Jersey.

We had been to another game exactly one year earlier when Michael had been an almost invisible figure. At that time, his TV show had been cancelled, and it had been awhile since he'd been able to make a movie. His book *Stupid White Men* was being held in the warehouses of HarperCollins. The publisher thought that the book needed to be rewritten to deal with post-9/11 sensibilities. It would take another few months of pressure to get the book into stores. Rosemary and I still have a copy autographed by him that says, "You guys may be the only people able to read this." Yeah, right! When it finally came out, *Stupid White Men* went to number one and became the best-selling nonfiction title of the year (selling more than even Rudy Giuliani's new book). Later that year, *Bowling for Columbine* was released and Michael was bigger than ever.

Now Michael was a celebrity, having made his controversial acceptance speech for best documentary at the Academy Awards just a few weeks earlier. Suburban New Jersey is mostly Republican and we were a little worried that he might be heckled. Instead, Michael was warmly greeted by several Nets fans, and Bill Walton, the Hall of Fame player turned network basketball announcer, came over to sit with us. Walton told Michael in a voice choked with emotion, "Keep doing what you're doing, man."

As we watched the Nets demolish the Pistons (it would be another year before Detroit won the championship), Michael recalled his incendiary speech at the Oscars. He was reassured by many people, including Rosemary and myself, who told him that his unambiguous antiwar rant had been the one thing that resonated with our concerns at that moment. But always sensitive to popular effectiveness and always incredibly hard on himself, Michael had mixed feelings about the tone of his remarks. "I forgot to lead with humor," he lamented.

Michael told us about early research on his next projects and his fascination with the bin Laden family's quick departure from the United States after the September 11 attacks, but the conversation quickly turned to the 2004 election.

All of us who supported Nader in 2000 had taken some shit from our Democratic friends, but no one more than Michael. Rosemary and I had recently been to a dinner party at which we exchanged heated words with a prominent left-wing journalist who absurdly speculated that Moore was on the take of the Republican Party. Michael told us that he had talked to Nader and urged him not to run, framing his reasons in the language of borscht-belt show business. "I told him, you've got to be able to read the room," said Michael, meaning the progressive community, "and the room does not want a third-party run in 2004. The room wants to beat George Bush." Michael mistakenly thought that he had convinced Nader to sit this one out.

Then the conversation turned toward the Democrats, who, we feared, just didn't have anyone charismatic enough to beat Bush. Could we get to someone and help them shape their message? It seemed unlikely. I felt that even with an Oscar, Michael wouldn't have much, if any, influence over a Democratic nominee, and I knew I wouldn't.

Once Democrats decide to run for national office, they seem to be instantly surrounded by some combination of the same old campaign "experts." Could someone larger than life, like Oprah Winfrey, be persuaded to run? Again, it seemed like a long shot. Finally, Michael turned to Kathleen and said, "We can't count on having a nominee who listens to us, but we can focus on Bush. That we can do."

I had met Michael years earlier, after *Roger and Me* came out, sitting next to him on a panel at an alternative-media event. I thought I had spoken pretty well about the need for the left to com-municate more effectively, and then I felt utterly dwarfed as I watched Michael blow the roof off the place. Like an Old Testa-ment prophet, he berated the left-wing culture for infighting, such as the squabbles at the Pacifica radio network, and he mocked the notion of trying to make political change without understanding the common language of mass media culture. He got a standing ovation from the very people he was exhorting to change their ways.

His effectiveness seemed validated by the nature of right-wing attacks on him. It was impossible to defend amoral corporations, such as General Motors and Nike, which Michael had so effectively skewered, so critics would go after Michael himself for making money or being hard to work with or having a big ego—as if such charges had anything to do with issues such as child labor practices.

Some progressives and liberals seemed to misunderstand Michael's work. I heard activists quibble about a detail or two in his films, as if they were position papers. Michael's gig, as I saw it, wasn't to replicate PBS documentaries, but to create easily understandable popular culture in which audiences can both laugh and cry while being exposed to progressive ideas, a function that literally no one in the political media can perform on such a grand scale. He is not a politician; he is an artist with political views. And Michael knows how to speak to kids. Bowling for Columbine was, after all, about the killing of teenagers.

Nothing prepared me, and nothing prepared America, for the impact of Fahrenheit 9/11. Having become attached to Michael's comic persona as a major element in his movies, I was taken aback at first by the severity of this one. But Michael "read the room" cor-rectly. There was a huge audience that hadn't been interested in his other work, yet yearned for an alternative narrative about events since 9/11. Although he touched on the Saudi/Bush connection,

Michael focused primarily on the human cost of the war; this elicited fewer laughs and more tears. As before, Michael's success was underlined by the nature of the criticism against him, which invariably focused on nuances of his description of the bin Laden's departure, and on his decision not to mention the barbaric nature of Saddam Hussein's regime. Even assuming these were errors, that still leaves the 98 percent of *Fahrenheit 9/11* for which Michael's critics had few, if any, responses.

Within months of the film's release, polls showed that as many Americans had seen it as had listened to Rush Limbaugh — and Limbaugh had been building an audience for more than a dozen years. In the impressionistic emotional language that he masters, Michael Moore framed the case against George Bush better than Democrats or progressive media had done in the previous three and a half years.

After the election, some centrist Democrats tried to stigmatize Michael. Former Clinton chief of staff Leon Panetta said, "The party of FDR has become the party of Michael Moore, and that doesn't help the party." Will Marshall, president of the Progressive Policy Institute, the think tank of the Democratic Leadership Council, said, "Let's let Hollywood and the Cannes Film Festival fawn all over Michael Moore. We ought to make it pretty clear that he sure doesn't speak for us when it comes to standing up for our country."

It was surreal for a deficit hawk such as Panetta to attack an advocate for the working class such as Michael Moore on the basis of Franklin Roosevelt's legacy. Marshall served on the board of the Committee for the Liberation of Iraq, an organization cochaired by Joe Lieberman and John McCain whose aim was to build bipartisan support for the invasion of Iraq. What they dislike about Michael Moore is that he, like most actual Democrats, opposed the Iraq War. We stand up for our country by trying to dissuade it from policies which we think will increase the likelihood of terrorist attacks, and which we feel weaken America. The reason the pro–Iraq War Democrats single out Moore is precisely because he was so effective in conveying his opposition.

In the divide between the progressive campaign and the Kerry campaign stood Ralph Nader. Although Michael Moore thought he had gotten through to Ralph, the buzz around him early in the election cycle was that he was going to ignore "the room" and run again. It seemed like there was hardly a conversation among people on the political left that didn't include some brainstorming about how to get him to drop out. One by one, the prominent people who had supported him in the past privately counseled him not to run, but with no better results than Michael.

Just before Christmas, 2003, after a mailing from Nader that seemed an awful lot like a prequel to an announcement of a new campaign, I got a call from one of his aides asking if Rosemary and I would host an event for him to talk to former supporters. We declined—unless Nader would announce he wasn't running for president again, in which case we'd be happy to help his public-interest work.

The next day, Nader himself called and spent almost an hour fending off my arguments against running. He obviously had practice. I agreed with him that most of the blame for Gore's defeat rested with Gore. But there was no question that Bush's supposed margin in Florida was a tiny fraction of Nader's vote total, and no one seriously believed that Nader took as many votes from Bush as from Gore. Whatever his past rationale, there could be no question that he would be perceived as helping Bush in 2004 if he ran. Finally, I appealed to his sense of his own legacy. If he didn't run, he would be seen as a statesman and as the leader of the left. Otherwise, he would delegitimize himself among most of his supporters and be seen as an egotist. Nader replied sourly, "No one paid any attention to me during the Clinton administration. Only when I ran did the media start giving my ideas exposure again." He felt he would be irrelevant if he didn't run.

I realized with profound sadness that Nader, whose career had epitomized the value of public-interest work, now felt that work was beneath him. Was he a prisoner of his bitterness about how he was treated by Clinton and Gore? Had he become addicted to the level of media attention that only presidential candidates get?

A month or so later, Robert Greenwald wanted me to take one more shot at Nader. If he was concerned about having a platform, why couldn't a bunch of us try to get him a radio and/or TV show? I spoke to people at Pacifica and Air America about the radio side. The response was immediate. If he wasn't a candidate, of course they'd give him a show—daily, weekly, whatever he wanted. I dutifully called Ralph and told him about these opportunities, and that Greenwald and others felt TV was probably a viable possibility as well. Nader dismissed it out of hand. "I'm not a journalist," he said contemptuously. He had boxed himself into a self-destructive position which could also be destructive to the country.

For months afterward, many progressives hoped that Ralph would use his visibility to advance various issues and at the last minute pull out and urge support for Kerry. Early in the campaign he met with Kerry, said the senator looked "presidential," and urged him to choose Edwards as his running mate. However, as the campaign went on, he turned his venom toward Kerry, for not opposing legal challenges to Nader's ballot status in various states, and Edwards, for being insufficiently vigorous in his advocacy of punitive damages in civil litigation.

In August, Michael Lerner put together a conference call in which Nader spoke to me, Lerner, Ann Lewis from the Kerry campaign, Congresswoman Lynn Woolsey, a California progressive, and David Cobb, who was running on the Green Party line Nader had used in 2000. (The Green Party chose Cobb over Nader, in part because Cobb was willing to publicly acknowledge that Kerry would be a better president than Bush. That Nader couldn't even claim that he was building an actual third party made his 2004 run all the more absurd.)

Nader talked about the corporate influences on both parties and lamented that environmental, feminist, labor, and minority groups supporting Kerry were not "pushing him to take stands in support of their issues. The Democrats feel they can get away with anything when it comes to dealing with progressives, because they believe that we have nowhere to go but them."

After listening to Ralph delineate various progressive issues that Kerry was ignoring, such as electoral reform, I took a deep breath, determined not to get overly emotional or disrespectful, and said my piece: "There's a lack of logic and common sense in ignoring the impact and importance of this particular presidential election. It's a false premise to say that one can't care about who is president of the United States on one hand, and be for a progressive movement that is to the left of the Democratic Party on the other. I don't think that those ideas are mutually exclusive. I think that one can disagree with many parts of the Democratic Party platform, as I do, and still see clearly and unequivocally that it's better to have Kerry appoint Supreme Court justices, better to have him running our foreign policy, and better to have him as president on every single issue that's important to progressives, than George Bush."

For most of the year, those who knew Nader best had cautioned against too public a confrontation with him. Nader's pride was such that he would never back down if challenged directly. But as the election grew near, all back-channel and personal efforts had failed to budge him. Thus, Nader's most prominent supporters on the left, including Jeff Cohen, Noam Chomsky, Barbara Ehrenreich, Ben Cohen, Phil Donahue, Jim Hightower, Cornel West, the Black

Congressional Caucus, Bonnie Raitt, Tim Robbins, Michael Moore, and Howard Zinn, wrote a public letter in which they urged "support for Kerry/Edwards in all swing states" because "removing George W. Bush from office should be the top priority in the 2004 presidential election." Stone Gossard of Pearl Jam similarly told AlterNet, "Ralph was proven wrong, in terms of his theory that there's no difference between the [major party] candidates."

The coup de grâce was administered by Michael Moore on his website one day before the election: "After the debacle of 2000, the Democrats got smart and abandoned the conservative wing of their party. That's why eight of the nine Democrats in the primaries this year were from the liberal wing. Ralph should take credit for that and declare victory. It's so sad that he doesn't realize the good he's accomplished. But for reasons only known to him, he's more angry at the Democrats than he is at Bush. He has lost his compass. I worry he has lost his mind."

Ultimately, Nader only got about half a million votes in 2004, around one-fifth of what he drew in 2000, and he did not affect the outcome in any state.

The week after the election Nader called me, unrepentant. He claimed that he had forced issues into the media that were ignored by Bush and Kerry. I still felt that his race had been a terrible mistake. Even though he hadn't affected the outcome this time, he *might* have, and if he hadn't run in 2000, the 2004 race might have been Gore's reelection effort.

Nonetheless, Nader still had intellectual acuity. "We tried to show Kerry how to soundly beat Bush by giving him all these issues on a silver platter," he said with a morbid chuckle. In a vain attempt to get media attention, Nader had sent ten volunteers dressed as waiters to Kerry headquarters to "serve up" the ideas, literally on platters. "They're hopelessly decadent," Nader complained. "Jesus, Bush is the worst president in modern history and the Democrats couldn't beat him. Why couldn't Kerry at least have been for the living wage? In Florida the ballot initiative to increase the minimum wage by one dollar, up to $6.15, won with 72 percent of the vote despite Jeb Bush's opposition. Kerry wouldn't support it." Nader sighed and resumed his tirade: "When I had dinner with Kerry two years ago, when he told me he was going to run for president, I told him, 'Don't get in the clutches of the campaign consultants because all they want is the 15 percent of the ad buy.' And the last time I saw him he said, 'I have the best campaign consultants anyone ever had.'"

Part of the dynamic that led to the extraordinary opening week for *Fahrenheit 9/11* in June 2004 was the support of a new entity with leaders largely unknown to other progressive leaders, and unconnected to either Democratic Party institutions or the leftist public interest world. It sprang from passionate individuals whose expertise was grounded in the language of the Internet, and it was a major catalyst for much of the revitalized progressive energy. Its very name announced that it was part of a new era which would connect with teen spirit in a way that old political structures no longer could: MoveOn.org.

In early 2004, David Fenton, the lion of progressive PR, had a dinner party at his New York apartment for Eli Pariser, one of the partners in MoveOn. The group was originally created in northern California by Wes Boyd and Joan Blades, who had made millions of dollars on screen savers for computers and who organized an Internet campaign to counteract attempts to impeach Bill Clinton. A couple of years later, Pariser got so many responses to emails he was writing opposing Bush's plan for war in Iraq that he was unable to handle all the traffic, and he hooked up with MoveOn. The combination quickly yielded an extraordinary organizing and fundraising vehicle for progressive causes. There was something about the moral clarity and simplicity of the MoveOn website, combined with an intuitive grasp of how to empower its growing membership, that created a kind of Internet magic. One of the early indications of the power and commitment of MoveOn was when its members contributed hundreds of thousands of dollars to Paul Wellstone's 2002 senatorial campaign within days after he voted against the Iraq war resolution. Over the course of the next year, MoveOn would raise millions in small contributions, a mass progressive fundraising base that had eluded Democrats since the McGovern campaign more than a quarter of a century earlier.

When I met later with Fenton and Pariser to discuss the possibility of political concerts in 2004, Eli uttered a sentence that I had never heard from anyone in progressive politics before: "We're not worried about money."

MoveOn motivated their members to contact legislators. One of my favorite parts of their website was a section called "Recent MoveOn Victories" in which they would congratulate their members on email campaigns that led to successful votes on issues like limiting destruction of old-growth forests, congressional condemnation of torture, protection of overtime pay, and more.

The purpose of Fenton's dinner party was to introduce some members of the older New York progressive community to Eli. It was remarkable how many major left-wing New York leaders had never met the force that had suddenly unleashed a groundbreaking organizing mechanism for progressive activity. One of my fellow middle-aged lefties asked Eli, who had recently turned twenty-three, what he had done before he started at MoveOn. Eli paused for a moment, as if surprised by the question, and answered quietly, "I was in college."

One of MoveOn's most compelling projects was their sponsorship of a series of speeches by Al Gore. Gore had epitomized the establishment Democratic Party until his loss in 2000. Curiously liberated by his decision not to run for president in 2004, he was re-born as a progressive firebrand. His speech on May 26, following the revelations of torture at the Abu Ghraib prison in Iraq, was the best that any Democrat made on the subject. John Kerry would have been wise to adopt its tone of moral outrage:

> George W. Bush promised us a foreign policy with humility. Instead, he has brought us humiliation in the eyes of the world.
>
> He decided not to honor the Geneva Convention, just as he would not honor the United Nations, international treaties, the opinions of our allies, the role of Congress and the courts, or what Jefferson described as "a decent respect for the opinion of mankind."
>
> How did we get from September 12, 2001—when a leading French newspaper ran a giant headline with the words "We Are All Americans Now," and when we had the goodwill and empathy of all the world—to the horror that we all felt in witnessing the pictures of torture in Abu Ghraib?
>
> How dare they blame their misdeeds on enlisted personnel from a Reserve unit in upstate New York. President Bush owes more than one apology. On the list of those he let down are the young soldiers who are themselves apparently culpable, but who were clearly put into a moral cesspool. The perpetrators as well as the victims were both placed in their relationship to one another by the policies of George W. Bush.
>
> How dare the incompetent and willful members of this Bush/Cheney administration humiliate our nation and our people in the eyes of the world and in the conscience of our own people. How dare they subject us to such dishonor and disgrace. How dare they drag the good name of the United States of America through the mud of Saddam Hussein's torture prison.

Any progressives who get discouraged about the future can further take heart from the unlikely story of Air America. I had gotten to know Jon Sinton in the early eighties when he was an influential radio consultant who advised dozens of stations on which rock records to play. As the years went by we discovered that we shared an interest in progressive politics. After Rush Limbaugh became a phenomenon, Jon developed an interest, which eventually became an obsession, with creating a liberal talk-radio alternative. I remember meeting with him and Jim Hightower during the early nineties to try to convince the Texan populist to do a Rush-style program. Hightower demurred and said he would rather do commentaries than take phone calls.

In 2002, Sinton met Sheldon and Anita Drobny, Chicago-based philanthropists with a similar vision. Over the years Sinton had become convinced that because of the proliferation of conservative talk radio, in order to be successful, liberal talk radio would need to be situated in a friendly environment. "You wouldn't have a classical music show on a hard-rock station," he said. He developed the ambitious notion of a seven-day-a-week, twenty-four-hour-a-day liberal network. Thus Air America was born, with Sinton as its president. Building a radio network from the ground up was harder than anyone imagined. It took weeks for them just to get the system running well enough to broadcast telephone calls.

Air America faced enormous obstacles. Many stations questioned whether there was an audience for liberal talk and whether entertainers with no radio background such as Al Franken could cut it in this arena. It soon became clear that in order to get distribution for unorthodox programming, they would need to acquire some radio stations on which to prove the concept, and this would require additional funding. And once they got on the air, they had a dispute with the owners of their Los Angeles and Chicago outlets, who abruptly dropped their programming. The Drudge Report ran rumors that they were going out of business. A few months later, when one of their funders failed to deliver, they had to reorganize the board of directors, and again rumors flew about their demise.

Somehow they held on. Audience response to their programming attracted new investors, including Doug Kreeger and, most notably, Rob Glaser, founder of RealNetworks, who also became chairman. Carl Ginsburg ran operations while Sinton worked on expanding the network's reach. At their shabby offices on Park Avenue and 34th Street, the enthusiasm of the staff was infectious. I visited the Janeane Garofalo show shortly after the ratings showed her winning her time slot in New York. After a brief period as a hot commercial actress in the mid-nineties, Garofalo had a more difficult time finding roles. When Robert Greenwald cast her as Anita Hoffman in his bio pic of Abbie Hoffman, she discovered her inner activist. She joined Artists United to Win Without War and was incredibly generous with her time when asked to support progressive causes. Some conservative pundits had predicted career damage for antiwar actors, but Tim Robbins and Sean Penn had both won Academy Awards for *Mystic River*, and now Janeane was paid to be herself five days a week on the radio. "This is the best job I ever had," she said, beaming, as she sat behind the microphone about to launch into another tirade against the Bush administration.

Al Franken was the franchise player. His celebrity as a best-selling author made him a media magnet, and he approached his three-hour daily show with a ferocious concentration. Deconstructing Rush Limbaugh's excesses, responding in detail to daily Republican spin, and becoming a vehicle for progressive think tanks, he established a unique niche in the American political conversation. "Al was treated like a rock star at the Democratic Convention," Janeane told me. As a veteran writer and cast member of *Saturday Night Live*, Franken, like Michael Moore, believed in "leading with humor." He compiled some of the comedy highlights of his first few months on the air into a CD called *The O'Franken Factor Factor,* which we released on Artemis.

"The typical talk-radio listener," Sinton told me, "listens for twenty minutes. A large proportion of Al's audience listens for the entire three hours, which is literally unheard of."

As Sinton reflected on the network's position in November 2004, he had reason to be excited. Air America was now in forty markets, including Boston, Philadelphia, Miami, Charlotte, Portland, Seattle, San Francisco, Phoenix, and New York. Los Angeles and Washington, D.C. were about to be added (the latter would debut with a Franken broadcast from D.C. on inauguration day in January 2005). They finally had enough money to provide traffic feeds to local stations, a critical feature to be perceived as a "real" local radio station. "We beat WOR [a venerable New York talk-radio station]," Sinton exulted, "and Franken crushed O'Reilly and Sean Hannity." They were only .6 of a ratings point behind WABC, the talk-radio leader that broadcast Limbaugh. The turning point in getting more stations were the ratings in Portland, Oregon, where they debuted at number three in the market among twenty-five- to fifty-four-year-olds.

Randy Rhodes, the on-air personality with the most talk-radio experience, was getting great afternoon drive-time ratings everywhere, and beating Rush Limbaugh head-to-head in his home market of West Palm Beach, Florida.

And then there was Garofalo and her broadcast partner Sam Seder. "The amazing thing about Janeane," said Sinton, "is that she has brought youth to talk radio—you never know if she's gonna have Eddie Vedder or Susan Sarandon. Talk radio usually dies at night because adults leave it for TV. Janeane is the first person since Larry King left radio to be a 7-10 radio phenomenon."

Most importantly, the network was working as a whole. By September 2004, Air America's station in San Diego, KLSD (the initials stand for "Liberal San Diego"), was the number-one rated radio station among twenty-five- to fifty-four-year-olds, with an average of 100,000 listeners in the San Diego market during any given quarter-hour.

"People said we were gonna be too boring, nuanced, and highbrow," Sinton said, recalling the early response to his sales pitch. "It turns out we have a very good audience composition—younger than traditional talk-radio audiences."

Another creative person who figured out how to connect the dots involving new technology, traditional media, and the rapidly developing progressive political subculture was Robert Greenwald, my partner in RDV Books, an independent publishing company we cofounded in 2002 with my father Victor. As I have discussed, Robert had been a leading producer of movies for television and was also a longtime progressive activist, having created Artists United to Win Without War with Mike Farrell. For the film *Unprecedented*, about voting irregularities in Florida in the 2000 presidential election, Robert served as executive producer, working closely with directors Joan Sekler and Richard Perez. Next, Robert himself produced and directed *Uncovered*, an exposé of the fraudulence of the Bush administration's proported reasons for the war in Iraq, using former CIA officials such as Ray McGovern and Mel Goodman and the soon-to-be-famous State Department alumnus Joe Wilson.

"My strategy was to not let the traditional gatekeepers slow me or the film down," recalled Greenwald, who marketed *Uncovered* through the Internet via sites such as MoveOn, Buzzflash, and AlterNet, and sold an extraordinary 150,000 DVDs. "As a result of these collaborations, we were not dependent on gatekeepers or middlemen controlling our access to the public, and we were able to move the film lightning-quick to those who wanted it and would use it in battles for change. This was never possible before."

He followed this by creating *Outfoxed*, a biting analysis of the conservative bias of Fox News; in addition to the Internet relationships, he promoted this film with the help of public interest groups such as the Center for American Progress and Common Cause. (*Outfoxed* sold 170,000 DVDs.) The same year, Robert was the executive producer of *Unconstitutional*, a critique of the Ashcroft Justice Department, made in conjunction with the ACLU. ACLU executive director Anthony Romero glowed when he talked about Greenwald: "Robert, in doing this film, helped the ACLU revamp its communication operations, and it also strengthened the relationship between our national office and our affiliates. We had over seventy-five screenings organized by our affiliates. It's been shown on the Sundance Channel, and we got back all of the money we put into the movie and actually made some."

Laurie David, wife of *Seinfeld* creator and HBO auteur Larry David, has become one of the leading Hollywood progressive activists. Her primary cause has been environmentalism, but in the spring of 2004, her focus, like so many other progressives around the country, was on defeating President Bush.

Laurie organized an event at the Ethical Culture Society in New York to introduce two intertwined organizations, both created to take advantage of a loophole in the McCain-Feingold campaign-finance law. While there were limits on positive ads, there were no limits to what organizations (which soon become known as 527s) could do in terms of negative advertising or voter registration. The Media Fund, which was run by former Clinton aide Harold Ickes, produced TV ads. ACT, run by the AFL-CIO's Steve Rosenthal, focused on voter registration and get-out-the-vote efforts in primarily Democratic areas in swing states.

"People are going to hear about a plan," said Laurie in her intense New York accent, "and this plan will work, and if people don't help this plan they can never complain again about George Bush."

I hastily agreed to make some calls, not wanting to be listed among the non-helpers.

The auditorium at the Ethical Culture Society contained an impressive crowd of over a thousand liberal movers and shakers, including Michael Moore, Al Franken, Jon Tisch, Jann Wenner, Tom Freston, and Harvey Weinstein. On stage, David, Ickes, and Rosenthal were joined by the powerful head of the hospital workers union, Dennis Rivera, and Ellen Malcolm, the creator of Emily's List, the most prominent feminist PAC.

They made a coherent presentation about the need and the opportunity for a heavily funded independent campaign.

The feel-good mood was jarringly broken when the floor was opened to questions and Russell Simmons complained about the exclusion of African Americans and anyone who communicated with young people from the proposed effort. Russell said that the ads and outreach efforts would seem "corny" to young people and minorities. Ken Sunshine, who had helped organize the event, got into a shouting match with Leyla Turkkan, one of Russell's consultants. Kenny was campaign manager and chief of staff for former New York mayor David Dinkins and has worked closely over the years with Reverend Jesse Jackson and other African American leaders. He was incensed that the organizing committee was being called racially insensitive.

An item ran in the *New York Post*'s widely read gossip column, Page Six, the following day. I felt that Russell's confrontational approach might not have been the best way of making his point, but the fact is that he and his group, the Hip-Hop Summit Action Network, should have been made a part of the organization from the beginning.

I was asked to try to mediate, so a few weeks later, Ken Sunshine and I met with Russell, Ben Chavis, Leyla Turkkan, and Alexis McGill at Russell's offices on Seventh Avenue, which also house his clothing company, Phat Farm. Chavis had been a controversial figure when he was the executive director of the NAACP because of the organization's financial problems, and he was later associated with Louis Farrakhan, which even for left-leaning American Jews like myself is hard to swallow. However, in his incarnation as the executive director of the Hip-Hop Summit Action Network, Chavis has been brilliant, effective, and focused. He described conservative opposition to their work succinctly. "The right wing fears the influence of hip-hop translating into political power, and they attack it every time there's a glimmer of a political connection. Rap baiting. Race baiting. Same thing. Hip-hop transcends race in America—that's the greatest fear of the right wing: a generation who would dare to transcend racial division and embrace a vision of a new America that is more inclusive." Apparently, the latest version of the liberal establishment was disrespecting them as well.

Meeting with Russell Simmons always involves a combination of theater, humor, and serious business. Eating a vegan sandwich from Subway, Russell asked his entourage if his orange shirt matched his orange sneakers. The next minute he was doing a phone interview with KMEL, the powerhouse crossover hip-hop radio station in the San Francisco/Oakland area. "I got a tax cut," he told the interviewer. "What do I need a tax cut for?" He exhorted the DJ, "You have credibility and power with your audience. When Bush and Cheney or Rumsfeld says something, people aren't sure. When you say it, people believe you."

Once these preliminaries were dispensed with, Russell turned to the business at hand. Chavis and Simmons described their efforts earlier in the year to register voters in Philadelphia, which helped reelect the Democratic mayor, John Street, in a tough campaign. The Hip-Hop Summit Action Network organized events with Power 99, the hip-hop station in Philly. They recruited rappers Will Smith and Wyclef Jean, among others, to appear at a rally where they registered 11,000 in one day and were credited by Governor

Rendell with registering a total of 80,000 in the days immediately following the event.

"People were in tears with emotion at these rallies," Russell told us. "Kids were going home and getting their parents to register as well."

Steve Rosenthal from the AFL-CIO, who was running ACT, had carried out the actual registration at the Philadelphia events. Chavis was miffed that Rosenthal had subsequently refused to share the email list he had collected with the Hip-Hop Summit Action Network, which was responsible for drawing the crowd. In addition to the patronizing nature of such a practice, it isn't practical. "Getting out the vote is as important as registering people!" shouted Russell. "How will they know what kind of emails to send people? What if they send corny emails?"

Kenny and I looked at each other to acknowledge that they shouldn't have been treated this way. Now it was clear why Russell had been so upset at the Ethical Culture Society meeting.

Chavis added that Rosenthal didn't understand that hip-hop isn't all black. He hadn't wanted them to register young whites because research told them that young whites might vote for Bush. Russell expounded on what to me was the obvious flaw in this "conventional wisdom" tactic: "White hip-hop fans aren't like other whites—they're choosing to identify with black culture."

Kenny agreed to enlist Dennis Rivera on these issues. A meeting soon took place between Russell, Chavis, and Rosenthal, and everything was worked out for the groups to collaborate more closely.

A few months later, Alexis McGill, at Russell's suggestion, went to work for P. Diddy, heading up his Citizen Change voter registration effort that coined the phrase "Vote or Die." In TV interviews, Diddy sat at a desk with the old-fashioned sign, "The buck stops here." He said, "The hip-hop nation is 40 million. I call them the forgotten ones. Politicians ignore us because they think we won't vote. When we do vote we'll have more power than the National Rifle Association or the Christian Coalition." After the election, when reporters asked if he was disappointed in the results, P. Diddy calmly responded, "I think it's obvious that the youth voter turnout increased. This was a community that was going the other way, getting disinterested. We were effective enough to turn them around."

In the spring, Kelly Curtis, manager of Pearl Jam, and Jenny Toomey of the artists-rights organization Future of Music Coalition, organized a meeting of many of the top music managers. To the extent that anyone "controls" what musical stars do in concert, it's the managers. Various political groups had been trying to organize concerts related to the election, but the managers wanted to organize themselves.

The meeting at the Soho Grand Hotel in New York City was an extraordinary collection of managers, who are iconoclasts by nature and had been, prior to that moment, highly resistant to collaboration. The group included Bertis Downs (REM), Jon Landau (Bruce Springsteen), Coran Capshaw (Dave Matthews Band), Simon Renshaw (Dixie Chicks), Alexis McGill, Bob Titley (leader of a Nashville group called Music Row Democrat), and around twenty-five others. Everyone exchanged ideas of how their clients could best express their feelings during the campaign. Some wanted to avoid endorsing John Kerry and focus on voter registration, and others wanted to focus on congressional races. At the end of the afternoon, Al Franken made an impassioned speech about the importance of the presidential race.

Kelly and Jenny asked me to become a third board member of Air Traffic Control, an organization created to coordinate information about election-related concerts, big and small. By Election Day, over 3,000 such performances had taken place.

The highest profile of these was a tour featuring Springsteen, REM, Pearl Jam, the Dixie Chicks, and sixteen other artists that played a dozen shows, many of them in battleground states. MoveOn.org was the sponsor of the tour and greatly expanded their email list. ACT was the financial beneficiary, receiving around $15 million in profits from the shows.

One question which came up in planning the concerts was what role British artists could play. I was of the opinion that they should tend to their own backyard, rather than try to influence the American election. For one thing, I don't think that Americans like it when people from other countries lecture them on politics. Moreover, the United Kingdom, through the actions of Prime Minister Tony Blair, has been the number-one enabler of George Bush's war on Iraq. Not only did Blair support the war and send British troops, who themselves were killing and dying in Iraq, but he had repeatedly made himself available to American television to help sell the war to the American people. When weapons of mass destruction were not found, he was equally unrepentant.

Blair also seemed to have found his inner baby-boomer snob. The July 19 *London Evening Standard* reported an anti-crime speech in which Blair attacked the "swinging sixties," when, the prime minister said, "a society of different lifestyles spawned a group of young people who were brought up without parental discipline, without proper role models, and without any sense of responsibility to others. All of this was then multiplied in effect by the economic and social changes that altered the established pattern of community life in cities, towns, and villages."

Yeah, those were the good old days, not like the morally upright British society of today in which young soldiers are sent to war against the wishes of a majority of its citizens for reasons known only to those who plan behind closed doors! Where, I wondered, were the efforts by British artists to replace Tony Blair? Where were the songs and concerts protesting Britain's participation in the war?

The first Rock for Change show took place in Philadelphia the day after the first Kerry/Bush debate, so, as James Taylor said, the artists all "had a spring in our step."

I went to the last of the shows, in Washington, D.C. on October 11, which was simulcast on the Sundance Channel. Outside were a handful of Republican picketers with signs like, "Bruce Springsteen Saddam Aid 2004," counterbalanced by mock "Billionaires for Bush" leafleters who urged the throngs of rock fans not to vote, "just leave it to the billionaires."

James Taylor told the audience, "I really hate when people say, 'Don't change horses in midstream.' What if your horse can't swim?" Springsteen played a spirited (though for him, abbreviated) set including "No Surrender," which Kerry had used in his primary campaign, and, with guest star John Fogarty, "Fortunate Son," which Edwards had used. Bruce stalked the stage like a preacher, exhorting the crowd, "I want us all to be washed by the waters of democracy tonight. For all you swing voters out there—it's October 11, what are you waiting for? A guy misleads us into war—he loses his job!" He talked about the issues he felt were important to the country: the environment, health care, and, most emotionally, a living wage. Kerry and Edwards, Bruce said, respected the values connected to those issues. "And remember," the Boss concluded, "the country we carry in our heart is waiting for us."

Since 1992, Rock the Vote has never been able to compete with people's image of it. In reality they have a staff of half a dozen on off years and little more than double that during an election cycle. Yet there are thousands of efforts to register young people around the country, and many local leaders assume that Rock the Vote has a staff of hundreds to service every need for information, videos, celebrities, and media coverage.

The organization and their new executive director, Jehmu Green, rose again in 2004. Combining online organizing, bus tours, and various events, Rock the Vote registered more than 1.3 million voters.

On September 28, the *New York Times* published an editorial criticizing local electoral agencies who refuse to let students vote where they go to college. Rock the Vote had started working on this issue in late 2003 when they took rapper Q-Tip to a town hall meeting with the Congressional Black Caucus, and they followed it throughout the year, building with petitions, websites, press conferences, and grassroots efforts.

The rock political group with "edge" was PunkVoter.com, the brainchild of Fat Mike, from the punk-rock group NOFX, and his cohort Scott Goodstein, the group's political director who enlisted more than 200 punk bands. "Rock the Vote is into telling kids to vote," Mike said to me. "I'm into telling kids—fuck George Bush. That's what moves punk fans." Over the course of the campaign, PunkVoter created two "Rock Against Bush" albums, with songs from Green Day, Sugarcult, Bad Religion, and others, which sold several hundred thousand copies, each containing strong partisan attacks on Bush, focusing especially on economic inequity and civil liberties.

Goodstein explained, "I've been upset with my parents' generation talking about how great activism was—and how it wasn't great anymore. And I was upset with the weakness of progressive leaders. This year we wanted to put a backbone out there."

Stimulated by former Reprise president Howie Klein, PunkVoter launched an Internet campaign complaining that the clothing chain Urban Outfitters was selling a "Voting is for Old People" T-shirt. Although the T-shirt was probably intended as a joke, the message from PunkVoter was that cynicism is not cool. Within weeks the shirt was withdrawn.

PunkVoter commissioned musician Justin Sane from the band Anti-Flag to write an op-ed piece attacking the cynical divisiveness of congressional resolutions on flag burning that ran in Madison, Wisconsin's *Statesman* and Seattle, Washington's *Post-Intelligencer.*

At a Rock Against Bush press conference, the group focused on media bias and showed *Outfoxed.* Their twenty-one-city Rock Against Bush Tour started in Portland, Oregon, in conjunction with the Oregon AFL-CIO. In Florida they honored Gloria Steinem at an event with Young Voter Alliance and Florida Alliance of Planned Parenthood Affiliates. Goodstein was proud of the cross-generational collaboration. "Gloria was very real and very credible to our audience, even though she wasn't on the surface a natural ally. There was nothing weird about her and Anti-Flag being on stage together. Kids were calling their parents on cellphones." Another successful combination was an event in Cleveland with janitors from Local No. 3, 90 percent of whom were African American women. Goodstein proudly noted that they were singing "This Land Is Your Land" along with Tom Morello of the rock bands Rage Against the Machine and Audioslave.

With proceeds from album sales, PunkVoter spent more than $400,000 on full-page print ads in alternative magazines in swing states, urging punk fans to turn out and vote against Bush.

The war in Iraq and the election also touched and inspired many artists who were not part of any organized tour.

Linda Ronstadt was booed and asked to leave Alladin Hotel in Las Vegas after saying she was dedicating "Desperado" to Michael Moore. Tom Waits wrote several political songs, including "Day After Tomorrow," which is about a letter home from a soldier in Iraq. Keb Mo released an album called *Peace . . . Back By Popular Demand.* Other artists with political songs included John Fogarty ("Déjà vu All Over Again"), Loudon Wainwright ("President's Day"), Talib Kweli ("Beautiful Struggle"), Green Day (*American Idiot,* an album that debuted at number one), and John Mellencamp

("Walk Tall"). Rapper Jada Kiss, in his number-one song "Why?" had a line which asked, "Why did Bush knock down the towers?" In interviews, Kiss said he didn't think that Bush literally knocked them down but that he was responsible because of his inaction against terrorism—kind of a hip-hop-hyperbole version of ideas expressed by Richard Clarke in his book *Against All Enemies: Inside America's War on Terror*. Perhaps the most powerful political song was "Mosh" by Eminem, which was released just before the election.

For Artemis, Steve Earle wrote an intensely political album, *The Revolution Starts Now*, which included a tongue-in-cheek love song to Condoleezza Rice ("Condi") and a plaintive poetic song, "Rich Man's War." (Jonathan Demme, whose summer feature remake of *The Manchurian Candidate* was rich with contemporary political subtext, directed a music video of "Rich Man's War" which aired shortly after the election, a reminder that although the election was over, the war was not.) Steve also began hosting a weekly radio show on Air America called "The Revolution Starts Now."

Howard Stern had developed an audience of twenty million ardent radio fans based on his insistence on saying exactly what he, and his audience, were thinking—using virtually uncensored, crude humor and a willingness to stick it in the faces of the snobs. Until 2004, Stern's politics were libertarian Republican. He had endorsed Republican Christie Todd Whitman for governor of New Jersey, George Pataki for governor of New York, and Al D'Amato for U.S. senator from New York. And in the early stages of the Iraq War, Stern told his audiences that he supported President Bush. All of this changed in January 2004 when Stern came back from vacation, having read Al Franken's book *Lies and the Lying Liars Who Tell Them*, and said he'd had an "epiphany" and was now an "anyone-but-Bush guy."

Within weeks, Clear Channel, the nation's largest owner of radio stations, had dropped the Stern show on the basis that it was too vulgar for their audiences. Around the same time, Infinity Broadcasting, who owned the flagship station where Stern broadcast, was hit with heavy fines from the FCC because Stern allowed profanity and the word "nigger" to be broadcast when uttered by a listener calling in to the show. (Although some African Americans do not like Stern's macho white-guy persona, it should be noted that for years his cohost has been a black woman, Robin Quivers).

Since Stern had been consistently vulgar for more than a decade, there were two theories about the timing. The conventional wisdom held that the FCC was cracking down on radio stations because of the adverse public and media reaction to the Janet Jackson breast-flashing incident during the last Super Bowl halftime show. Others felt that Stern was singled out because of his overnight conversion to a fierce critic of George Bush. Stern himself relentlessly insisted that he was the victim not only of prudishness, but of politics.

Not long before the election, Stern, with unerring PR panache, announced that as soon as his current contract was over, he would escape the regulation of the FCC and its chairman whom he despised, Michael Powell. He signed a long-term contract with the satellite radio service Sirius, which shortly thereafter announced that it was hiring Stern's longtime corporate mentor, former Infinity Broadcasting CEO Mel Karmazin. Just as the opening of FM radio was part of a general cultural expansion in the 1960s, many people felt that satellite radio would add to the variety of programming, reversing the trend brought about by the radio consolidation of the 1990s.

In the last several elections, *Saturday Night Live* had provided the most relevant comic commentary on the races. Although that show continued to spoof the candidates, the comic zeitgeist in 2004 had moved to Jon Stewart's *Daily Show*. Stewart carefully positioned himself as a comedian and did indeed make fun of both

Democrats and Republicans. He interviewed Republican chairman Ed Gillespie and Henry Kissinger, as well as Democrats like Bill Clinton and John Kerry, and he made fun of leaders of both parties with a glee that revealed his main agenda—getting the biggest laughs possible. But Stewart, unlike most of his comic predecessors, was willing to take a stand. He made it clear that he wanted Kerry to beat Bush.

Stewart also became a fierce critic of the political media. When he appeared as a guest on CNN's *Crossfire* (after his show's book, *America (The Book): A Citizen's Guide to Democracy Inaction*, had gone to number one on the nonfiction best-seller list), conservative Tucker Carlson tried to bait him for giving Kerry softball questions like, "How are you holding up?" Stewart responded with an aggressive critique of the format of *Crossfire*: "Calling it a debate format is like calling pro-wrestling a sporting event."

When Carlson came back with an attack on Stewart's own interviewing technique, Stewart ridiculed the idea that a serious news channel would compare itself to a comedy news show. Stewart pointedly added, "You're on CNN. The show that leads into me is puppets making crank phone calls."

Carlson replied, "I think you're a good comedian. I think your lectures are boring." Stewart snapped back that Carlson was "a dick." The thirteen-minute CNN segment with Stewart was downloaded or streamed from the Internet more than 1.5 million times, surpassing the viewership of *Crossfire* itself.

Stewart's tart, skeptical look at politics rang true to many young people, but the fact that he found politics worthy of humor also made the statement that he thought it mattered. In doing so, he made politics more hip to the audience of Comedy Central, the network that broadcast his show.

On HBO, Bill Maher's *Real Time* also fused comedy and politics, but with a more overtly progressive edge than either Stewart's show or Maher's previous one, *Politically Incorrect*. Dennis Miller, formerly an HBO and *Saturday Night Live* star, had moved to the right and was a big supporter of George Bush, so he brought his wise-ass, vaguely intellectual comedy directly to a cable news channel, CNBC.

For the first time since comedy came to cable television, politics was competing with sex as fodder for laughs.

As TV comedy addressed one under-serviced part of the political market, the indie book world served another. Dan Simon, president of Seven Stories Press, a leading progressive independent book company, had published several books by MIT professor Noam Chomsky, but Chomsky had never had as big a best-seller as *9-11*, a series of the professor's lectures criticizing U.S. foreign policy under both Clinton and Bush. Simon told me that he thought the book sold so well—several hundred thousand copies, more than ten times a typical Chomsky title—because of the timing (it was one of the first books published after September 11 on the subject), the title, and the absence of progressive politics in the debate on network and cable news, or, for that matter, in most of the leading national newspapers and magazines.

Following *9-11* and the spectacular success of *Stupid White Men*, bookstores were becoming a significant alternative medium to millions of disenfranchised progressives. This laid the groundwork for commentators such as Molly Ivins and Jim Hightower to publish their most popular works to date, and for policy books by Richard Clarke, Joe Wilson, and Scott Ritter to find large audiences—and then echo back onto the mass media.

At RDV we published a book by former Nirvana bass player Krist Novoselic called *Of Grunge and Government: Let's Fix This Broken Democracy!* Krist was straightforward about his support of Kerry and his opposition to the war, but his book and much of his public-interest work focus on long-term electoral reforms, such as instant run-off voting, designed to make minority views part of the government process.

Several Democratic and progressive funders were finally waking up to the vast web of conservative think tanks and activist groups funded by the likes of Richard Mellon Scaife and the Coors family. Many important new endeavors, some mainstream Democratic and some progressive, were launched to counteract the "vast right-wing conspiracy." Former Clinton chief of staff John Podesta started the Center for American Progress, which helped produce Greenwald's *Outfoxed*, and which provided daily spin on Al Franken's Air America show, but, more significantly, was engaged in the long-term work of incubating progressive ideas and figuring out how to get them into the system. Simon Rosenberg's New Democratic Network was trying to reinvent moderate Democratic politics in a way that could include minorities and progressives, and David Brock's Media Matters for America developed a rigorous critique of the conservative news media. The *American Prospect*, a magazine launched in 1990 by liberal writers and thinkers Robert Reich, Paul Starr, and Robert Kuttner, had originally printed 2,500 copies per month. By late 2004, with the addition of editor Michael Tomasky and the growing market for progressive policy ideas, the circulation was up to 60,000.

Not surprisingly, those activists who were thinking long-term had the shortest depressions after the election. PunkVoter's Scott Goodstein was filled with enthusiasm to build on what his new group had accomplished. "It wasn't really about Kerry. It was this overwhelming feeling that something has to be done. Everybody realizes that the real work begins after the election. The possibility of the draft, the war in Iraq is still going to be happening."

After the election, PunkVoter's Fat Mike wrote an email missive called "Still Not My President" that read:

Senator Kerry today said that now we need to come together and heal as a nation. FUCK THAT. We as a community have to take care of each other and respect each other because apparently our current government has no interest in that. They do not care about gay people, they do not care about sick people, they do not care about black people, they do not care about poor people, they do not care about the rest of the world, they do not care about our environment, and they especially don't care about a woman's right to choose. We may have lost the battle, shit, we may have lost the war . . . but we are not losing our minds. WE ARE RIGHT . . . THEY ARE WRONG . . . just because we seem to be the minority doesn't mean we come together with them. We continue to fight . . . and drink . . . and try to have a good fucking time. That's my plan anyway, thanx to you all, Fat Mike.

CHAPTER 16

The Kerry Campaign

People say George Bush is a cowboy. Well, what's a cowboy but a guy in a white hat, getting things done for the downtrodden? People say he shoots quick. Well listen, sometimes you have to do that, you have to be decisive. Kerry never projected that.

—Gene Hadley, a voter from Columbus, Ohio, as quoted in the *New York Times*, November 4, 2004

I N FAIRNESS TO JOHN KERRY, the Democrats were faced with an incredibly difficult task in 2004. No sitting president has ever been denied reelection during wartime. The wars that drove Harry Truman and Lyndon Johnson not to seek reelection had killed and wounded far more Americans than the Iraq War by November 2004.

Any Democrat would have faced enormous obstacles in 2004. September 11 had given Bush the mantle of father-protector to a lot of Americans. After all, Rudy Giuliani had approval rates in the low forties at the time of September 11, and he was overnight transformed into the beloved Prince of the City. If Gore had been president on September 11 (and this is where reflections on Nader's role in 2000 are particularly painful), he would have inherited the authority and respect that comes with being in office during a crisis, and discussion in 2004 might have been about a realignment that favored the Democrats.

Moreover, the conservative media really was a formidable problem. Although liberals were scratching their way into the national conversation in corners of the culture, they had nothing to compare with Fox News or Sinclair Broadcasting.

The issues related to September 11 drove the 2004 election, and among the Democrats running for president, the person who defined the primary campaign in its early months was not Kerry, but Howard Dean.

Of all the silly things said about Howard Dean, the silliest was that he became popular *because* of the Internet. What made Howard Dean popular was that he spoke passionately against the war in Iraq and expressed his opposition with a tone of indignation. He perfectly reflected the anger most Democratic activists had with their supposed national leaders who had ignored their base and supported the administration. Of course, once this message started resonating, the Internet *was* indispensable to Dean, in terms of raising money and organizing his constituency.

Dean was not the only candidate who opposed the war, but for a time he came to embody opposition to it in a way that the other antiwar candidates did not. Reverend Al Sharpton and former senator Carol Moseley Braun were against it, but they did not make either foreign policy or homeland security a centerpiece of their candidacies, which instead revolved around economic issues. Moseley Braun, while intelligent and well liked, never created a rationale for her campaign. Sharpton would consistently make the most incisive and funniest comments on an assortment of issues and emerged with his national status greatly enhanced, but he never got a foothold in any of the primaries. Sharpton had entered the race in a clear effort to take the place of Reverend Jesse Jackson as the symbolic voice of African Americans, poor people, and others who were locked out of the corridors of power. Yet Sharpton never achieved the status of Jackson, in part because the latter had already been such a pioneer, and in part because, unlike Jackson, he could not unite African Americans. For example, Jackson's son, Congressman Jesse Jackson Jr., himself an influential national leader, chose not to endorse Sharpton but to support Howard Dean. To use Michael Moore's metaphor, "the room" did not feel the need for a symbolic minority candidate in 2004, but for one whose success would measure the depth of Democratic opposition to the war.

Dennis Kucinich was the congressman who had actually organized Democratic war opposition in the House of Representatives in October 2002. Nearly two-thirds of House Democrats voted against the resolution, despite the fact that House Democratic leader Richard Gephardt supported the administration. Kucinich had years of credibility as a progressive and a detailed series of cutting-edge ideas on every imaginable issue. Although his supporters considered that depth an asset, it created a campaign that seemed more like a shopping list of left-wing positions than a vehicle for a plausible president. Kucinich had one other strike against him: He announced his candidacy long after Dean had become the name-brand antiwar candidate. Jeff Cohen, who was communications director for Kucinich, recalled, "We got dwarfed by the Dean upsurge—he got into the race almost a year before and he had the antiwar energy."

Kucinich made a spirited, though ultimately unsuccessful, attempt to get media attention. He lined up benefit concerts by rock singers Willie Nelson, Michelle Shocked, and Ani DiFranco. On Kucinich's website, he wrote "An Open Letter to the Hip-Hop Community," which said in part: "I do not claim to know the names of the top ten greatest MCs of all time. I do know what it is like to live on the wrong side of American society. I am the oldest of seven children, and I grew up in the inner city of Cleveland. My family was often the only Caucasian family living in a community of color. Having been homeless, I know poverty all too well." He asked his supporters to hand out campaign fliers at the premiere of the movie *Seabiscuit*, comparing his own underdog candidacy to that of the famous race horse.

Like Sharpton, Kucinich was able to use the campaign to establish himself as an important progressive voice with an expanded constituency. But during the primaries, to the public and to the media, it was Dean, not Kucinich, who reminded them of Seabiscuit.

In addition to the timeliness of his antiwar message, Howard Dean had another advantage over the other antiwar candidates: He did not sound like a politician. Perhaps it was the fact that he had been a doctor, not a lawyer like most politicians. Perhaps it was his intuitive attraction to teen spirit. Dean had announced his campaign by saying it was "for the young and young at heart." Whatever the reason, Dean's confrontational clarity set the tone for the Democratic primary season.

Dean had arrived at my office at Artemis Records in early 2003 with one of his advisors, David Bender, a gay activist I have known since the 1980s who had written a book with David Crosby about political concerts. Dean had endeared himself to the gay community by signing a bill in Vermont legalizing civil unions, and he took some pride in the political courage it had taken. He spoke knowledgeably about how to move toward a national health care system. But he was most excited when he talked about the response he was getting to his position on Iraq. "The fact that I'm against the war is really turning people on," he said, with the gleeful expression of a kid who has found a cookie jar.

In March, he and Bender went to a gathering in New York organized by the Meetup Internet site that had previously been used primarily for singles to meet each other. "We were expecting a hundred people, and there were about six hundred people—spilling into the street. It was definitely Iraq." Over the next several weeks, Dean's campaign exploded.

Dean's supporters, for a time, gave him extraordinary momentum. Every time a centrist Democrat complained that Dean was too far to the left or was too much like George McGovern, donations would flood Dean headquarters. When Dean gave what was viewed as a weak interview on *Meet the Press*, and was ridiculed by many political columnists, he got yet another enormous influx of cash. His supporters had coalesced, in part, because of rage at the smug pro-war Democratic establishment, and they were not daunted by the early carping.

But antiwar Democrats, like all Democrats, wanted to beat George Bush, and as the Iraq War got worse and Bush's popularity went down, victory seemed more plausible. Many Dean supporters became concerned that Dean was not up to the task. There were too many signs, as Marge Tabankin said, that "Dean didn't know what he didn't know." Michael Moore could never take Dean seriously after he referred to contemporary Russia as "the Soviet Union" in an interview with Chris Matthews.

Bender had set up a lunch with California State Senator Sheila Kuehl at which she said, "I decided I want to support someone from the Democratic wing of the Democratic Party—and that's why I'm supporting you." Dean started using the line in his speeches, not knowing, and therefore not acknowledging, that it had originated with the late Senator Paul Wellstone. The omission irritated many of Wellstone's supporters.

"Howard would bristle at being told he didn't know things," Bender recalled in a phone conversation after the election. "When Trippi would ask him to get media training, he refused to do it. Trippi wanted him to humanize himself. Howard was a doctor, but he could have been an accountant, as far as what he revealed about his own experience."

Bender took a deep breath as if to consider how much he wanted to say, and then plunged forward: "Howard's accelerated success affected his equilibrium. As we say in rock and roll, he was getting high on his own supply. He didn't pace himself. He didn't realize he'd be exhausted by the year end. He over-scheduled himself. He never took downtime. By December he had flat-lined. He was giving the same speech from back in the spring. In conversations, he was reciting stump lines instead of interacting."

When I had met with Dean I told him that I considered Al Sharpton a serious rival for progressive votes, and Dean rolled his eyes. Vermont had few African Americans and Dean's lack of experience with racial issues would prove to be a problem. In various speeches he had been saying that Democrats needed to reach out to "the kind of guys who have the confederate flag on their pickup trucks." Many people agreed that Democrats needed to reach out to working-class whites, and in the context of his speeches, audiences understood what he was talking about. But once it was taken out of context and subjected to the glare of the media, many African Americans were offended by it.

At a Rock the Vote/CNN debate at Boston's Faneuil Hall in November, one of the first questions to Dean came from a young African American man who told the governor that the confederate flag reference was very painful to him due to the legacy of slavery. Instead of apologizing, Dean defensively insisted that because of his support for civil unions for gays and lesbians in Vermont, he had proved that he did not have any tolerance for bigotry. This non-apology gave fodder for both Sharpton and Edwards to lecture him, and Dean came across as insensitive, thin-skinned, and politically unsophisticated.

After Dean lost in Iowa, he made the manic concession speech that was endlessly played on cable TV and which became known as "the scream." But the scream did not kill Dean's candidacy, it acknowledged its death. As Dean himself later said, because of the primary schedule and the yearning of Democrats to coalesce around a candidate, "Whoever won Iowa was going to win the nomination." Iowa Democrats, most of whom were against the war, knew that and were paying close attention to every nuance of the campaign, and backed away from Dean.

Because of the roller-coaster nature of Dean's race, it is easy to forget what a brilliant visionary he was. He came from a state with a population smaller than that of Brooklyn and with no elite support. Gary Hart's campaign in 1984 was considered one of the great dark-horse leaps forward in modern politics, but Hart was far better known nationally in 1984 than Dean was in 2004.

Not only was Dean smart enough to see through the Washington propaganda for the war, he also had a distinctive emotional style and an intuitive sense of how to reposition Democratic ideas. He was the first candidate in a generation to create a genuine grassroots following and build a totally independent funding base. As Bender says, "At his best, Howard knew and could express that it wasn't about him, but about a movement. He changed the debate. He gave us pride in being Democrats." It is not surprising that while tiresome centrist Democratic pundits were writing about moving the party to the right, Dean out-organized all of his rivals and, as this book went to press, emerged as the front-runner to lead the Democratic National Committee. His history of budget-balancing and moderation as a governor, combined with his credibility among antiwar grassroots activists and young people, make Dean the perfect figure to drag the Democrats into the future.

Senator Joe Lieberman, my cultural nemesis, stridently supported Bush's foreign policy and generally ran as an overt non-liberal. He never became a factor in any of the primaries. I had a perverse moment of ego gratification when, in response to a query from the

Washington Post, a "spokesman" for Lieberman said that the senator hadn't read my book, but "doesn't feel it's necessary to respond to the political analysis of a record producer. Suffice it to say, he shouldn't give up his day job."

Senator Bob Graham of Florida opposed the war on the theory that Bush was not tough enough on terrorism. He lacked the emotional and moral clarity of Senators Byrd and Kennedy, but as the former chair of the Senate Intelligence Committee, he had enormous insight into the flaws in the Bush foreign-policy team. Unfortunately, Graham was the least poetic of public speakers, expressing his indignation in a singsong cadence that made it hard for all but the most devoted C-SPAN viewers to follow. One of my business partners had a fundraiser for Graham, and in a stunningly awkward moment, the candidate sang his own campaign song a cappella. If this was meant to show he had a common touch, it failed.

As Dean's campaign began to fray at the edges, there was a big flurry of excitement about former general Wesley Clark. But Clark got started too late. He acknowledged that he had been a Republican who had voted for Ronald Reagan and George Bush Sr., and his affirmation of Democratic positions on domestic issues seemed a bit glib. It was indeed exciting that a flesh-and-blood general was against the war, and this position alone may have convinced Michael Moore and Madonna to support Clark. If he had entered the race as early as Dean, and developed a deeper connection with Democrats, the race might have been quite different.

Richard Gephardt had a long and noble track record of fighting for core Democratic economic values. John Edwards had a compelling stump speech about the inherent unfairness in "two Americas." However, they both chose to support Bush's foreign policy uncritically during a year when Democrats passionately disagreed with it. At least John Kerry had a history of defying foreign-policy conventional wisdom. Once antiwar primary voters decided that

Dean was unelectable, Kerry, among those who had voted for the war, was the only one whose background hinted that he might, if elected, do something different.

I have long had a soft spot for John Kerry. He played a genuinely important role in the protest of the war in Vietnam. He met with John Lennon and was photographed with him. He was an outspoken opponent of the Reagan administration's policies in Central America. He was a strong leader on environmental issues. And he had resisted when Lieberman tried to draw him into bashing teen culture.

Once Dean had, in essence, disqualified himself, it was easy to see why Iowa Democrats chose Kerry. Shortly before the Iowa caucuses, Ted Kennedy was at our house for an event to support the *American Prospect* and made a cogent and impassioned case against the war. Journalist Eric Alterman pointedly asked Kennedy why, if he was so offended by the war, he was supporting John Kerry. Kennedy, with deep emotion, snapped back fiercely, "Listen, that was one vote, and I disagreed with him on it. But I've worked with John Kerry for twenty years and I'm telling you that he's the right man to be president." Soon after, Kennedy went to Iowa and campaigned tirelessly for Kerry. When Kerry won Iowa, I shared the feelings of the subsequent Democratic primary voters who wanted to quickly coalesce around a candidate rather than have extended turmoil.

Despite the energy injected into the race by the Dean campaign and MoveOn.org, many Washington Democrats were counseling Kerry to focus on the same centrist middle-aged and elderly undecided voters who had ultimately eluded Gore. In *Rolling Stone* in April, Democratic strategist James Carville said, "We're supposed to give great homage to the youth vote, but I don't see any significant mobilization among young people in the country right now. The youth vote is less important than the elderly because old people actually vote."

In terms of his appeal to young people, Kerry shared some of Bill Clinton's enthusiasm for the entertainment culture. In high school he had been in a rock band called the Electras, and he was still known to occasionally pull out an electric guitar. In March he told MTV, "I'm fascinated by rap and by hip-hop. I think there's a lot of poetry in it. And I think you'd better listen to it pretty carefully because it's important." From the point of view of the pop-culture audience, Kerry was only helped when Rush Limbaugh mocked him for those comments. The MTV Kerry special got a 1.6 rating. The best Clinton had gotten, at the peak of the 1992 campaign, was a .6.

Kerry's dilemma was that the primary reason for all this interest in the election was the war in Iraq. But Kerry had voted for the war resolution. Then he (and John Edwards) voted against $87 billion for funding the war because he preferred a version in which the cost was paid by taxes on the wealthy. It was not unreasonable for the political media to interpret the latter vote as a response to the enormous traction Howard Dean was getting in the polls.

In the months since the war started, Bush's policy had taken a pounding as his claims that there were weapons of mass destruction in Iraq and a link between September 11 and Saddam Hussein turned out to be false. In his convention speech, Kerry said he would be a president who would "never lead the country into war because we want to, but because we have to." Bush defiantly and, it turned out, cleverly began asking on a daily basis whether, knowing what he knew now, Kerry would have supported the war—and whether, as Bush put it, the world would be safer if Saddam Hussein were still in power.

Of course, a lot of progressives wanted an answer to the same question. Michael Moore called James Carville, by then a Kerry campaign advisor, and suggested that the candidate needed to define himself on Iraq in a "dramatic and compelling way." "I told him," recalled Michael, "that Kerry should say, 'Mr. President, I, like 70 percent of the American people, believed you and believed Secretary Powell. I wanted to believe our commander in chief; but you didn't tell the truth, and you let us down.'" Alas, Kerry did no such thing.

Instead, shortly after the Democratic Convention, Kerry answered Bush's question and said that, knowing what he knew now, he still would have voted for the war. I remember reading it on one of the Internet news sites and feeling my heart sink. For a minute I tried to pretend that he hadn't really said it, or that it was some hideous misunderstanding. But Kerry had been psyched out again, and it was as if one could feel air leaving a balloon.

It is impossible to imagine a national Republican betraying their base that way. But more to the point, it deprived Kerry of having a coherent alternative idea on Iraq, which suggested he did not have an alternative philosophy on the war on terror.

Scott Ritter, the former U.S. marine and U.N. arms inspector who had predicted before the war that no weapons of mass destruction would be found in Iraq, felt that this was the defining moment of Kerry's campaign. Ritter had spoken to Kerry prior to the war and prepared a memo for his staff.

"I am a Republican and voted for Bush in 2000, and a lot of my friends are Republicans," Ritter told me after the election, "and when it became clear that there were no weapons of mass destruction, that the war had not been necessary for our security, a lot of people questioned Bush and were willing to consider another man as president."

Ritter continued, his voice choked with emotion: "People would have forgiven Kerry if he had just admitted that his first vote was the wrong vote. The inanity of his position is that Kerry said he would win the war. What's that mean? He said he would build a consensus of other nations. Around what? The world rejected the war because there wasn't the evidence that Iraq was a threat. How could he have convinced them, since no threat existed?"

As Maureen Dowd would write in the New York Times, "When Mr. Kerry says it was about the *way* the president went about challenging Saddam that was wrong—rather than the fact he challenged Saddam—he's sidestepping the central moral issue . . . It was wrong for the president to pretend the dictator was a threat to our national security, to drum up a fake case on weapons and a faux link to Al Qaeda and to divert our energy . . . away from the real enemy. It was wrong to take Americans to war without telling them the truth about why we were doing it and what it would cost. It wasn't the *way* W. did it. It was *what* he did."

A few weeks after the 2004 election I met with one of the senators who had bucked the Democratic leadership and voted against the war. He confided, "When we were privately discussing what to do about the resolution the administration gave us, the single most eloquent person who spoke in our caucus *against* the idea of going to war was John Kerry. He had been there. He knew it was a mistake. Most of us did. But then Daschle said to all of us that we had to vote for it, that it would be political suicide otherwise. So most of the Democrats, including Kerry and Edwards and Daschle himself, voted for it on the theory that it would help them win."

Kerry similarly muddied his Vietnam history. Although he was obviously a brave soldier and commander, Kerry was just one of thousands of Americans who won combat medals. What made John Kerry famous was the soul of his political career: after having served with such distinction, he took a leadership role in opposing the war. That opposition earned him many enemies among those who could never admit the mistake made by both the Johnson and Nixon administrations. Kerry's most famous line in his testimony to Congress was, "How do you ask a man to be the last one to die for a mistake?"

Yet in his campaign, and particularly at the Democratic Convention, Kerry's emphasis was overwhelmingly on his heroic service, with little mention of his opposition to the war. It was inevitable that Republicans would find anti-Kerry Vietnam vets. Some of them had been dogging him for years. Because his narrative didn't emphasize his opposition, it didn't offer a rebuttal to his enemies. Moreover, his experience in Vietnam would have tracked perfectly with the situation in Iraq. He could have said he didn't want another generation of Americans dying for a mistake.

Karl Rove, the mastermind of Bush's victory, spoke after the election of his successful effort to mobilize the conservative Christian base. But while sending continual reassuring signals to this base, Rove also echoed his mentor Lee Atwater in sending messages to libertarian Republicans and independents. It was no coincidence that two of the major Republican Convention speakers, Rudy Giuliani and Arnold Schwarzenegger, were pro-choice, pro–stem cell research, and pro–gay rights.

A small but vocal group of Republican rockers emerged in media stories. Gene Simmons of KISS said he was supporting Bush because of the war on terror: "When you have rodents, hire an exterminator." Bush also won support from Alice Cooper, Ted Nugent, Kid Rock, and even Johnny Ramone, who, when inducted into the Rock and Roll Hall of Fame wearing his trademark torn jeans and black leather jacket, said, "God bless President Bush." Republican National Chairman Ed Gillespie appeared on MTV's biggest show, TRL, and Dana Mozier, who formerly worked for the gangsta rap group NWA, was quoted as saying, "The Republican Party is more accepting than most people think."

At the Republican Convention, actor Ron Silver got his revenge on the Hollywood left, saying, "Even though I am a well-recognized liberal on many issues confronting our society today, I find it ironic that many human-rights advocates and outspoken members of my own entertainment community are often on the front lines to protest repression, for which I applaud them, but they are usually the first ones to oppose any use of force to take care of these horrors that they catalog repeatedly."

Then came the "swift boat ads," which falsely claimed that Kerry

did not deserve his Vietnam War medals. Kerry, in an eerie echo of
the Dukakis campaign, was late in responding to the attacks, and
then reacted in a bombastic but oddly impersonal way.

On September 13, Rosemary and I attended a small fundraiser in
New York for Barack Obama, who was on his way to being elected
senator in Illinois. Obama's keynote speech at the Democratic Convention had been one of its highlights. He has a plain-spoken gift for
evoking an idealistic vision of government that was both inspiring
and maddening, because of the fact that Kerry would not rise to that
level of connection.

In front of the smaller group, Obama's low-key but eloquent remarks again touched on the concept that the ideal of citizenship is
to care about other people's families in addition to one's own.
Obama also talked about the need to address spiritual issues.

When it came time for questions, they were all variations on the
same theme: Why couldn't Kerry explain as well as Obama what he
stood for? Asked about the swift boat ads, Obama answered, "I
think if he had done a five-minute press conference right away expressing his disgust, and really showed it in his face, that would
have been it." Referring to a supposed Democratic counterattack
from "Texans for Truth," who were raising questions about Bush's
National Guard service, Obama said, "I think it's kind of lame."

That day, the New York Post quoted Mario Cuomo on the im-
pending debates. "It's going to come down, in the end, to how well
Kerry can get his message out. The question is: Can he do it every
day without using sentences with three commas in them? He's
good with words in the Senate, but that's different than talking to
a TV camera." The next day, Kerry went on the Don Imus Show,
but afterwards the radio host, who was supporting Kerry, banged
on a table and lamented, "I still don't know what his position is on
Iraq."

The determined good soldier Michael Moore sent an email telling the left to stop whining about Kerry and help:

Dear Friends,

Enough of the hand-wringing! Enough of the doomsaying! Do I have to come there and personally calm you down? . . . Bush gets a bounce after his convention and you would have thought the Germans had run through Poland again. Yes, they caught Kerry asleep on the swift boat thing. If I hear one more person tell me how lousy a candidate Kerry is and how he can't win . . . Dammit, of COURSE he's a lousy candidate—he's a Democrat, for heavens sake! That party is so pathetic, they even lose the elections they win! What were you expecting, Bruce Springsteen heading up the ticket? Guys like him don't run—and neither do you or I. People like Kerry run . . . Buck up. The country is almost back in our hands. Not another negative word until Nov. 3rd! Then you can bitch all you want about how you wish Kerry was still that long-haired kid who once had the courage to stand up for something. Instead of the wailing and gnashing of your teeth, why not hold out a hand to him and help the inner soldier/protester come out and defeat the forces of evil we now so desperately face. Do we have any other choice?

Yours,

Michael Moore

Chicago University professor Stanley Fish wrote an op-ed in the *New York Times* in which he described an exercise he did in a freshman writing class: Students analyzed excerpts from speeches by Kerry and Bush and voted on which candidate did a better job of presenting their ideas. Fish explained that Bush had speeches with almost perfect topic sentences ("We are succeeding") and clear supporting paragraphs. Kerry used confusing rhetorical devices such as this one about the outsourcing of jobs: "That's bad enough, but you know there's something worse, don't you?" Fish, who supported Kerry, complained that Kerry was "asking people to respond to a point he hasn't made yet and, even worse, by saying 'don't you?' he is implying they should know what the point is before he makes it. As a result the audience is made to feel stupid." Fish's class voted 13-2 that Bush presented his ideas better.

The next week Kerry was interviewed by Diane Sawyer, who asked him if the Iraq War was "worth it." He made several stabs at a response without ever quite answering her beyond saying, "It depends on the outcome ultimately." The next day, Bush advisor Karen Hughes effectively mocked that answer: "I guess that means if we win it was worth it, if we don't it wasn't. That's leadership, isn't it?"

Kerry rebounded when he won the first debate with Bush. The negative advertising had lowered expectations so much that his cool, commanding, and articulate demeanor came as a welcome surprise. The time limit for answers forced Kerry to speak in more declarative sentences with fewer of the "commas" that Cuomo had worried about. Bush was at his worst, petulant and repetitive. Yet the boost from the debate seemed to reignite a weird sense of complacency in Kerry's campaign. A *Washington Post* headline read, "As Bush pumps up his base, Kerry aims for the middle." But what "middle" was he going for? Kerry, in thrall to Washington advisors, avoided making a passionate case for government. He implausibly said his health care plan wouldn't be a new government program. He barely focused on the adverse effects of globalization on working people. He abandoned his line about "Benedict Arnold corporations" that outsourced jobs. (Kerry's Wall Street advisor Roger Altman told Arianna Huffington that he had gotten Kerry to drop that "unfortunate language." It was even excised from Kerry's website.) Kerry failed to make critiques of Bush's policies, like those made by Richard Clarke about the president's pre-9/11 terrorism plan. Kerry avoided the point that Al Gore had made about the link between administration policies and the Abu Ghraib prison scandal in Iraq.

In the final debate, Kerry again undercut his own credibility by gratuitously mentioning Dick Cheney's lesbian daughter Mary Cheney in answer to Bob Schieffer's question about whether homosexuality is a choice. Since John Edwards had made a similar reference in his debate with Dick Cheney, it appeared that the campaign had decided that this would help them politically. Democrats said that this was justified because Bush and Cheney were hypocrites for wanting a constitutional amendment banning same-sex marriage, given their own closeness to gays.

But Kerry and Edwards were also being hypocrites. It was widely believed that in the 2000 election large numbers of conservative Christians had decided not to vote for Bush because of his drunk-driving arrest when he was a young man. The Kerry/Edwards campaign made a calculated attempt to remind bigoted people that there was a gay in the Republican family in hopes of a similar dampening effect on their opponents' turnout.

Kerry was not really opposing homophobia in that moment, he was trying to exploit it. (His campaign manager Mary Beth Cahill admitted as much in the post-debate spin room when she said that Mary Cheney was "fair game.") Thus, the Democrats lost the moral high ground on this issue and gave some credence to Dick Cheney's scripted but effective line, "He'll say anything to win," which hit Kerry squarely where he was already weak.

As the election grew closer, Rock the Vote created a petition on their website to protest a rumored draft. They revealed a Pentagon memo showing a discussion of the draft in early 2003 between the Pentagon and the Selective Service, opining, "This is a real issue and deserves real answers." They urged young people to send faux "draft cards" to their friends to focus on the fact that the U.S. military was "stretched to the breaking point and the candidates need to tell Americans what they are going to do about it."

RNC Chairman Ed Gillespie sent a letter to Rock the Vote telling them they "have an obligation to immediately cease and desist from promoting or conducting your 'Draft' campaign." He called it a "malicious political deception." Rock the Vote's Jehmu Green was thrilled that she had provoked this reaction and wrote back: "I have news for you: Just because President Bush, Vice President Cheney, and Secretary Rumsfeld, or for that matter Senator Kerry, say there is not going to be a draft does not make it so. Just because Congress holds a transparently phony vote against the draft doesn't mean there isn't going to be one. Anyone who thinks that the youth of America are going to take a politician's word on this topic is living on another planet."

In October, the Bush campaign unveiled their best TV spot, "Ashley's Story," which featured a teenage girl from Ohio whose mother had been killed at the World Trade Center on September 11. Bush had been photographed hugging her at a campaign rally. In the commercial, Ashley Faulkner says, "He's the most powerful man in the world and all he wants to do is make sure I'm safe, that I'm okay." Her father adds, "What I saw was what I want to see in the heart and soul of the man who sits in the highest elective office in our country." "Ashley's Story" was the most expensive ad buy of the campaign. It was corny. It bore no relation to the truth of how Bush's presidency related to the protection of Americans from terrorism. But as good commercials do, it created an emotionally compelling illusion.

The final week's political stories that dominated the media were the missing cache of dangerous weapons from Iraq and a new Osama bin Laden videotape. Both Kerry and Bush hated bin Laden and neither were in favor of losing dangerous weapons.

And then it was over.

* * *

I wish that Kerry had won and I think he would have made a fine president, but I am not surprised that he lost, which, perhaps, is why I was less depressed than a lot of my friends. Yes, the election result was deeply disappointing to anyone who cares about opportunities for poor people, the rights of women and gays, civil liberties, the environment, and an alternative to the neocon foreign policy of American Empire.

But it's important to recognize that despite the results of the election, progressive populist energy is greater than it has been for decades. Conservatives have worked tirelessly on changing public opinion since the 1960s, transforming the political reality in society so that Clinton felt he had to adopt many conservative ideas to get elected; so that Newt Gingrich and Jerry Falwell and Rush Limbaugh were accepted as serious thinkers in polite society; so that Democratic congressional leaders believed it was wise to ignore the vast majority of their constituents and support Bush's war in Iraq.

In Rick Perlstein's book *Before the Storm: Barry Goldwater and the Unmaking of the American Consensus*, he describes the early stirrings of the conservative movement that was created to fight the liberal establishment. In 1958, Brent Bozell, who helped edit his cousin William Buckley's magazine, *National Review*, wrote a memo to conservatives in which he discussed the need to influence the ideas of millions of people. "A conservative electorate has to be created," Bozell exhorted his compatriots.

The silver lining of the 2004 campaign is that, unlike any election in my lifetime, the campaign left many progressive footprints, an infrastructure of activists, media, and organizations that have at long last begun the work of creating a true progressive electorate.

Air America's Jon Sinton has used focus groups for decades to help guide radio programming, but he cautions, "Focus groups are like a rearview mirror. They can tell you where people have been, but not where they're going." They can measure what words people like to describe Social Security privatization and what words they hate—but they do not measure so well what constitutes "leadership." The job description of progressive political leaders must include the ability, either learned or natural, to communicate with the cultural heart of America.

Although John Kerry was no Barry Goldwater (either in the good or the bad sense), the progressive campaign catalyzed by MoveOn.org, Michael Moore, and Howard Dean—along with a general revulsion against the excesses of the Bush administration—mobilized millions of people, not just to vote, but to become activists. They have passion, a moral imperative, and commitment.

Steve Earle played an election-night show at the New York City rock club CBGBs at which Jonathan Demme filmed a music video of Earle's song "Rich Man's War." "I'm bummed out at the results of the election," Steve said, when he called me from his tour in Germany the following week, "but from my experience as a recovering addict, I believe that real change takes a long time." Steve, whose interest in the election was driven by his opposition to the war, gained heart from the depth of worldwide antiwar sentiment that was undiminished by the election results.

Joe Uehlein of the AFL-CIO said, "We're trying to figure out what we need to do differently, but one good thing that happened is that we had 150,000 new activists who worked with us during the election. We have to keep them motivated."

Gloria Totten, executive director of the Progressive Majority, also felt cautiously optimistic. Supported by the most progressive members of the U.S. Congress, the organization had focused on recruiting candidates for statewide office in Washington State, Wisconsin, and Pennsylvania to create a "farm team" for the future. "We had firefighters, nurses, and rank-and-file union leaders," Gloria told me two weeks after the election. Very few of their candidates had run for office before. Out of one hundred state legislative candidates, their farm team won forty-one races, and Gloria stressed, "Most of the others we knew we would lose but we wanted to build people for the future." For 2005, Progressive Majority is adding Arizona and Colorado to their areas of focus, and they plan to have a presence in ten states by 2006. "I'm amazed at the energy behind what we're doing," said Gloria, buoyed by several post-election house parties she had convened in Southern California to support their work. "My whole rap has been that we can't put everything we have into one man running for one office, even if that's the presidency. We're grooming progressive leaders, so if one guy doesn't click with voters we're not completely screwed. We are one year into a ten-year plan to take control."

The *Nation*—whose circulation has increased from 100,000 to 170,000 during the Bush years—was drawing so many new subscription requests in the weeks after the election that they expected to be at 180,000 by the end of the year, by far the largest circulation in the magazine's 139-year history. Katrina vanden Heuval, the magazine's editor, reflected, "Unlike 1972, when Democrats were wiped out everywhere, in 2004 there is an emerging progressive infrastructure capable of standing and fighting. Progressives should build on those structures put in place in this last cycle and redouble their commitment to economic justice, peace, and environmental movements that can make real change."

At the ACLU, membership at the beginning of the Bush administration was slightly under 300,000; by the end of 2004 it was close to 450,000.

Perhaps even more significant were the hundreds of thousands of unaffiliated volunteers. Mary Marcus, a native of Louisiana who now lives in Santa Monica, felt compelled to "do something to help the country," and went to Las Vegas with two busloads of people for get-out-the-vote work before the election. There were ninety volunteers in her group and, with the exception of two group leaders, none of them had ever worked on a campaign before.

"It was a very mixed group of people," Mary recalled. "There was an engineer from Boeing, a woman whose son was serving in Iraq." The biggest issue that motivated most of them was the war, but many were also concerned with other issues, such as women's rights and the environment. "It was just a general sense that we have to do something to keep our country from sliding downhill," Mary recalled. Enku Geyaye, an assistant dean of students at UCLA, also made the trip to Nevada. Although discouraged by the final stages of the Kerry campaign, she said that several volunteers she worked with were organizing to influence congressional races in 2006, as well as to help reinvent the DNC. "We're all emailing each other trying to figure out what we can do next."

For me, the best antidote to pessimism was an electoral map I printed out from the website MusicforAmerica.org that showed, in red and blue, how the various states would have gone if those under the age of thirty had been the only ones voting. Kerry would have easily won with 375 electoral votes, taking not only Ohio and Florida, but also Virginia, West Virginia, Missouri, Arkansas, Colorado, Iowa, and North Carolina. It is very clear where the future is for progressives. Goldwater conservatives never had it so good.

CHAPTER 17

To My Fellow Former Hippies

My self-image was as a young person. Up comes this younger generation.
I think they are ignoring my sincere, honest, and absolutely profound ad-
vice. And that struck at my self-image.
—Socialist Michael Harrington, as quoted in Jim Miller's book
Democracy in the Streets, describing his confrontations with "new
left" radicals in the 1960s

O NE OF THE BAD THINGS that happened to the left in
the sixties was that the older generation never really embraced the "new left." Jack Newfield, who passed away at
the age of sixty-six in December 2004, was older than most hippies;
he had been one of the founders of SDS, the most prominent radical group of the sixties, and was quick to criticize the excesses of
that era. "Drugs replaced politics for a lot of people," he lamented,
citing such crazy and destructive developments as Yippie leader Jerry
Rubin's reference to Sirhan Sirhan, Robert Kennedy's assassin, as a
"freedom fighter." But Newfield also acknowledged the many mistakes made by the older left-wing intellectuals and leaders, many of
whom had lived through harrowing conflicts with American com-

munism and who wrongly feared that sixties protesters would be co-opted by communism.

Newfield pointed out that leftist nitpicking of progressive artists is not new. When Phil Ochs sang "Love Me, I'm a Liberal" at a peace rally in 1965, the legendary radical journalist I.F. Stone missed the humor of the song and shouted, "There are good liberals and there are bad liberals! Liberalism is not our enemy!"

In his memoir, *Somebody's Got to Tell It: A Journalist's Life on the Lines,* Newfield recalled that during the drafting of the SDS "Port Huron Statement," the defining document of sixties radicalism, Socialist icon and author Michael Harrington bitterly railed against the young activist Tom Hayden for being insensitive to the authoritarian evils of communism, ultimately causing a breakdown of relations between many of the older leftists and the student leaders. Newfield remembered, "I told Mike we were rebelling against the void of the 1950s but that he was still living in the 1930s," reflecting the fact that the Communist Party was virtually irrelevant to the new left of the 1960s.

Years later, Harrington regretted his dismissal of the younger radicals, a rejection which had left the new generation unsupported, depriving them of wisdom and advice that might have helped them avoid some of the destructiveness that tarnished the successes of the sixties progressive movements.

In 2005, too many leaders on the left and in the Democratic Party continue to see politics through the prism of the sixties and seventies. The 1968 Democratic Convention took place *thirty-seven years ago.* It's time to let it go.

The enormous explosion of grassroots activism in 2004 eliminated all doubt that a new generation of progressives has emerged. As in the 1960s, there are two dimensions to this new constituency—on the one hand, generational and cultural, and on the other, ideological. Most Democratic Party leaders supported Bush's decision to go to war in Iraq and the major tenets of the president's foreign policy, disagreeing only on tactics. Most actual Democratic voters, however, opposed the war and are not inclined to trust the same self-styled "wise men" who supported it (and who, for the most part, supported the Patriot Act) to make good foreign policy and anti-terrorism decisions.

In the wake of John Kerry's defeat, establishment Democratic voices such as the Democratic Leadership Council and writers for the *New Republic* shamelessly blamed the defeat on grassroots organizations like MoveOn.org and communicators like Michael Moore. They got it exactly wrong. In terms of financial support, the grassroots efforts led to an expansion of the Democratic National Committee's donor base from 400,000 in 2000 to 2.7 million in 2004. It was the votes of young people that prevented a landslide Bush reelection on the scale of those by Nixon and Reagan.

Wes Boyd, one of the leaders of MoveOn.org, explained the group's future mission in an interview with Salon: "Leaders are like the whitecaps on the tops of waves. They're stuck in a particular political context, and it's unreasonable to expect them to change that context. MoveOn's goal is to broaden the wave so that a future leader will have an easier time of it."

Although veterans of the sixties have to defer, when appropriate, to youth, we also have to complete our own destiny. Baby-boom satirist Joe Queenan, in his book *Balsamic Dreams: A Short but Self-Important History of the Baby Boomer Generation*, criticizes our generation for underachievement. But this is a form of cop-out as well. We're not dead yet! While supporting and encouraging teen spirit, we should also emulate the continued focus and passion of people like Harry Belafonte, who remains highly effective and politically engaged at age seventy-five; Jimmy Carter, who won the Nobel Peace Prize at seventy-nine; and Ramona Ripston, who runs the Southern California ACLU well into her seventies. The final judgment of the sixties generation will come not now but in twenty or thirty years. We do not have the luxury of either resting on our laurels or wallowing in self-loathing.

The left must learn to communicate in ways that, as President Bush says, "the boys in Lubbock can understand." Unless it connects with a mass constituency, progressive politics is like the proverbial tree falling in a forest that no one hears. Professors and critics can and should have rarefied taste, but political activists must learn to speak the language of the people, not solely the "Latin" of the political elite.

One does not have to agree with the policies of Ronald Reagan or Newt Gingrich or George W. Bush to appreciate their tactical strengths. One morning over coffee, several months before his eightieth birthday, Norman Lear, the creative genius behind *All in the Family* and *Maude*, told me that during the course of several decades, not a single organization, political candidate, or public official had been seriously interested in his thoughts on how to communicate through television. As Norman was grumpily reflecting on this, he suddenly interrupted himself with a smile. "You know, there was one guy who I could really talk to. Ronald Reagan. I had great meetings with him. He really listened to what I was saying and tried to answer. When I wrote him letters about the Christian right, even if he had other people write the responses, at least the responses were specific, not those form letters. Unfortunately," Norman laughed wistfully, "I disagreed with Reagan on just about everything, but ironically he was the one guy who actually engaged me."

"Most people in Washington, including those on the left," observes Sidney Blumenthal, former aide to President Clinton, "love the idea of America—which is the ideals, the symbols, the monuments, and the history books—but they don't like actual Americans very much. Americans are those gross people who go to shopping malls and watch television."

This is an indulgence the left cannot afford. Bob Dylan's message of four decades ago still rings true: "You better start swimming or you'll sink like a stone, for the times they are a-changin'."

Let's swim.

Index